Safety, Danger, and
in the Family and C

This book provides an analysis of the meaning of safety and security across the contexts of community and public life, throughout the life span, and within a therapeutic framework, examining threats and the strategies for coping with them.

The book starts in Part I with a discussion of general safety and security concepts in the socio-cultural context. Part II of the book details the role of a sense of security in psychological assistance, psychotherapy and supervision, while Part III centres on safety and security at different life stages. Drawing on the tenets of modern attachment theory and trauma theory, chapter authors address questions of safety, danger, and protection for both individuals and groups, across a variety of fields of knowledge and expertise. Themes such as loneliness, play and exploration, evil and forgiveness, health and death, and spirituality and healing are discussed as practice examples, learning points, and tips.

A wide range of health and social care professional practitioners will find this book useful in exploring social, interpersonal, and psychological aspects of safety and security.

Szymon Chrząstowski, PhD, is a lecturer at Warsaw University and has his independent psychotherapy practice. He specialises in attachment narrative therapy and his research focuses on safety/security as an everyday experience. He resides in Poland and Portugal.

Arlene Vetere, PhD, is a clinical psychologist and systemic psychotherapist, supervisor and trainer. She is Professor Emeritus of family therapy and systemic practice at VID Specialized University, Oslo, Norway. She resides in the UK.

'The texts in this book are both touching and enlightening. We comprehend through this volume how our basic needs for security and safety are intertwined with culture, politics and the influence of anthropocentrism on nature. We zoom in from the global level to the community, and then to family relations. The foresight and the courage of editors and authors must be highlighted. I wish this book a wide readership as it is an extremely rich and precious compendium for further thinking and acting.'

Maria Borcsa, PhD, *Professor in Clinical Psychology at the*
University of Applied Sciences Nordhausen, Germany.
Past President of the European Family Therapy
Association (EFTA)

'"The times they are a-changin"', Bob Dylan sang. We live in a world of unprecedented adversity and unpredictability at a global scale. This book compels psychotherapists to think, reflect and act in adversity (climate changes, migration, pandemics, war) across different contexts (global, community, and couple-family). To face this challenge, one must navigate safety and security, as proposed by the Editors. Arlene and Simon guide us through a most wonderful voyage in a systemic-attachment ship where some authors share ideas to fight people's vulnerability. An inspirational, useful, and respectful expedition.'

Ana Paula Relvas, PhD, *Professor of Clinical Psychology, Faculty of*
Psychology and Education Sciences, University of Coimbra, Portugal

'We live in a world with a desperate need to understand and ameliorate dangers at every level of human life. This fascinating book is rooted in the extensive experience of Arlene Vetere in family violence and the shared base with her co-editor Szymon Chrząstowski in attachment narrative therapy. It coordinates the rich experience of its diverse authors in progressive contexts of the world, the community and the family. The book offers a sophisticated and carefully coordinated understanding of the wide ramifications and considerations of safety and security at each level of context. This structure will equip readers to understand the sources of danger at each level and to know what resources are available or could be mobilised for people and communities.'

Peter Stratton, *Emeritus Professor of Family Therapy, Leeds, UK*

Safety, Danger, and Protection in the Family and Community

A Systemic and Attachment-Informed Approach

Edited by Szymon Chrząstowski and Arlene Vetere

Routledge
Taylor & Francis Group

LONDON AND NEW YORK

Designed cover image: © Getty Images

First published 2024
by Routledge
4 Park Square, Milton Park, Abingdon, Oxon OX14 4RN

and by Routledge
605 Third Avenue, New York, NY 10158

Routledge is an imprint of the Taylor & Francis Group, an informa business

British Library Cataloguing-in-Publication Data
A catalogue record for this book is available from the British Library

ISBN: 9781032311104 (hbk)
ISBN: 9781032311098 (pbk)
ISBN: 9781003308096 (ebk)

DOI: 10.4324/9781003308096

Typeset in Times New Roman
by Newgen Publishing UK

Contents

Contributors

Bogdan de Barbaro, Poland, independent practice

Daniel Bąk, UK & Poland, Pink Therapy, London & Centre for Social Queer Studies, Institute of Applied Social Science, University of Warsaw

Bibi van den Berg, Netherlands, Leiden University

Magdalena Budziszewska, Poland, Faculty of Psychology, University of Warsaw

Chip Chimera, UK, independent practice

Szymon Chrząstowski, Poland & Portugal, Faculty of Psychology, University of Warsaw & independent practice

Rudi Dallos, UK, University of Plymouth

Andy Glossop, UK, Oxfordshire County Council

Myrna Gower, UK, independent practice

Ben Grey, UK, Department of Psychology, Sport and Geography, University of Hertfordshire

Lydia Guthrie, UK, independent practice

Åse Holmberg, Norway, VID Specialized University

Per Jensen, Norway, VID Specialized University

Barbara Józefik, Poland, Jagiellonian University Medical College

Katarzyna Lubiewska, Poland, Faculty of Psychology, University of Warsaw

Kalina J. Michalska, US, Department of Psychology, University of California, Riverside, CA

Jordan L. Mullins, US, Department of Psychology, University of California, Riverside, CA

Laura Ogi, UK, Oxfordshire County Council

Olivia Polisano, UK, Oxfordshire County Council

Rebecca Stancer, UK, University of Plymouth

Tara Vassallo, UK, Institute of Education, University of Plymouth

Arlene Vetere, UK and Norway, VID Specialized University

Jennifer Wallis, UK, Doctorate in Clinical Psychology, University of Southampton

Jo Wilson, UK, Team Leader Family and Bereavement Support, Helen and Douglas House

Safety, danger, and protection across different contexts

Editors' introduction

This book is about safety – how we understand psychological security, its development over time, its loss, and our attempts to recover it. The book analyses the various meanings of personal and interpersonal safety and security in the different life contexts of the home, the community, and in the wider world around us all. The international authors are researchers and psychotherapists working with different groups of people in different life contexts. They discuss many kinds of threats to security and safety and the strategies we develop for coping with them, at social, institutional, interpersonal, family, and personal levels.

Existential issues and questions have always been at the heart of psychotherapeutic practices, and never so more poignantly than now, as we emerge from the global COVID-19 pandemic. Themes of loneliness, safety, play and exploration, evil and forgiveness, health and death, spirituality and healing have always been with us, but the pandemic has intensified our awareness of how such existential issues impact in our daily lives. Safety and protection, comfort and reassurance, in the face of relational and external dangers, preoccupy our therapeutic practice and inform our research activity, but still there remains a theory-policy gap in many of our community and social institutions and workspaces. There are different approaches to psychotherapeutic intervention, but we still need common ground and a shared language for therapeutic dialogues around safety. The existential issues seem crucial as they are both isomorphic with practitioners' and clients' perspectives and often will interweave in a shared resonance.

The authors draw on key theoretical frameworks, such as modern attachment theory, systemic, narrative, and trauma theories to help organise, clarify, and enrich their reflections on these existential questions of safety, danger, and protection in their areas of expertise. For example, safety in schools and in residential care, for staff, pupils, and residents; safety for refugees in their journey of migration; safety in couple relationships and for older adults and their grown-up children; safety in the child protection process – how do parents see danger for their children; safety for practitioners; safety in hospital intensive care units; the neurobiology of the felt experience of safety in significant relationships; climate safety; and safety and

DOI: 10.4324/9781003308096-1

protection in the context of homophobia and other abusive social discourses, practices, and contexts. We do not wish to stretch the application of attachment theory to relational dangers that emerge and exist in these various life contexts, but where there are people, and where fear and dangers are present, then the need for protective strategies is activated – both individually and collectively. And this is what we wish to explore in this edited text – how do we build and support robust and inter-dependent communities in the face of both everyday relational dangers and in extraordinary times.

We hope that the ideas expressed in our book are universal enough to help everyone involved in developing psychological security across many different contexts. Attachment theory states that a sense of security arises from interactions between people who are close to one another. Thus, a sense of security is possible even if people's surroundings are beset by all sorts of difficulties. These external threats, on the other hand, can have a circular effect on a sense of security. They can take it away and destroy it, a fact that psychotherapists are well aware of when working with people who have experienced various kinds of danger. Threats to a sense of security are not just experiences or narratives but can also constitute a real force that destroys a person, family, or society. On the other hand, our surroundings, in the broad sense of the word, mostly people, but also the physical neighbourhood, can also help in building a sense of inner security, which is the foundation that allows a person, their family, or community to flourish.

We came up with the idea for this book during the SARS-COVID-19 pandemic. This was at the time of a global threat that not only had a negative impact on the psychological functioning of many people around the world but was also a period when close to 7 million people died (WHO, January 2023), leaving their closest friends and family suffering greatly. Such suffering triggers our compassion and respect. And then, as this book was starting to materialise, Russia invaded Ukraine. While writing this introduction, there was already an estimated 6,755 Ukrainian civilian fatalities (424 of whom were children). We can discuss the figures portraying these threats at great length but they will never be complete and exhaustive. As Wiesława Szymborska, the Polish Nobel Prize-winning poet, wrote in her poem "A Large Number":[1]

> Four billion people on this earth,
> but my imagination is the way it's always been:
> bad with large numbers.
> It is still moved by particularity.

We too, as psychotherapists, are still "moved by particularities", which is why we are not going to focus on figures in this book, despite being fully aware of just how important they are – hence the reference. The Ukrainian border is only 200 km away from Warsaw, where one of the editors of this book was born. Because of the very proximity of the war, war is not just another piece of news but also a threat. The war in Ukraine is just one of the ongoing armed conflicts around the world.

Nevertheless, this war and the COVID-19 pandemic show just how fragile a sense of security can be for those of us living in Europe, often considered to be a particularly safe continent, and how valid the issue of protection against different kinds of threats is and will continue to be.

The book's chapter authors have outlined various ways to strengthen a sense of security. A golden thread runs throughout the pages of this book, suggesting that one remedy for feelings of insecurity is to develop close relationships based on trust, and also belonging to a community that respects both separateness and autonomy and, at the same time, supports dependence. Security is both a value and a right. This has already been emphasised in Article 3 of the Universal Declaration of Human Rights, that every human being has the right to security of person. The very fact that the Declaration is being invoked here constitutes an act of political choice. Thus, the study of a sense of security and writing about it is also our ethical choice. We believe that fostering security not only constitutes the foundation of our work but also one of the core values informing personal decisions. What we want to show here is that fostering such security does not have to involve over-simplified and populist recipes. Rather, it demands constant thought and reflection that we hope this book will facilitate and support.

We are also aware that we have not discussed all aspects of safety and security in this book. Some topics regarding security have already been discussed extensively in the existing literature. We therefore decided against devoting a chapter to polyvagal theory and discussing the basic assumptions of attachment theory or systemic thinking. We did not want to edit an academic textbook but rather a book that would prove useful to different people interested in this topic, and especially practitioners who are supporting the building of a sense of security for their clients. We wanted this book to be more inspiring than exhaustive. Both of us are practising systemic psychotherapists, that is why we did not want to venture beyond the boundaries of our competencies, which, in effect, led us to limit the scope of topics discussed in this volume. While working on the book, we wanted to avoid focusing on psychological safety solely from a European perspective. Unfortunately, we have failed to do so. This is definitely a topic for another collection.

We hope our book will complement existing publications on safety and security. The field of security studies is still evolving, having initially focussed on a global or state-centric approach to security, particularly the military aspect. Increasingly, however, more attention is being paid to the non-military aspects of security, as well as to the security of individuals. A good example of this is *The Phenomenology of Human Security and Insecurity*, edited by Juhani Laurinkari (2022). This book contains the results of a long-term research project conducted by the University of Eastern Finland. For us, the phenomenological perspective is important, but here we shall focus primarily on the systems approach and attachment theory.

As joint editors of this volume we wanted to briefly illustrate our personal positioning on questions and experiences of safety to make clear our motivations and intentions for addressing the issues of safety and security.

Arlene Vetere: My parents were economic migrants, leaving post-war Britain for a new life in Canada. They found neither economic security, job security, nor secure accommodation. As a child, I attended 13 different schools as a consequence of frequent moves in search of employment. Yet, as two parents they kept my younger brother and me safe. They created a context in which we could grow and thrive, with a felt sense of comfort and safety. My father was killed when I was 11 years old. My mother struggled as a lone parent, especially financially. Emotionally, we had all had our world turned upside down, but we all felt the continuing bond in our love for our father, her husband. These were early lessons for me in the significance of dependable and embodied safe connections with close others, which later in life translated into a wish to understand how to promote feelings of safety in families and local communities. My professional career culminated in establishing an independent family violence intervention service to assist family members in stopping their violent behaviour (Cooper & Vetere, 2005).

Szymon Chrząstowski: There were several reasons why I wanted to tackle the topic of psychological security. First, fostering clients' sense of security is critical in the approach that I identify with as a psychotherapist – attachment narrative therapy. This is why I focussed my thoughts and attention on what it means to feel secure. The more time I spent exploring the topic, the more questions emerged. These questions led me to initiate research on a sense of security and to engage in theoretical discussions with my supervisor and the co-editor of this book, Arlene Vetere. Thus, this book was borne from a collaboration between the supervisee and his supervisor. I feel safe under the supervision of Arlene, and this safety is the foundation of the reflexivity that ultimately led to this book coming about.

Another aspect of my interest in a sense of security is associated with the broader social context in which I find myself. I currently divide my time between two countries: Poland and Portugal. Poland is a country whose most recent history has been defined by the Second World War, which has also affected the lives of my own family. The way I see it, as in the case of many Polish families, the impact of wartime experiences was not recognised or discussed thoroughly enough in my family, which is why it exerted an even greater effect on the way we adapted and continue to adapt to various kinds of threats (both on an individual and more general level). At the same time, Poland is currently a country where its social and political processes are a cause for concern to many, and which do not allow certain groups, particularly marginalised ones, to feel fully safe.

Portugal is a place that is rapidly becoming my second home. It is here that the Carnation Revolution broke out – two years after I was born – which triggered the process of democratisation in the country. Despite its many problems and difficulties, Portugal for me has become a welcoming "land of brotherhood", as Zeca Afonso sings in "*Grândola, vila morena*". It was this song that was broadcast on the radio on 25 April 1974, signalling the beginning of the aforementioned revolution. Portugal, then, gives me a sense of security. While my Polish roots help me identify and understand the influence of various kinds of threats, my life in

Portugal allows me to perceive, albeit from a certain distance, how these dangers affect me and my way of experiencing myself and other people.

And, finally, a sense of security is also a recurring topic in my own personal experiences. My grandparents became my main attachment figures when I was a small child – these same (grand)parents who found it difficult to build a sense of security for their own children, probably because of their wartime experiences. I have been very fortunate because throughout my life I have encountered many supporting and loving people who have helped and continue to help me feel safe. It is thanks to these positive experiences with the people closest to me that I have learnt to foster my own sense of security and to share it with those close to me and with my clients.

Thus this edited book is intended to be an invitation to reflect on the "obvious". The COVID-19 pandemic appears to have shown us that the obvious is not always obvious, and there is a constant need to care about safety and security. From this perspective, a lived sense of safety and security is less a state and more a continuous action – both for individuals and their relationships. We believe that such reflection helps to protect us all against dangers to our safety and security – on social, intra-familial, and individual levels.

Note

1 Szymborska, W. (1995). *View with a Grain of Sand: Selected Poems.* Orlando: Harcourt, a Harvest Original. Translated by Stanisław Barańczak and Clare Cavanagh.

References

Cooper, J., & Vetere, A. (2005) *Domestic Violence and Family Safety: A Systemic Approach to Working with Violence in Families.* Wiley.

Laurinkari, J. (Ed.). (2022). *The Phenomenology of Human Security and Insecurity.* Metropolis Verlag.

World Health Organization. (2023). Weekly epidemiological update on COVID-19. www. who.int/

Part I

Safety and security in the world

Chapter 1

The need for safety and security

Bibi van den Berg

Safety and security: Controlling risk

Safety and security are important preoccupations in our modern times. Whenever we open a newspaper or watch the news, we encounter stories of hazards and crises leading to harm to humans or the things they hold dear. From chemical spills and forest fires to international conflict and cybersecurity incidents, there is a strong focus on the many ways in which human safety and security may come under pressure as a result of natural or man-made forces. There are several reasons why it is worthwhile to question this focus on safety hazards and security. For one, this focus is relatively recent. There is ample evidence from history that shows that in former times people tended to think very differently about the fact that life was fraught with hazards. So, what has changed? Our strong focus – some would even label it an obsession – with safety and security is surprising in light of evidence that shows that, in fact, at least in the Western world, we live in safer times than all of our forebears before us. What explains this preoccupation, then?

In this chapter I will argue that the answer to this question is that safety and security are foundational conditions for human beings in order to thrive, and that we have existential concerns over our safety and security precisely *because* our lives have gradually become so much safer in recent centuries. To understand how this dynamic has developed over time, we will begin by tracing its historical origins.

A comparison with the past

Underneath our concerns over safety and security lies an acute awareness of the notion of *risk*. Our bodies and minds, the objects around us, the systems that we are part of, and the values that we hold dear: all of these have vulnerabilities, weaknesses. Therefore, there is a chance they may be damaged or destroyed (cf. Furedi 2008): weaknesses in our bodies may give rise to disease, just like vulnerabilities in computer systems may be exploited by hackers, or weak spots in a dam may lead to a flood. At the same time, it is important to note that vulnerabilities *may* give rise to harm, but they need not necessarily do so.

DOI: 10.4324/9781003308096-3

We can quantify and calculate risks, according to many risk scholars, by multiplying two factors: the chance or likelihood that the risk may arise, and the (set of) consequences or the impact it may have once it does (cf. Paté-Cornell 2012; Zio 2018). Most importantly, in our current interpretation of risks human beings have the potential to intervene in their potential occurrence. Crises and hazards may be averted through human interventions, especially when we understand their root causes and know how to protect the 'targets' they may harm. Of course, some risks are easier to mitigate than others – it is easier to thwart the dangers of falling down the stairs than it is to influence the eruption of a volcano. Having said that, one of the core characteristics of our modern vision of risks is the assumption that there is always at least *something* that human beings can do to reduce the likelihood of risks materializing or their impact, or both. Risk, therefore, is part of a worldview that places the agency of mankind, and its will to control, at its heart.

This conception of risk is relatively new. It only emerged at the end of the Renaissance, with the dawn of modernity. This is not to say that people throughout history were not aware of the hazards they faced. Until the end of the Middle Ages, people were very aware of the fragility of life. Diseases, natural disasters, famines, and conflicts happened all the time. Villages were destroyed by fires or floods, people died of malnutrition or lack of food, and crime and war were rampant. Life expectancy was much lower than it is today. However, several scholars note that for much of history, people did not think about all of these hazards in terms of *risks* (Bernstein 1998; Cutter 1993; Lupton 2013). Rather, they believed that their lives and futures were determined by the gods, by fate, or by other mechanisms outside their control. Hazards befell people for reasons unbeknownst to them, and were labelled as destiny or divine intervention. This is not to say that people simply underwent the bad things that were happening to them. They had numerous customs and habits to try to thwart bad things from materializing, ranging from offerings to the gods to going on pilgrimages and adhering to superstitions (Lupton 2013).

What sets the interpretation of crises and disasters by our forebears apart from that in our time is the idea of the *manageability* of risk, of being able to identify and quantify risks, and to develop responses to risks. Our forebears in the Middle Ages appeared to attempt to 'tame fate' using their habits of offerings to the gods and going on pilgrimages. By contrast, we seek to 'tame hazards' themselves.

What changed?

What happened at the end of the Renaissance to bring about this change? Risk scholars point towards several developments that collectively enabled humanity in early modernity to start thinking about risks as something to be calculated and managed. First and foremost are developments in the science of mathematics, more specifically the development of probability theory (Bernstein 1998). Statistics facilitated the growth of predictive thinking: an ability to make claims about the likelihood of (repeat) occurrences of particular events in the future in a way that was literally unthinkable until that point in time.

The importance of this development cannot be overstated. Because of these developments in the field of mathematics, people now had the possibility to start thinking in terms of chances: what are the odds that so-and-so will happen? What are the odds that I will have plentiful crops this year? And, what choices can I make to influence the odds so that I'll have more crops? It also facilitated new ventures in the field of business. During the Age of Discovery (15th–17th century), European countries set out to discover the world, building ships to develop new trade routes, to colonize new territories, and to map the world. Trade on a global scale like this is what Bernstein calls 'a risky business' (Bernstein 1998, 21): ships could be lost at sea, new products from the other side of the world might not appeal to the public, and high investments needed to be made beforehand, building ships and sending them off with a crew for travels that might take years. Using bookkeeping, combined with elementary statistics and probability thinking, enabled these traders to engage in forecasting (Bernstein 1998). This, in turn, contributed in a significant way to the expansion of European trade. Risk, in this form of trade, was actively and consciously engaged with in the act of trading itself, but at the same time it was also contained, managed, through numbers and administration.

A final element in bringing about the change in thinking about risk at the end of the Renaissance is the introduction of a new number system in Europe. It is because of this new number system, the Arab number system, that developments in bookkeeping and probability theory could take place. The Arab number system, which arrived in Europe in the 12th and 13th centuries as a consequence of the Crusades, functioned as a key technology without which advances in mathematics and business were impossible. Until that time, people used Roman numerals, and doing math with letters is very challenging: even doing elementary calculations, such as subtraction or addition, was already quite complicated. When the Arab number system found its way to Europe, people needed 'only ten digits, from zero to nine, to perform every conceivable calculation and to write any conceivable number' (Bernstein 1998, 33). Thus, new levels of mathematical thinking were facilitated, which, in turn, enabled Europeans, for the very first time, to think about the world around them in terms of probabilities, and in terms of possibilities of influencing the future.

Natural versus man-made risks

Until the end of the Renaissance, the majority of hazards that human beings faced were natural in their origins: fires, storms, floods, viruses, food gone bad, risks due to bad weather and so on and so forth. War and crime were a serious source of risk of course as well, but other than those human-induced risks, almost all other hazards were external in the sense that they occurred outside human beings' influence.

At the end of the Renaissance, a new realization of thinking in terms of risk gradually materialized. Thus, human beings slowly started seeking a sense of control over risks: they became aware of the fact they could try to intervene in the likelihood of the occurrence of disasters, or that they might be able to influence the impact that hazards would have. Here we witness the birth of a long and ever-expanding tendency to work towards improving safety and security in our life-world.

All throughout the Age of Enlightenment (17th and 18th centuries) and the Industrial Revolution (second half of the 18th century), scholars and engineers started thinking of ways in which they could make life safer and more secure in a variety of different domains. Great improvements were made in the field of construction, so that buildings could withstand weather events, and were better insulated against the cold. Significant steps were made over the centuries in food safety, by improving food hygiene, preventing food contamination, and adding substances to improve the quality and durability of food. In agriculture similar improvements were made: crops became sturdier and more resistant to bacteria and viruses, so that the risk of crop failure went down, and agriculture was intensified to yield higher gains. Developments in medicine and hygiene of course played a vital role as well. Life expectancy went up dramatically because of discoveries with respect to the transmission and control of diseases, and the role of personal hygiene in preventing illness (Riley 2001). Cures were found for viruses that used to wipe out large portions of the population in the past, and vaccines were developed to inundate human beings against others. At the same time, financial support systems were developed to help people protect themselves against windfall. Governments designed pension plans and the financial sector developed savings and investment plans to help people insulate themselves financially against the hazards of life – and, fair is fair, to take more risk, be more adventurous with their money as well. And then there was an array of technological innovations that were created over the centuries to make life safer, easier, and more comfortable. These ranged from industrial systems for the production of goods and services, to critical infrastructures for electricity, water, and sanitation, transport, and telecommunication, to consumer technologies.

All of these inventions were created to increase control over the risks we face as human beings, to protect us against the many hazards that could befall us. All of them combined have led to the fact that the likelihood of dying from the cold, from bad food, from an epidemic, and even from natural hazards or wars has been reduced dramatically. However, at the same time, humanity has discovered that every insulation we created, every protective mechanism we developed, also carried its own risks. Nuclear power provided us with a source of highly reliable, clean energy, but nuclear incidents have a very severe and long-lasting impact. Concrete has become one of the most important building materials because of its sturdiness and the protection it offers, but it has a high environmental footprint and it contains radon, an element that is released gradually over time, and may cause cancer. Bug sprays that were developed in the middle of the previous century to help improve the protection of crops and fight malaria were banned decades later after the discovery of the fact that they may damage unborn children and cause cancer. Antibiotics have enabled humanity to fight common diseases and infections, but using too much of them makes bodies resistant, thereby increasing our susceptibility to new and mutating viruses. These examples show that in the past centuries human beings have developed a wide array of protective and insulating artefacts and systems that shield them from the hazardous, random nature of life.

But in the process, they have also created an explosion of new, man-made risks. Some risk scholars call these societal hazards (Bankoff 2012), others call them manufactured uncertainties (Beck 2006) or manufactured risks (Giddens 1999). What these terms share is an acute awareness that mankind has created novel risks, hazards that are a direct result of the innovations it has brought forth, alongside the 'classical' natural risks that these innovations often seek to combat.

An objectively safe world?

Man-made risks aside, it is clear that through the development of myriad technologies, systems, and techniques over the past centuries, human beings have eliminated some of the random hazards that befell them in past times, and have, in fact, increased their control over (particular types of) risk. Some scholars argue that, objectively speaking, our lives are pretty safe and secure indeed – especially in comparison to those of our forebears (Pinker 2018; Rosling, Rosling, and Rönnlund 2018). Establishing whether or not we live more safe and secure lives of course hinges on how we measure security and insecurity. What constitutes a 'secure' world? What constitutes 'insecurity'? One standard that is often used for measuring the risk of specific types of hazards is to look at mortality rates for specific hazards (see Figures 1.1 and 1.2) and life expectancy (see Figure 1.3).

Figure 1.1 Deaths in state-based conflicts per 100.000 since 1946.

Source: Data from Pettersson et al (2021) Organized violence 1989–2020, with a special emphasis on Syria and Lacina and Gleditsch (2005) Monitoring Trends in Global Combat: A New Dataset of Battle Deaths via Our World in Data.

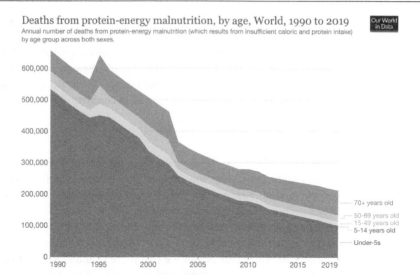

Deaths from protein-energy malnutrition, by age, World, 1990 to 2019

Annual number of deaths from protein-energy malnutrition (which results from insufficient caloric and protein intake) by age group across both sexes.

Figure 1.2 Deaths from malnutrition per age group.

Source: Data from Global Burden of Disease Collaborative Network. Global Burden of Disease Study 2019 (GBD 2019) Results. Seattle, United States: Institute for Health Metrics and Evaluation (IHME), 2021 via Our World in Data.

https://ourworldindata.org/famines

From these figures, one can draw several conclusions. The number of deaths as a result of armed conflicts, such as wars between nation states or civil wars, fluctuated over time since the Second World War, but since the beginning of the new millennium it has been low. Second, the death rate as a result of malnutrition is also declining steadily, due to increased food production and, as a consequence, food security. Finally, life expectancy has gone up dramatically in the previous century and continues to rise globally. All three figures appear to confirms the 'safe(r) world paradigm'. We may conclude that, objectively speaking, at least for essential parameters such as these, our lives are more secure than those of generations before us. At the same time, we have seen that in our times risks are a source of concern. We worry more about the risks that surround us. What explains this worry?

Our preoccupation with unsafety and insecurity explained

When answering this question, a first thing to note is the fact that whenever we speak about safety and security, we express a concern over the *absence* thereof. National security does not refer to a state of peace, but to concerns over threats to that peace, just like child safety or food safety refer to concerns over a lack of safety in relation to children or food stuffs respectively. Similar to the domain of health – where we tend to speak of 'health' when in fact we mean 'sickness' or at least 'absence of health' (Luhmann 1990) – in the field of safety and security, when

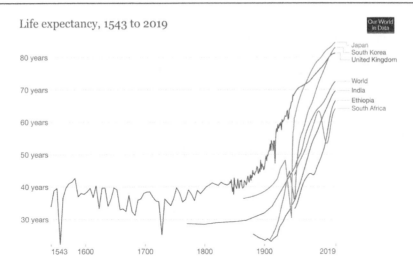

Note: Shown is period life expectancy at birth, the average number of years a newborn would live if the pattern of mortality in the given year were to stay the same throughout its life.

Figure 1.3 Life expectancy in different countries between 1543 and 2019.

Source: Data from United Nations, Department of Economic and Social Affairs, Population Division (2022). World Population Prospects 2022, Online Edition; Zijdeman et al. (2015) (via clio-infra.eu); Riley, J. C. (2005). Estimates of Regional and Global Life Expectancy, 1800–2001. Population and Development Review, 31(3), 537–543. www.jstor.org/stable/ 3401478 via Our World in Data.

we use these key terms, we do not generally refer to a state in which our bodies, possessions or the values we hold dear *are* well-protected and sheltered, but rather to the fact that they *should* be, and either are not, or are under threat of losing that state. When we speak about safety and security, in fact, we mean the *opposite* of safety and security: *insecurity* and *unsafety*.[1]

What explains our increased preoccupation with risk, and with safety and security? When delving into this question, we encounter an interesting paradox: as we have gained more control over our life-world in the past centuries by developing protective mechanisms and insulations from hazards and harms, at the same time we have become much less tolerant to risk in general. Our perception of increased control has led to a stronger aversion of all instances when that control appears to be undercut or suspended, that is, in moments of crisis, when hazards materialize, when humans or their belongings come to harm. This lack of tolerance vis-a-vis risk is most apparent when there is a failure in the protective mechanisms that we have created ourselves. Because we have been so successful at pinpointing dangers and threats, and at devising countermeasures against them, we have become less tolerant of the randomness of life, of the fact that accidents happen and that we cannot ban safety and security incidents fully.

Our preoccupation with safety and security, in fact, really is a preoccupation with our ability to control, and the consistent realization that that control is incomplete.

This is also clearly visible in our treatment of politicians, experts, and crisis managers whenever incidents materialize. In crises big or small, audiences inadvertently tend to ask 'could someone have known this was going to happen?', 'could it have been prevented?', 'who is responsible?', and 'who is to blame?'. Scholars label the societal attitude underneath these questions a 'zero-risk society' (Slovic 1987), a society in which citizens see risks and dangers all around them, but expect that these risks and dangers will be addressed in such a way that no harm can befall us anymore.

The irony of living in a zero-risk society is that while people in such a society demand that risk should be eliminated from their life-world, at the same time citizens are, in fact, more afraid than ever before. They are so keenly aware of all the many vulnerabilities of life that as a consequence, they feel incredibly insecure and vulnerable – perhaps more so than any generation before them. While increased knowledge and awareness of risks helps us increase protections against many hazards and potential harms, the other side of the coin is that the same knowledge appears to breed fear and insecurity. Risk-awareness is, in fact, a double-edged sword.

Security and safety as a state of normalcy

In 1994 the United Nations Development Programme (UNDP) defined a number of key indicators of safe and secure societies (United Nations 1994). These indicators focus on economic security, food and health security, environmental security, and personal, political and community security (Orencio et al. 2016). Most Western countries score highly on all or almost all of these indicators. According to the UNDP's Human Development Index in 2021–2022 (HDI)[2] Western countries almost all fall in the category of 'very high human development'. In these countries, moreover, the population's self-reported life satisfaction in 2020 was the highest in the world, as is shown in Figure 1.4.

To all intents and purposes, therefore, human beings living in Western countries generally live safe and secure lives – especially, sadly, in contrast to human beings living in (certain) other parts of the world. In Western countries, one could argue, safety and security are 'normal' for individuals, or even more strongly put: being safe and secure is *the norm*. Safety and security form the foundation, as it were, upon which they can engage in their everyday activities. Phrased differently, one could claim that in Western countries, security and safety are what we could call the 'state of normalcy'. On any average day, as human beings go about their daily routines, security and safety are absent from their thinking. They trust that they can navigate reality – both in a literal and a figurative sense – without coming to harm (bodily or otherwise). In the words of Barry A. Turner, under normal conditions people tend to operate on the basis of a set of beliefs about the world and about the hazards that it may contain which are 'sufficiently accurate to enable individuals and groups to survive successfully in the world' (Turner 1976, 381). Under normal conditions human beings go about their lives based on a sense of security, resting assured that things are peaceful and safe. This state of normalcy is the backdrop against which they engage with the world around them, and the other people in it.

Self-reported life satisfaction, 2020

"Please imagine a ladder, with steps numbered from 0 at the bottom to 10 at the top. The top of the ladder represents the best possible life for you and the bottom of the ladder represents the worst possible life for you. On which step of the ladder would you say you personally feel you stand at this time?"

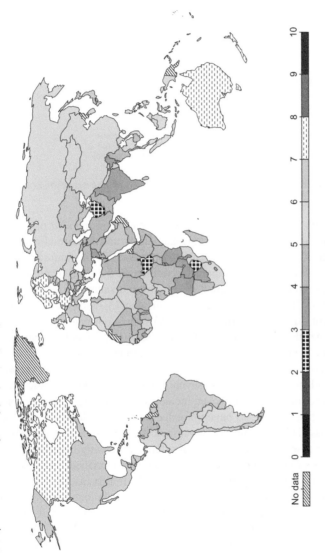

Note: The value shown in a given year is the average of that year, the previous year and the following year.

Figure 1.4 Self-reported life satisfaction of the world's population in 2020.

Source: Data from Helliwell, J.F., Layard, R., Sachs, J.D., De Neve, J.-E., Aknin, L.B., and Wang, S. (eds) (2023). World Happiness Report 2023. New York: Sustainable Development Solutions Network via Our World in Data. https://ourworldindata.org/happiness-and-life-satisfaction.

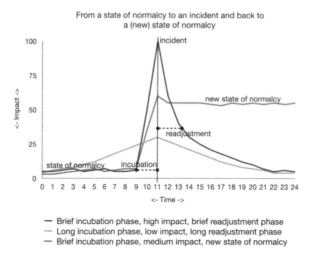

From a state of normalcy to an incident and back to
a (new) state of normalcy

— Brief incubation phase, high impact, brief readjustment phase
— Long incubation phase, low impact, long readjustment phase
— Brief incubation phase, medium impact, new state of normalcy

Figure 1.5 The five phases of temporary cessation of the state of normalcy.

However, this state of normalcy may sometimes be *suspended* or *disrupted*. At such a moment, an incident of some kind materializes, and the normal state of security and safety is turned into one of unsafety and/or insecurity. The figure below provides a schematic depiction of the temporary cessation of the state of normalcy, which generally goes through five different phases: from a state of normalcy (1) into an incubation phase (2), which culminates in an incident (3), and is followed by a phase of readjustment (4) before returning to a (new) state of normalcy (5) (Figure 1.5).

In the image, the state of normalcy ends because an incident materializes (at $t = 11$). This incident leads to a situation that is insecure or unsafe – or to a situation that is perceived as such. Moreover, it has a certain impact, which is expressed on the y-axis. Incidents may have a very severe impact (the red line), or a lower one (the yellow and the orange line). Moreover, incidents arise in different ways: sometimes, they materialize suddenly and have immediate impact. In this case, their so-called incubation phase is brief. Think of, for instance, a car accident or a terrorist attack as examples in case: here the cessation of safety and security is sudden and the sur-prise element is strong. Alternatively, incidents may materialise gradually over time, and/or their impact may only be noticed gradually. In this case, we may speak of a 'creeping crisis': a crisis that is slow-burning, that has 'a long incubation time and may keep simmering long after the 'hot phase' of the crisis is over. It does not have a clear beginning or ending' (Boin, Ekengren, and Rhinard 2020, 120). Examples of creeping crises are the COVID-19 pandemic or climate change: both have led to deep and extended senses of unsafety and insecurity at a crisis level. Neither came about suddenly; rather these crises crept up on us, and still managed to surprise us.

Once an incident materializes, the next phase emerges: that of readjustment, of returning to a state of normalcy after the heat of the incident has cooled down. Similar to the incubation phase, the adjustment phase can be brief, as is the case when an accident happens with minor impact, or long, when a crisis is protracted or the impact is wide-ranging and severe. Moreover, some incidents alter socio-economic reality to such a degree that a return to the previous state of normalcy is no longer possible. Think for instance of the disruptive force of the 9/11 terrorist attacks or the 1929 stock market crash: those were followed by a *new* state of normalcy after the readjustment phase ended, rather than a return to the state of normalcy from before.

Safety and security as fundamental human needs

We have seen that for most human beings in Western countries, a state of being safe and secure is a state of normalcy. The final question that needs answering is what the implication of this state of normalcy is. When seeking to understand the reasons why human beings work hard to make their life-world more safe and secure *and* why they are less and less tolerant when harms and hazards materialize in that secure(d) life-world, it turns out that both findings point to the same origin. Safety and security are fundamental requirements for human experience, they fall in the category of 'basic needs'. As a matter of fact, following the work of Abraham Maslow, when human beings' needs for safety and security are not fulfilled to a sufficient degree, they cannot blossom in other areas (Maslow, 1943, 379). In his hierarchy of needs, Maslow pointed out that safety is essential for human thriving: it follows immediately after the most elementary needs, called the physiological needs, which include breathing, eating and drinking, sleeping, homeostasis, and sex. In Maslow's line of reasoning, the categories of basic needs are consecutive in the sense that human beings can only focus on the 'higher' needs, once the 'lower' needs are met to a certain degree. For instance, he writes, when human beings consistently go hungry, they will have little room for anything else in their minds but to focus on finding sustenance. Once the most elementary needs of eating, drinking etcetera are met, then the next need on the list is being safe and secure. Here, too, a certain level of stability needs to be met before higher needs, such as loving and belonging, or self-development come into play. Society plays a crucial function in providing this sense of safety and security, according to Maslow: 'society ordinarily makes its members feel safe enough from wild animals, extremes of temperature, criminals, assault and murder, tyranny, etc. Therefore, in a very real sense, he no longer has any safety needs as active motivators. Just as a sated man no longer feels hungry, a safe man no longer feels endangered' (Maslow 1943, 379).

Note that Maslow's hierarchy of needs does not make a clear distinction between whether or not human beings *are* objectively safe, or whether they *perceive* themselves as being safe. For the topic at hand, however, this is a highly relevant distinction: as we have seen, there are many facts and figures available that appear to prove that we are living in safer times than any generation before us. At the same time, many people experience high degrees of anxiety and fear in general, and we have increasingly become less and less tolerant to risks, to harm and to hazards. This raises that question of whether or not we have managed to satisfy our need for safety and security sufficiently, even if, to all intents and purposes, the outwardly appearance is that this is certainly the case.

The answer to this question is that both are true. We *have* in fact managed to make our lives more safe and secure in the past centuries. At the same time, however, we also live in highly dynamic times. Since the Industrial Revolution, the pace of innovations has picked up, and our life-world is changing dramatically with every generation. The rise of digital technologies and globalization have strengthened that trend. And this dynamism leads to anxiety. As Anthony Giddens explains, when human beings find themselves in environments that are highly dynamic, they become 'obsessively preoccupied with apprehension of possible risks to [their] existence, and paralysed in terms of practical action' (Giddens 1991, 53). It is not surprising, therefore, that there is such a strong focus on safety and security in our times. They are basic needs, and while we work hard to fulfil these needs, at the same time the dynamism of our age entails that risks are still abundant and the fulfilment of our need for safe and secure lives, in that sense, is insufficiently met. This explains why we live relatively safe lives, especially in comparison to our forebears, but unfortunately, the fast pace of change in our times leads to a high perception of uncertainty. *Being secure* and *feeling secure*[3] apparently are two separate things.

Being secure versus feeling secure? A need for more research

In recent decades, several subfields within psychology have made inroads into shedding light on the role of interpersonal relationships, motivations, and attitudes to help explain this contrast. Two topics merit attention in this regard. First, there is the consistent finding that human beings have a deeply seated 'belief in a just world' (Lerner 1980): a need to believe that the world in which they live is just, in the sense that people in this world get what they deserve – good behaviour is ultimately rewarded, and bad behaviour is punished in some form or other (cf. Dalbert and Donat 2015; Furnham 2003; Hafer and Bègue 2005). This belief is an important motivator for positive behaviour. What is most striking for the current topic at hand, is that individuals actually tend to believe in the existence of *two* parallel worlds (Lerner 1980; Hafer and Bègue 2005): one in which they live themselves, with their close circle around them, and one which is more at a distance, occupied by human beings further removed from them socially, economically, physically, or a combination thereof. The former world is a just one, in which justice prevails and order and structure are respected. By contrast, in the latter world bad things may befall good people and vice versa. While many people would consider this to be unjust, in principle, by dividing the world into an immediate environment that is just, and a further removed reality that is not, people may relegate 'cases of injustice to another sphere of existence, thus reducing their relevance to [their] own environment' (Hafer and Bègue 2005, 145). Although it is challenging to do so, it would be worthwhile to test empirically whether or not individuals' sentiments about safety and security pertain predominantly to their own close-by reality, or rather to the further removed world where injustice is rampant.

A related strand of research in psychology on attachment theories also embraces the idea of a division between two worlds, here called the personal and the socio-political world. This strand of psychology uses this distinction between two different worlds to get a better understanding of safety and security in interpersonal relationships (Murray et al. 2021). According to Murray et al. the personal relational world is one in which individuals choose to be close to particular people and become (partially) dependent on them, for instance on their partner, friends, or friendly co-workers. The socio-political world, by contrast, is made up of people that are imposed on individuals, but with which a relationship with some degree of dependence exists nevertheless. Think for instance of one's employer or teacher, fellow citizens or politicians. In both worlds (inter)dependencies exist, and in both worlds it is important for individuals that there is level of certainty with respect to other parties' behaviours: being able to predict the behaviour of others is important to human beings, because it makes them feel safe. Now, in reality, of course, the behaviour of others is *not* always predictable. As a matter of fact, in both worlds, individuals will sometimes display unexpected behaviours: partners, friends, presidents, and employers may all act out of character sometimes. Research has brought up a fascinating finding: when unexpected behaviour emerges in individuals' personal world, they seek to restore their sense of safety by investing in their socio-political world, and when uncertainties emerge in individuals' socio-political world, they seek solace in their personal world (Murray et al. 2021). For instance, when disappointed by close friends or a partner (personal world), individuals may go out to seek new acquaintances (socio-political world), and when individuals worry over the socio-economic or political situation in their home country (socio-political world), they may seek to accommodate for that lack of safety by investing in their close relationships (personal world). One could label this system as a 'normative risk regulation system', to borrow a phrase from Holmes and Murray (2007, 164).

Similar to the belief in a just world, then, here too we find a distinction between a world that is closer by, and one that is further removed. And here, too, we see this distinction is used to somehow accommodate for risks or hazards, as a means to balance feelings of unsafety. What this research line in psychology so far has not addressed yet, however, is the tension between *being* secure and *feeling* secure. If we live in a world that is increasingly objectively secure, as this article has suggested, then why is it that feelings of anxiety have risen nevertheless? This strand of research in psychology has focused on the ways in which individuals 'repair' feelings of unsafety by focusing on another world. However, using Murray et al.'s 'social-safety system' approach, it would be worthwhile to investigate how the reality of living in an increasingly safe world has a bearing on the (strong) feelings of insecurity that we have seen emerging in the Western world in recent decades. Both strands of psychological research would enable us to shed more light on the impact of the experience of unsafety and insecurity in our modern times.

Notes

1 For a conceptual discussion on safety and security, see Van den Berg, Hutten, and Prins (2019) and Van den Berg, Prins, and Kuipers (2021).
2 The Human Development Index is calculated using factors in three key dimensions: (1) life expectancy, (2) knowledge (years of education), and (3) standard of living (GNI).

For more information, see https://hdr.undp.org/data-center/human-development-index#/ indicies/HDI

3 'Felt security' has been studied in the context of attachment theory in psychology. See for instance (Bowlby 1982; Baldwin 2007; Holmes and Murray 2007; Mikulincer and Shaver 2007).

References

Baldwin, Mark W. 2007. 'On Priming Security and Insecurity.' *Psychological Inquiry* 18 (3): 157–62.

Bankoff, Greg. 2012. 'Historical Concepts of Disaster and Risk.' In *The Routledge Handbook of Hazards and Disaster Risk Reduction*, edited by Ben Wisner, J. C. Gaillard, and Ilan Kelman, 37–48. Abingdon, NY: Routledge.

Beck, Ulrich. 2006. 'Living in the World Risk Society.' *Economy and Society* 35 (3): 329–45.

Bernstein, Peter L. 1998. *Against the Gods: The Remarkable Story of Risk*. New York: John Wiley & Sons Inc.

Boin, Arjen, Magnus Ekengren, and Mark Rhinard. 2020. 'Hiding in Plain Sight: Conceptualizing the Creeping Crisis.' *Risk, Hazards and Crisis in Public Policy* 11 (2): 116–38.

Bowlby, John. 1982. 'Attachment and Loss: Retrospect and Prospect.' *The American Journal of Orthopsychiatry* 52 (4): 664–78.

Cutter, Susan L. 1993. *Living with Risk*. New York: Wiley.

Dalbert, Claudia, and Matthias Donat. 2015. 'Belief in a Just World.' In *International Encyclopedia of the Social and Behavioral Sciences*, edited by J. D. Wright, 2nd ed., vol. 2: 487–92. Oxford, UK: Elsevier.

Furedi, Frank. 2008. 'Fear and Security: A Vulnerability-Led Policy Response.' *Social Policy & Administration* 42 (6): 645–61.

Furnham, Adrian. 2003. 'Belief in a Just World: Research Progress over the Past Decade.' *Personality and Individual Differences* 34: 795–817.

Giddens, Anthony. 1991. *Modernity and Self-Identity: Self and Society in the Late Modern Age*. Stanford, CA: Stanford University Press.

———. 1999. 'Risk and Responsibility.' *The Modern Law Review* 62 (1): 1–10.

Global Burden of Disease Collaborative Network. Global Burden of Disease Study 2019 (GBD 2019) Results. (2021). Seattle, United States: Institute for Health Metrics and Evaluation (IHME).

Hafer, Carolyn L. and Laurent Bègue. 2005. 'Experimental Research on Just-World Theory: Problems, Developments, and Future Challenges.' *Psychological Bulletin* 131 (1): 128–67.

Helliwell, J. F., Layard, R., Sachs, J. D., De Neve, J.-E., Aknin, L. B., and Wang, S. (eds). 2023. World Happiness Report 2023. New York: Sustainable Development Solutions Network

Holmes, John G. and Sandra L. Murray. 2007. 'Felt Security as a Normative Resource: Evidence for an Elemental Risk Regulation System?' *Psychological Inquiry* 18 (3): 163–67.

Lacina, B. and Gleditsch, N.P. (2005). 'Monitoring Trends in Global Combat: A New Dataset of Battle Deaths.' *European Journal of Population* 21 (2–3): 145–116.

Lerner, Melvin J. (ed.) 1980. 'The Belief in a Just World.' In *The Belief in a Just World*. Boston, MA: Springer, 9–30.

Luhmann, Niklas. 1990. 'Technology, Environment and Social Risk: A Systems Perspective.' *Industrial Crisis Quarterly* 4: 223–31.

Lupton, Deborah. 2013. *Risk*. 2nd ed. Abingdon, UK: Routledge.

Maslow, Abraham. 1943. 'A Theory of Human Motivation.' *Psychological Review* 50 (4): 370–96.

Mikulincer, Mario and Phillip R. Shaver. 2007. 'Reflections on Security Dynamics: Core Constructs, Psychological Mechanisms, Relational Contexts, and the Need for an Integrative Theory, Psychological Inquiry.' *Psychological Inquiry* 18 (3): 197–209.

Murray, Sandra L., Veronica Lamarche, Mark D. Seery, Han Young Jung, Dale W. Griffin, and Craig Brinkman. 2021. 'The Social-Safety System: Fortifying Relationships in the Face of the Unforeseeable.' *Journal of Personality and Social Psychology* 120 (1): 99–130.

Orencio, Pedcris M., Aiko Endo, Makoto Taniguchi, and Masahiko Fujii. 2016. 'Using Thresholds of Severity to Threats to and the Resilience of Human Systems in Measuring Human Security.' *Social Indicators Research* 129: 979–99.

Paté-Cornell, Elisabeth. 2012. 'On "Black Swans" and "Perfect Storms": Risk Analysis and Management When Statistics Are Not Enough.' *Risk Analysis: An Official Publication of the Society for Risk Analysis* 32 (11): 1823–33.

Pettersson, T., Therése Pettersson, Shawn Davies, Amber Deniz, Garoun Engström, Nanar Hawach, Stina Högbladh, Margareta Sollenberg, and Magnus Öberg (2021). 'Organized Violence 1989–2020, with a Special Emphasis on Syria.' *Journal of Peace Research* 58 (4): 12–25.

Pinker, Steven. 2018. *Enlightenment Now: The Case for Reason, Science, Humanism and Progress*. London: Allen Lane – Penguin Random House UK.

Riley, James C. 2001. *Rising Life Expectancy: A Global History*. New York: Cambridge University Press.

Rosling, Hans, Ola Rosling, and Anna Rosling Rönnlund. 2018. *Factfulness: Ten Reasons We're Wrong about the World – and Why Things Are Better than You Think*. First edition. New York: Flatiron Books.

Slovic, Paul. 1987. 'Perception of Risk.' *Science* 236 (4799): 280–85.

Turner, Barry A. 1976. 'The Organizational and Interorganizational Development of Disasters.' *Administrative Science Quarterly* 21 (3): 378–98.

United Nations. 1994. *Human Development Report 1994: New Dimensions of Human Security*. New York: Oxford University Press.

United Nations, Department of Economic and Social Affairs, Population Division (2022). World Population Prospects 2022, Online Edition.

Van den Berg, Bibi, Pauline Hutten, and Ruth Prins. 2019. 'Security and Safety: An Integrative Perspective.' In *International Security Management: New Solutions*, edited by Gabriele Jacobs, Ilona Suojanen, Kate Horton, and P. Saskia Bayerl, 13–27. Cham: Springer. https://doi.org/10.1007/978-3-030-42523-4_2

Van den Berg, Bibi, Ruth Prins, and Sanneke Kuipers. 2021. 'Assessing Contemporary Crises: Aligning Safety Science and Security Studies.' *Encyclopedia of Crisis Analysis*. Oxford: Oxford University Press. https://doi.org/10.1093/acrefore/9780190228637.013.1733

Zio, Enrico. 2018. 'The Future of Risk Assessment.' *Reliability Engineering & System Safety* 177: 176–90.

Zijdeman et al. (2015) (via clio-infra.eu); Riley, J. C. (2005). Estimates of Regional and Global Life Expectancy, 1800–2001. Population and Development Review, 31(3), 537–543. www.jstor.org/stable/3401478

Chapter 2

Looking for a safe self in a dangerous world

The place of psychotherapists: citizens – observers – beacons

Barbara Józefik and Bogdan de Barbaro

Introductory remarks

When writing our outline in 2021, we named it "A seemingly safe world." We believed we could focus on describing the circumstances affecting the social security level in terms of political and cultural changes occurring in Poland, with biological security (for a healthy and long life) and psychological security (for personal development) remaining in the background. We wanted to distinguish between inconspicuous (authentic) and apparent security. We assumed that a basic condition of inconspicuous social security is a system of state organization and its institutions, guaranteed by politicians' actions and citizens' activity, protecting the rights of citizens to take decisions in their own lives, without resigning from actions helping the common good, and following the principles of solidarity and care. We assumed inconspicuous security appears when conflicts in the social sphere are developmental, respect for the Other dominates in social relations, and the adherence of legal rules is guaranteed. Meanwhile, the narratives created by politicians do not lead to a zero-one distribution.

We intended to describe the phenomena of "apparent security" to show that, through politicians' actions, it is possible to designate the external, real, or false enemy, the Other, nominated as a stranger, and the conviction widespread in society that the authorities protect citizens against this enemy. Simultaneously, this leads to legitimizing restrictions in human rights under the apparent defense of state sovereignty and traditional values. Such apparent security is concentrated on ad hoc political goals, consists of building narratives contradicting the facts, and weakens the country's cultural and economic development and its political security.

We wanted to present, based on phenomena appearing in Poland, among others, political manipulation, with the victim being part of Polish society. In accordance with the systemic perspective, these phenomena are connected with processes occurring in the globalized world. Cultural consent for post-truth (in politics and public debate), impunity regarding the online distribution of hate and fake news, and the mutual drifting apart of liberal and conservative views of the world, are the circumstances that create – not only in Poland – apparent security. Russian aggression towards Ukraine, presented as a strategy for building security, is a

DOI: 10.4324/9781003308096-4

vivid example. We are experiencing how shameless lies support post-truth, hate is realized through war crimes, and attempts at deliberation between various groups change into hostile attacks and aggressive liquidation of differing versions (online censorship and forcing others into silence). Obviously, these phenomena appear outside Poland. However, a war has started in Poland's neighbor, and the technological revolution and life in cyberspace mean that the division into local and global is increasingly blurred. Therefore, the following reflections will concern both worldwide phenomena and local ones in Poland.

There are many reasons why, from a global perspective, the situation is currently (fall 2022) considered extremely dangerous and there is good reason to feel threatened.[1] The threat of nuclear weapons being used is growing, the economic consequences of the conflict are severe, and the sense of insecurity is present both in public and the therapy office. By understanding the sense of security as a feeling of experience and related to *what will be*, it is possible to indicate many circumstances showing the situation is serious and rightly causes deep concern. This does not mean that, during real danger, there are no mechanisms operating to maintain apparent security. Looking for the inconspicuous is therefore even more important. Thus, we will refer to both aspects in our work using our experience. The text's first author is a female clinical psychologist and psychotherapist who has worked with families and adolescents for years. The second author is a male psychiatrist working with psychotic patients and providing family and couples therapy. We are both closest to a systems approach and social constructionism, including attachment theory and a psychodynamic perspective, and are committed to working against social exclusion.

The issues' complexity and range restrict the reflections to selected phenomena, appearing at various levels, which according to systemic thinking influence one another. We begin by illustrating the general context and indicating those aspects that we believe are important when considering a sense of security linked with social, political, cultural and economic processes. We then move on to the local Polish historical and present perspective and finally look for actions that can provide hope.

General context: danger on a global scale

The threat of global war

Russia's war with Ukraine is significantly destabilizing the global economy, causing economic and political tensions, and threatening the spread of armed conflict. Many Western governments and societies remain in a dramatic conflict requiring specific solutions regarding the level of engagement and endangering their economic interests. It is unclear what the public mood in Europe will be in the coming months, whether the solidarity on display, resulting in a deteriorating material situation, will not contribute to crises in the idea of a cooperating Europe. We are almost helpless witnesses to a situation in which one man, probably supported to a large extent by the public, initiates a war, bringing with him suffering and death to countless victims. We are witnessing the ineffective actions of international institutions, such as the UN Security Council and the Court of Justice of the European Union, which do not have the tools to stop invasions and military actions.

The threat of climate catastrophes

The threat of climate catastrophes has not prompted politicians to take decisive and consistent steps. It's no coincidence that mainly young people and even teenagers (e.g., Greta Thunberg) are most involved in the struggle to change public consciousness, pressurizing politicians. They call for changes that decelerate the ongoing processes, which have irreversible and hard-to-imagine consequences.

Cognitive threat: indistinguishable truth and lies

Narratives based on post-truth are increasingly dominant in social and political discourse. The boundaries between event, fact, and opinion are increasingly blurred. Thus, the level of citizens' understanding of an otherwise complex reality decreases (Markowski, 2019). Citizens' minds are increasingly ruled by journalists (the so-called fourth power, although it sometimes seems to be the "first power"), ensuring the information is sensational and does not violate the recipient's existing map. This is a consequence of immersion in the consumer culture, for which sales and the associated profit – in this case viewing figures and the associated capabilities – are the basic values. The polarization of narratives reinforced by the filter bubble (Pariser, 2010) results in growing aggression, tension, and even hatred. Those representing professions that could be effective signalers of current and escalating threats (philosophers, ethicists, psychologists, climatologists, political scientists, historians and even psychiatrists) have too little influence on citizens who prefer simplistic knowledge. There is, as Tom Nichols (2017) puts it, an "agony of knowledge." The teaching of rationality and dialogue is disappearing.

Liberal democracy on the defense

Nationalist, populist, and xenophobic tendencies are growing in many countries (including those recently characterized by openness and liberal democracy). This may be a coping mechanism for the confusion, helplessness experienced facing the complexity and incoherence of reality in a globalized world, for expressing dissent and seeking a foothold by appealing to constructs of community, such as nations. The culture war threatens the sense of security both for conservatives, seeking security in protecting the status quo, and liberals (with programs containing universal freedom, which often is utopian and has apparent effects) (Deneen, 2018/2021). It is exceptionally difficult to have a forum (whether it be in journals, on television or the radio), where there can be a debate based on dialog, and not on annulment. The consequences are contradictory visions of reality, shared by followers ready to fight against facts, which are negated and interpreted within the framework of their system of convictions, despite the established legal regulations.

Postmodernism and its ethical-social consequences

Described by cultural anthropologists and philosophers as increasingly present this century, the values of hedonism, narcissism, and consumerism (sometimes described by scholars of neoliberalism as "Economy as a God") pose a serious threat to the individual's existential vulnerability and the idea of inter-personal and social cooperation that could counter the progressive anomie. The idea of cooperation remains in the dominant discourse in clear defiance of individualistic ideas appealing to narcissism and manic socioeconomic structures (Macdonald, Carabbio-Thopsey, and Goodman, 2022). A satisfactory and generally respected boundary between necessary fundamental civic freedom and socially harmful swagger ("everything goes") has not yet been found. For example, the challenge for those seeking to develop social security is the natural conflict between security and freedom, since protecting citizens condemns them to restrictions on their freedom.

Additionally, no satisfactory and generally respected ethical version has yet been found that can replace – during religious decline – the values that organize the individual's ethical horizon. This is reflected, among others, in the acceptance of persistent social inequality and a community, where 30,000 people die daily of starvation, spending money to conquer space.

Culture of neoliberalism and postmodernism

Here, we refer to the modern trends in psychology and psychotherapy, assuming the individual's responsibility for his fate. Medicine is similar: the individual takes full responsibility for health and long life by taking preventive measures, leading a healthy lifestyle, and eating properly. Thus, illnesses can be treated as personal culpable failures, something to be rather hidden, that cause embarrassment and do not deserve sympathy.

Additionally, many expectations and demands are directed toward the modern family, especially mothers, both from legal regulations formulating high childcare standards, and from psychology emphasizing the important bond that largely determines the developmental trajectories of offspring and related psychosocial functioning. We are dealing with a clash of two perspectives: traditional and postmodern, creating some confusion, intensified by existing social inequalities and differences in families' cultural capitals. It is difficult to consider both perspectives sufficient regarding the complex problems of modern times that are systemic in nature and require changes: different policies aimed at different problems. Assigning responsibility for solving dilemmas resulting from social-political-cultural change to the individual and family releases society and institutions from the effort of looking for functional solutions. A common denominator of such changes seems to be the victory of individualistic values over the values of empathy, cooperation, and solidarity within the liberal and neoliberal currents (Macdonald, Carabbio-Thopsey, and Goodman, 2022).

Thus, we are dealing with a possible global war, the looming climate catastrophe, cognitive chaos based on post-truth's triumph, and cultural patterns turning individuals away from cooperation, empathy, and concern for the vulnerable. The real challenge is taking action to foster a greater sense of social and individual security, either through responsible and care-driven policy actions at various levels implemented by different actors, or through activities to create a sense of apparent security among citizens.

Local Polish context

Historical perspective and damage to Polish identity

Reflection on Polish society's sense of security requires historical considerations. In the late 18th century, the great multi-ethnic, multi-national, multi-religious, and multi-cultural Polish-Lithuanian Commonwealth collapsed. It was incapable of development and maintaining its own structures, identity, and sense of security for its citizens, making it dependent on foreign states, their values, and their legal regulations. This created a peripheral space, delayed, and the Other became a stranger bringing danger (Sowa, 2012). Adaptation to the lost sovereignty, the assimilation of the partitioning powers' cultural elements (Russia, Prussia and Austria), and maintaining Polish mythology, as an adaptive mechanism, hindered long-term development, openness, and construction of a sense of pride and agency resulting from action and real influence. Consequently, there was a lack of constructive references, common symbols, which could build a strong identity (Poland regained its independence only in 1918). The experience of both world wars and 45 years of communism did not break these processes in all of society, confirming the theory of historians and sociologists regarding the existence of cultural memory. It has a long-lasting structure, storing the heritage of defined social groups and nations (Braudel, 1999).

Introducing the liberal democracy system in 1989, defined by the cultural and political elite as expected, bringing freedom and security, was not a joint project for all of society. For various groups, it became an excluding experience, and the predicted security was apparent, especially through the worsening material situation and the frequent loss of employment. Additionally, the traditional "Polishness – homeliness," connected with pre-modern cultural practices, being a subject of pride and an important element of identity, was challenged. Undermining Polish myths of suffering and sacrifice, confronting Western cultural patterns, and the need to adapt to the transformation became a threat, especially since liberal politicians' formulation of the "lagging behind modernity" narrative was associated with a policy of shaming groups remaining outside the neoliberal discourse (Czapliński, 2016).

The clash with the West's liberal culture created, and still creates, differences difficult to understand and assimilate for the traditional society functioning with a strong and conservative Catholic Church, which additionally defined the ongoing changes as threats that should be defended against and nowadays presents a strengthened xenophobic attitude. Initiated by Church representatives, the hostility to the politics of gender, emblematic for modern European culture, reinforced the emerging radically conservative discourse of hostility towards refugees, sexual minorities,[2] and restricting the right to abortion. In this way, the sense of security was threatened for many Poles.

Complex processes, reinforced by the narrative regarding the "loss of one's own culture in Europe" built by politicians and the Church hierarchy, shook the already brittle sense of identity in parts of society. The liberal elite's program, assuming individual identity development and security, was unsuitable for parts of society, expecting strong dependency to a community, the acceptance of responsibility for security and its provision, including material security. The response was support for the conservative parties, which accurately recognized these needs. However, by authoritarian rule, interfering in the constitutionally guaranteed judicial system, limiting the courts' and judges' independence, restricting individual rights and showing the Other as an enemy, in reality they offered society apparent security. Thus, a situation isomorphic to the family structure has occurred, where parents present the world as threatening, and control and limit their children's autonomy and freedom in the name of security. These phenomena, providing a description of the increasing populist and nationalist tendencies, not only appear in Polish society. They reflect, legible especially for systemic therapists, the above mentioned processes of globalization.

Sense of security in the current situation

Beyond Poland's eastern border, there is a war, with neither political scientists nor military experts predicting an imminent ending. The aggressor is Russia, a military and nuclear superpower without respect for the values accepted by Western nations. It attacks civilian targets, and breaks conventions generally accepted in the world. Unsurprisingly, the conflict evokes historical associations with past acts of violence in Polish-Russian relations, and activates traumas present in Polish national memory and transgenerational experiences. The latter, activated by the situation, are invoked in the psychotherapy office.

Simultaneously, despite being a frontier country with a potential threat for the sense of security, unequivocal support for Ukraine activated widespread social activity, civil solidarity, sympathy, and help. Consequently, Polish homes provided shelter to numerous Ukrainian refugees. Importantly, this happened through the spontaneous activity of citizens, months-long work of volunteers, and local government activities alongside the state's delayed and inadequate help. The activities resulting from accurate assessments of state institutions' apparent declarations protected against helplessness and fear, reinforcing the sense of subjectivity and empowerment.

This proactive attitude may explain the results obtained in the survey conducted between 2 and 12 May 2022. These were initially surprising because they show that, despite the war taking place just beyond our borders, the vast majority of those asked – 83 percent – believe that Poland is a safe country to live in (infosecurity, 2022). For the inconspicuous sense of security, the awareness of NATO and European Union membership cannot be overestimated.

So maybe it is not so bad ...

Nihil novi sub sole

Was the world ever safe and was ensuring a sense of security expected from past leaders? History shows that brutal conflicts, wars, genocide, regulations not providing basic human rights, the exclusion of whole ethnic groups, and social classes have been present for centuries. Stratification and the hierarchical structure of society meant that only privileged groups and individuals could build a sense of security unavailable for others. This was accompanied by natural disasters, low standards of living and medical care, and limited participation in the resources and achievements of given societies.

Beneficial changes

So, considering that it has long been dangerous and the problem of individual and collective responsibility remains a challenge, it is worth highlighting that, recently, beneficial global changes have also taken place. In other words: maybe it is not so bad, perhaps it is worth noting the positives. The Roslings (2018) wrote about this referring to a large amount of statistical data and research. These changes concern not only the economic, ecological, educational, and human health situation that they describe, but also many aspects of social life: a civil society is developing, the patriarchy is falling, social attention to the excluded and abused is increasing, as are ecological awareness and sensitivity towards animals. The average life expectancy is growing, and medicine is more effective against illnesses. This is happening thanks to, among others, the development of natural sciences, cultural studies, and gender studies researching ways of practicing femininity and masculinity in various social-cultural conditions. Consequently, legal regulations for equality regardless of gender, race, social origin, nationality, ethnicity, and sexual orientation are being introduced.

Awareness of the significance of biopolitics

Social awareness is increasing regarding the importance of analysis of bio power – power over biology, realized in the form of defined biopolitics (Foucault, 2011).

Nowadays, this covers increasingly more dimensions of human functioning subject to legal regulations. It concerns sexuality (e.g., permitted age of sexual intercourse, use of contraception measures), fertility (e.g., in vitro fertilization, abortion restrictions, or bans), regulations regarding relationships (e.g., age restrictions, homosexual relationships permitted or not), regulations concerning medical treatment and life support, and genetic standards (e.g., organ transplants), to name just a few. This means that, while thinking about security, we must, besides the global view, consider the situation from the individual perspective. Is it possible for a young woman or elderly person to feel safe? Is there access to health care and what is it like? To social care? For children, the elderly, the disabled? An equally important area is education, its level, availability, possibility of its continuation, and the lack of ideology. The situation in Poland in these areas is tense and unsatisfactory, although in the long term there is an opportunity for positive change due to the growing awareness of such matters, the actions taken by activists, experts, NGO workers, as well as pressure from interested social groups.

And so ..., what is possible?

What psychologists, psychiatrists, and psychotherapists can do

How, in respect of this great challenge facing the world, can (should) a citizen – a resident of this globe these days – behave? Where is the border between personal responsibility for creating a sense of security and the role of the state – politicians, local communities, religious communities, and professional groups, including psychotherapists?

The search for "how to live" has a long history, dating back to ancient times, and the thoughts of Epicurus, Epictetus, or Marcus Aurelius are valuable tips for many modern people. However, it is worth paying attention to the fact modern psychologists, psychiatrists, and psychotherapists increasingly and more boldly leave the confines of their offices and, risking accusations of being biased, speak on public issues (e.g., Robins and Post, 1997/2007; Lee, 2017). Goodman and Severson state that "might ethics also serve as a first psychology"[3] (2016, p. 9). Analyses of the political, economic, and social situation in today's world also appear, with the source and starting point being observations from psychotherapists' offices (e.g., Tweedy, 2017; Keval, 2016; Akhtar, 2018). Perhaps the essence of this perspective can be summarized using Samuels' words that "they [people] have to recognize that the human psyche is a political psyche" (Samuels, 2001, p. 21), and the *political* self he describes looks like a category organizing the narrative around the modern world. Slightly different, but also touching the same phenomena, Sugarman writes: "The Personal is Political" (2022, p. 14). The idea is to use psychotherapeutic knowledge as a perspective and tool for social criticism (Samuels, 2001). Postulating the inclusion of psycho-therapeutic and psychological knowledge in politics and action to increase social awareness of the active mechanisms, Samuels emphasizes the experience of clinical psychotherapists. He believes including it in social critique allows the influence of subconscious emotions and urges to be limited in social, political, and organizational life, and replaced by a "useful attitude" released from emotions (Samuels, 2001).

Increasingly often, psychotherapeutic knowledge is shared with society, presenting the mechanisms, consequences of politicians' actions. Consequences that not only move us away from mentalizing, understanding the complexity and magnitude of perspectives, but, on the contrary, aim to simplify, reinforcing fears, a sense of threat, and awakening xenophobia. We can find a wide range of works analyzing the functioning of social groups, social conflicts using the language of psychotherapy theory, psychoanalysis, and systemic theory. Erlich used psychoanalytical concepts to understand the phenomena of paranoia and hostility in groups and organizations (2016) and LaCapra analyzed the memory of trauma, its presentation, and the post-traumatic culture relating to Freud's theory (1998).

The works of Polish psychotherapists include Leder's book *Prześniona rewolucja* (*Sleepwalking the revolution*) (2014) analyzing the shape of Polish identity and the symbolic Polish revolution since 1939, based on Lacanian psychoanalysis. The author, analyzing Polish *imaginarium*, shows the historical events resulting in the murder of Jews and revolutionary changes in social relations perceived as external, carried out by "others," without recognizing the consequences of being a witness and participant of this process. He believes this transpassivity hinders the construction of Polish subjectivity, conscious influence of social reality and taking responsibility for the events, defining and experiencing Polish identity.

In a publication edited by Zajenkowska (2016), psychotherapists describe the current social processes in Poland, analyzing the emotions: embarrassment, humiliation, rage, hostility, dependence, convictions of grandeur, traumas that are non-verbalized, non-mentalized and intergenerational transmission of such experiences. Grzegołowska-Klarkowska (2016), discussing mourning after the Smolensk plane crash that killed the Polish president, his wife, and prominent political figures, shows how unfinished individual mourning, personalized and politicized, is part of the unfinished mourning of unaddressed national traumas. Her analysis corresponds with the thoughts of Prot-Klinger (2016), who, relating to the works of Freud, Klein, and Bion, analyzes mechanisms that activate themselves when social groups experience traumatic events caused by another group consciously subjecting them to suffering, helplessness, and humiliation, characteristic for military, ethnic, and religious conflicts. Not addressing the feelings of the victim: embarrassment, humiliation, a sense of guilt connected with the experience, and difficulty mourning the loss, results in the trauma being passed down to the following generations, creating a sense of dependence and co-building identity. It is not necessary to convince people about the importance of these matters both from an individual perspective and for all of Polish society.

Psychotherapists' reflections therefore concern such phenomena as trauma, racism, the exclusion of others and dehumanization, ethnic nihilism able to appear in a neoliberal climate, *shaming*, and other phenomena reducing subjectivity. The general tone of such analysis leads to the warnings (directed towards citizens, but also to psychotherapists): "be careful and sensitive to what is happening in the world," "not everything can be led to a subjective construct" (this last postulate of Sugarman seems to be an additional comment on social constructionists, op. cit., p. 21).

Social activity of psychotherapists in Poland

Since psychotherapy's development began, psychotherapists have observed a connection between the events in culture and society and what patients bring to the therapy office, and currently we expect them to perform actions to help social change (McCarthy and Simon, 2016). This challenge is particularly addressed to systemic therapists perceiving the connection between macro-structures (society), mezzo-structures (family), and micro-structures (individuals). Fifty years ago, Bateson (1972) showed the work of systemic therapists as practitioners should not be closed inside the office.

Polish psychotherapists, earlier only slightly active, have recently undertaken more steps to help social change. They publish their observations on civil sensitivity and the defense of universal humanistic values in professional journals (e.g., Bobrzyński, 2019). Despite the opposition of some psychotherapists (under the slogan of "let's leave politics to the politicians"), therapists discuss social issues as individual authors of mass-media publications, at Polish psychotherapy conferences, and also by publishing open letters. An example: an open letter critical of the Polish Bishops' Conference's stance towards LGBT+, discriminating against such people and suggesting reparative therapy. Or a letter against politicians' statements discriminating against and ridiculing trans-gender people. Psychotherapeutic associations place constant pressure on legal regulations to ensure, within refunded health care, the widest psychotherapy offer. In the pandemic, during heightened sanitary regulations, they intervened so parents could spend time with children in neonatal and pediatric wards. The great activity of psychotherapists, partially realized in NGOs, concerns the fight against violence towards children and neglect, whereas work has recently been conducted in various forms with refugees.

Ending

This is only a drop of protest in an ocean of injustice and evil, but it is worth justifying the attitude of protest with three old yet still relevant quotes. In the 2nd century, Marcus Aurelius advised: *If you see bad things happening around, then find some good act for yourself.* In the 18th century, Edmund Burke (1729–1797) said: *The only thing necessary for the triumph of evil is for good men to do nothing.* More recently, Martin Luther King warned: *It's not the violence of the few that scares me, it's the silence of the many.*

These words justify the sense of opposition against evil and the sense behind speaking up by those who, due to their profession, perceive the connection between what is happening on a social level and to individuals. Social awareness of hazards can provide material for "self-refutable theory," where the description of threats leads to the prevention of disasters. Rene Jules Dubos suggested (Gianinazzi, 2018): "think globally, act locally" to not leave matters to "run their own course." Psychotherapists may (and should) indicate the senselessness of *splendid isolation*, encourage experts' return and the distinction between events, facts, and opinions, discourage from simplified views of complicated problems, and raise awareness of the necessity to look after one's mind and to distinguish emotional reactions from reflections. The civil duties of psychologists and psychiatrists, as people rich in experience taken from the therapy office, should perhaps include warnings against inactivity, hostility, and xenophobia often activated by politicians, taking people from minority groups under protection, and distinguishing the threat "from-culture." The starting point for introducing changes influencing the sense of inconspicuous security should be whether social and cultural processes, occurring in a defined context, favor the building of a sense of subjectivity and guarantee the right of individuals to their own choices, as well as if these are respected. This invites citizens to actively participate in social life.

Such a view also means psychotherapists face an especially important and responsible task of signaling danger and co-creating a method to restrict the risk of catastrophes.

Notes

1 The situation is so dynamic that its presentation may constantly change. However, we believe it is a useful current description, even if it could be archival next weeks.
2 One Polish archbishop named the LGBT+ movement the "rainbow plague" in a sermon.
3 This is a paraphrase of Emanuel Levinas' theory (E. Levinas, Ethics as first philosophy. In. S. Hand (Ed.), *The Levinas Reader*. Cambridge, MA: Blackwell 1989): "Morality is not a branch of philosophy, but first philosophy."

References

Akhtar, S. (2018). Mind, Culture, and Global Unrest. Psychoanalytical Reflections. London: Routledge.

Bateson, G. (1972). Steps to an Ecology of Mind. Chicago: University of Chicago Press.

Bobrzyński J. (2019). Milczenie jest prawdziwą zbrodnią – głos psychoterapeuty w sprawach obywatelskich. Psychoterapia, 1, 5–17.

Braudel, F. (1999). Historia i trwanie. Przekł. B Geremek. Warszawa: Czytelnik.

Czapliński, P. (2016). Wojna wstydów. Teksty Drugie Teoria literatury, krytyka, interpretacja. 4/2016, Electronic version, URL: http://journals.openedition.org/td/4143

Deneen, P.J. (2018). Why Liberalism Failed? New Haven: Yale University Press.

Erlich, S.H. (2016). Envy and its dynamic in Organizations. In: R.H. Smith, U. Merlone, and M.K. Duffy (eds.), Envy at Work and in Organizations. DOI: http://dx.doi.org/10.1093/acprof:oso/9780190228057.003.0009

Foucault, M. (2011). Narodziny biopolityki. Wykłady z Collège de France 1978/1979. Warszawa: Wydawnictwo Naukowe PWN.

Gianinazzi, W. (2018). Penser global, agir local. Histoire d'une idée, EcoRev. Revue critique d'écologie politique, 46, 24.

Goodman, D.M. and Severson E.R. (2016). The Ethical Turn Otherness and Subjectivity in Contemporary Psychoanalysis. London: Routledge.

Grzegołowska-Klarkowska, H.J. (2016). Niedokończona żałoba. W poszukiwaniu facylitującego charyzmatycznego lidera. In: A. Zajenkowska (ed.), Polska na kozetce. Siła obywatelskiej refleksyjności. Sopot: Smak Słowa, pp. 87–110.

Heather M., Carabbio-Thopsey S., and Goodman D.M. (2022). Neoliberalism, Ethics and the Social Responsibility of Psychology. London: Routledge, p. 12.

INFOSECURITY24 (2022, June 09) https://infosecurity24.pl/bezpieczenstwo-wewnetrzne/polacy-nadal-czuja-si-bezpiecznie

Keval, N. (2016). Racist States of Mind. Understanding the Perversion of Curiosity and Concern. London: Karnac.

LaCapra, D. (1998). History and Memory after Auschwitz. Ithaca, NY: Cornell University Press.

Leder, A. (2014). Prześniona rewolucja: Ćwiczenia z logiki historycznej. Warszawa: Wydawnictwo Krytyki Politycznej.

Lee, B. (ed.) (2017). The Dangerous Case of Donald Trump. New York: St. Martin's Press.

McCarthy, I. and Simon, G. (eds.) (2016). Systemic Therapy as Transformative Practice. Farnhill: Everything is Connected Press.

Macdonald, H., Carabbio-Thopsey S., and Goodman, D.M. (eds.) (2022). Neoliberalism, Ethics and the Social Responsibility of Psychology. London: Routledge, p. 12.

Markowski, M.P. (2019). Wojny nowoczesnych plemion. Kraków: Karakter.

Nichols, T. (2017). The Death of Expertise: The Campaign against Established Knowledge and Why It Matters. New York: Oxford University Press.

Pariser, E. (2010). The Filter Bubble: How the New Personalized Web Is Changing What We Read and How We Think? London: Penguin Books.

Prot-Klinger, K. (2016). Społeczne konsekwencje nieprzepracowanej traumy. In: A. Zajenkowska (ed.). Polska na kozetce. Siła obywatelskiej refleksyjności. Sopot: Smak Słowa, pp. 111–142.

Robins, R.S. and Post J.M. (1997). Political Paranoia: The Psychopolitics of Hatred. New Haven, CT: Yale University.

Rosling, H., Rosling, O., and Rosling-Ronnlund A. (2018). Factfulness: Ten Reasons We're Wrong About the World – and Why Things Are Better Than You Think. New York: Flatiron Books.

Samuels, A. (2001). Politics on the Couch: Citizenship and the Internal Life. London: Karnac.

Sowa, J. (2012). Fantomowe ciało króla. Peryferyjne zmagania z nowoczesną formą. Warszawa: PWN.

Sugarman, J. (2022). The Personal Is Political. A Conversation with Jeff Sugarman. Interviewed by Mark Freeman. In: H. Macdonald, S. Carabbio-Thopsey, and D. M. Goodman (eds.), Neoliberalism, Ethics and the Social Responsibility of Psychology. London: Routledge.

Tweedy, R. (2017). The Political Self: Understanding the Social Context for Mental Illness. London: Karnac.

Zajenkowska, A. (2016). Polska na kozetce: Siła obywatelskiej refleksyjności. Sopot: Smak Słowa.

Chapter 3

When home becomes a threat

Polish experience of homo-, bi-, and transphobia

Daniel Bąk

Introduction

I am a Gestalt psychotherapist and supervisor. I was born in Poland, where I live and work. My mental health practice is international, primarily with clients and supervisees from diverse LGBT+ communities. I am also a gay cis-male.

As a child and young adolescent, I was an introverted, significantly obese, and anxious boy whose self-esteem was based solely upon educational and intellectual achievements. I was reared by pretty old parents who decided to raise their third child late. Both of them are World War II survivors with unresolved childhood and war traumas. I do believe they wanted to provide me with emotional safety and nurturance. However, apart from moments of loving care, physical connection, and emotional support, I also experienced a lot of rejection, emotional neglect, and taking mental and bodily autonomy from me. My family home was a shaky ground with no witnesses. The three of us – my parents and I – constituted a closed system with impermeable boundaries; my siblings were adults at that time, living on their own. An add-on to this interpersonal trauma of my family home was primary school. I used to be regularly bullied not only for being obese but also for my gender non-conforming behaviours. Other boys never wanted to choose me to play on their team and also called me a "faggot". Somehow I felt that in this pejorative way they had been naming and referring to my emerging sexuality, with which I could come out to myself only two decades later. Together, it placed me really low down the chain in my peers' hierarchy. After all, my childhood and adolescence coincided with the period of communism and early transformation to capitalism in Poland. Times were tough and challenging, which only made my situation worse. I was one of many Polish children experiencing parents who were emotionally and/or physically absent and absorbed with the demands of the changing world.

My childhood and adolescence experiences equipped me with rather insecure attachment adaptations. I entered early adulthood ranking really high on attachment avoidance and attachment anxiety dimensions. Only with the help of psychotherapists was I able to learn to relate in a more secure manner. In the end, being a

DOI: 10.4324/9781003308096-5

psychotherapist myself I have sufficient relational groundedness to become a secure attachment figure for my clients. However, in situations of significant psychological distress my attachment insecurities may still unveil themselves. Typically for the post-trauma responses, I may temporarily lose my sense of safety, not being able to experience my body and mind as fundamental supports. Thankfully, after years of therapy, I have got now my own ways to "be back".

I live in a country of political violence (Punamäki, 2021) directed at LGBT+ citizenry. Polish society is acutely polarised when it comes to political choices and emotional attitudes towards people having opposite voting preferences (Górska, 2019). From my personal standpoint this political split has fuelled hostility aimed at LGBT+ citizens, above all, hate speech (Soral, 2021). The societal homo-, bi-, and transphobic prejudices and stereotypes have been used by the right-wing president, government, and parliament to achieve their own political goals. Depending on *ad hoc* political needs, the governing bodies in Poland present LGBT+ community to the general society as sexually and mentally disordered people (likely paedophiles), destroyers of the family, devastators of the Catholic tradition, or ideological backers of the supposedly leftist EU. These right-wing populists have received enormous support from the Catholic Church in Poland (Tilles, 2020a, 2020c, 2021). In my opinion, polarisation processes between varied political forces (in cooperation with the Catholic Church) and LGBT+ citizens in Poland should be understood in the context of contemporary Polish history. In post-communist Poland not only right-wing, but also left-wing governments failed to provide human rights to the LGBT+ citizenry. Being recognised as one of the main pillars of Polish freedom after 1989, the Catholic Church was able to back such a situation significantly. Due to the entanglement between the Church and Polish politics, a religious and therefore also moral issue of gender and sexual diversity became a subject of the political conflict. In this way, the Church's impact has been severely stifling the LGBT+ emancipation processes for decades.

This practice of instrumentally used hate speech, purposeful prevarication, and calculated turning people against each other, implemented by the governing bodies and Catholic Church, results in the alarmingly poor social situation and a significant decrease in markers of psychological well-being among Polish LGBT+ citizenry. According to the latest report on the situation of LGBT+ people in Poland for 2019–2020 (Bulska et al., 2021), 52.9% of participants experienced a hate crime on grounds of their gender identity or sexual orientation; 45.0% of participants experienced cyberbullying; 43.9% of participants exhibited severe symptoms of depression (in the report for 2015–2016 it was 28.4%); 51.5% of participants (LGB data only) declared having suicidal thoughts (it was 42.8% in 2015–2016); 16.5% of participants experienced at least one episode of homelessness (no access to safe accommodation) – among them, for every tenth person (10.6%), that episode was longer than a year. Clearly, hatred sponsored by the Polish right-wing populists has reaped its harvest. In comparison to 2015–2016, the latest report shows a fall in trust – measured as increase in the percentage of people declaring complete lack of trust – in the government (from 71.6% to 88.4%), police (from 13.2% to 42.1%), and judiciary (from 10.4% to 21.9%). At the same time increase in trust – measured as increase in the percentage of people declaring a significant degree of trust or a lot of trust – in LGBT+ organisations (from 82.0% to 90.4%), other NGOs (from 66.2% to 70.6%), and the EU (from 67.6% to 82.8%) has been observed.

A tipping point for me, as a gay man with attachment struggles, was 2019/2020. In his homily in August 2019, the archbishop of Kraków, Marek Jędraszewski, used the phrase "the rainbow plague" to describe the current LGBT+ liberation endeavours in Poland, making an explicit connotation to the so-called red plague of Marxism and Bolshevism in Polish history (Ash, 2020). A similar dehumanising message was sent by Andrzej Duda to his electorate in his second presidential campaign in 2020 when he said: "They try to convince us that these [LGBT+ community] are people, but it is simply an ideology" (Tilles, 2020b). At that time my sense of belonging to Poland as my homeland collapsed. Not only was it about a concept of a home country, but also about the Polish society I wanted to distance myself from instantly. My fellow citizens voted for LGBT+ hatred-driven political parties in parliamentary elections thrice. I could not ignore this fact then and I am not ready to overlook it now. Clearly, in such – I dare to say – re-traumatising circumstances, my attachment adaptations learnt in childhood started informing my behavioural and emotional reactions. I reacted to the broader socio-political context as to the attachment figure that failed to deliver security to me, bringing the homophobia-driven dread instead. I felt rejected and threatened. In my perception of what happened, other Poles endangered my existence, took hope for the better future in Poland from me as a gay man. I answered with anxiety, then rage, additional English classes, and plans to leave the country in the future. However, I stayed, finally. I will stay as long as needed for family reasons. Still, on an everyday basis I have to look for internal and external support to stay emotionally grounded, with a sense of personal agency, and with the feeling that my close ones and I are safe in Poland. Nonetheless, not only does the attachment theory potentially help to understand what happens between me, the individual, and the broader field of state politics and society, but obviously it also explains the microscale of interpersonal dynamics. As a Gestalt therapist, I would say that at the contact boundary between me and the homophobic, patriarchal, and misogynistic Polish field, the embodied experience of my own homosexuality emerges. Attachment and identity processes seem to be intertwined (Carmen Joanne Ablack, personal communication, 7 September 2022). I cannot escape the reality that oppressive socio-cultural narratives in Poland inform, at least to some extent, the way I love and can be loved, date and can be dated, lust and can be lusted after, care in same-gender relationships and can be cared for by other men. Environmental, also institutionalised homophobia, and misogyny may result in marginalisation, discrimination, and bare physical violence. When internalised, these oppressive attitudes may hinder, or even devastate, sexual encounters and/or love relationships. Same-gender secure attachment and belonging in Poland may be difficult to achieve.

Society and culture as attachment figures and moderators

One of my therapy teachers told us during a workshop: "How you do one thing is how you do everything". At that time, being a rather unexperienced psychotherapist, I thought it was a simplistic statement, an obvious generalisation to be cautious with. Today I know we were just encouraged to look for relational patterns. The relational approach (Stawman, 2009) strongly informs my theoretical thinking as well as clinical practice. From the relational point of view, every exchange between the self and environment – being it the other person, an item, animal, idea, institution, and so forth, can be considered a relation. The relational repertoire in a given person, this set of means to be in the relation, is always limited. We repeat what we learnt, especially from our primary care givers. I understand attachment adaptations (some would probably prefer to call them "attachment styles") as a crucial part of this repertoire. From my clinical experience, attachment adaptations founded on the early relational encounters seem to be evoked every time when danger, safety, and belonging issues are at play. When I write "every time", it means that it does not have to be about particular people, or it does not even have to be about people at all.

When I go back to my own example previously described, I can see that I reacted to homo-, bi-, and transphobia of the contemporary Polish socio-political context accordingly to my learnt attachment adaptation. Can we consider the society or state being experienced as attachment figures by LGBT+ people? Can we regard such prejudicial features of the socio-cultural domain as homo-, bi-, and transphobia as moderators of the attachment relationship? I hypothesise to say "yes" to both questions.

The contact boundary – exchange that yields attachment

I find Kurt Lewin's field theory (1953) and a construct of the contact boundary (Perls, Hefferline, and Goodman, 1951/2006) probably the most profound theoretical developments in Gestalt psychotherapy. Together, they enable a broadened – not individualistic but relational – perspective on clients' issues brought to the consulting room. The contact boundary is Gestalt imagery depicting constant exchange between the organism and environment. According to the founders of the Gestalt approach in psychotherapy (Perls, Hefferline, and Goodman, 1951/2006), the contact boundary is a true locus of the self. The self is a quality that concurrently belongs to the organism and its environment. The self does not exist without this exchange. Neither does attachment. To come into being, attachment needs environmental stimuli as well as organismic responsiveness. The former for the infant are most often parental figures with the care they provide. However, the environmental aspect of the contact boundary is more complex. It includes everyone and everything that can reach the boundary and goes far beyond the essential dyadic relationships, for example, between child and father, or between sexual partners. As a result, the environment means all factors affecting crucial attachment relationships. Every attachment relationship is embedded in given societal, cultural, and political interconnected fields. From this perspective, there is no scenario that homo-, bi-, and transphobia present in the field are avoidable and do not inform attachment opportunities for children, adolescents, and adults. In her nested model of trauma and attachment, Jessica Fern (2020) analyses such multiple influences.

The nested model of trauma and attachment by Jessica Fern

Attachment and trauma are indivisible. Lack of safe, nurturing relationships can directly cause trauma. On the other side, the secure attachment can serve as a protective bulwark against trauma. In her nested model of attachment and trauma, Fern (2020) attempted to describe interconnectedness of these two phenomena:

> trauma and attachment wounds are not just an individual or relational experience. They also stem from the world we are in, where injustice and power imbalances still exist, and where generations of cultural and collective traumas have been unaddressed, all shaping and informing our experiences.
>
> (pp. 76–77)

She points to a few different levels of human experience being vital to understand intersections of attachment and trauma:

- Self – this level refers to the individual self, which has, for example, specific temperamental and genetic characteristic, attachment history, thoughts, feelings, skills, dislikes, longings, identities, and their own ways to perceive and interpret others.
- Relationship – this level refers to one's interpersonal experiences with their parents, siblings, friends, romantic and/or sexual partners, and so forth.
- Home – this level refers to the ways one's family interacted as a whole, and how the actual physical home influenced attachment.
- Local communities and culture – this level refers to places such as work, school, friends' houses, sport venues, religious or spiritual centres, online fora, and social media groups – communities and cultures outside the house.
- Societal – this level refers to the larger societal structures and systems people live in, above all political, legal, and economic systems, as well as religious institutions.
- Global or collective – this level refers to issues concerning protection of our planet – especially climate change, and also to collective traumas such as slavery, famine, war, genocide, subjugation of women, or persecution of homosexual people by the post-World War II psychiatry and psychoanalysis (APA, 2009). What happens at this level affects people directly involved at a given historical time, but the consequences permeate also to the next generations.

As Fern (2020) considers every level interacting and influencing the others, she presents them as nested with "Self" being the central one. Research and psycho-therapeutic narratives on attachment and trauma most often concentrate on the Self and Relationship levels. This focus is understandable. Relationships we are in shape our attachment adaptations. In return, these adaptations determine, to a considerable extent, our behaviours, feelings, thoughts, and perceptions that occur in relationships. Nevertheless, to have a regard only to the Self and Relationship levels seems to be unjustified reduction of our thinking about trauma and attachment development. Structural violence (Galtung, 1969), originating at the Societal level, might be a proper example. This type of violence means social processes such as heteronormativity, homo-, bi-, and transphobia, or cissexism, that produce and perpetuate inequalities leading to social exclusion of certain groups, for example, LGBT+ people. Consequences of such marginalisation, for instance, minority stress in LGBTs+ (Meyer, 1995) and its clinical repercussions, such as depression, anxiety, high suicidality, low self-esteem, substance abuse, eating disorders, or sexual disfunction (Grabski et al., 2019; Mijas et al., 2021), penetrate further to the levels of "Local Communities and Culture", "Home", "Relationship", and finally – "Self". The following fictitious clinical vignette illustrates multiple influences on attachment adaptation in the LGBT+ client.

The client is a 31-year-old Polish gay white cis-male, describing himself as a non-practicing Roman Catholic. During the first session, he presents with severe depression (Self level). In childhood, he experienced conditional parental acceptance. All his gender non-conforming behaviours and interests were verbally punished, sometimes with temporary contact withdrawal afterwards. He learnt to hide his emerging gendered self as well as sexual fantasies about other boys – in adolescence, and men – later in life. Especially his mother used to be really vocal about "dirtiness" of Pride Marches and "putting children to jeopardy from homosexuals" by local governments' approval of such gatherings. The message he took from the relationship with parents was that his maleness and gayness do not deserve a loving bond. That way the insecure attachment adaptation arose (Relationship level). In primary and secondary school this message was only strengthened. The client was called a "faggot" or "pussy", and laughed at. Moreover, he was sometimes slapped in the face, "to prove his weakness and inferiority to him" – that is what perpetrators kept saying to him. There was no strong reaction from teachers and he decided not to tell parents about violence at school. He did not expect help (Relationship level). Furthermore, the client had two siblings – a sister a year younger and a brother two years older. Both were gender conforming children and adolescents. The brother was favoured by the father (Home level). The client felt he could not compete with his brother for father's love and attention (Relationship level). As a boy, the client was extremely religious, attended masses regularly, participated in religion classes at school, and absorbed the Catholic sexual ethics as a result (Local Communities and Culture level). He entered adolescence equating sex and sexuality to a sin, homosexuality being the greatest of them (Self level). The client has been identifying himself as a gay man only for two years now. Earlier he had spent a few months in a facility delivering so-called "conversion therapy" to homosexual people that wanted to be heterosexual. That "therapy centre" (in quotes since homosexuality is a normative sexual identity; conversion practices should not be called a therapy; they are considered harmful and unethical – De Groot, 2022) was religiously informed and associated with the Catholic Church (Local Communities and Culture level). Conversion attempts at the centre were founded on the theoretical claims typical of the 1950s through the 1970s of the 20th-century psychiatry that pathologised homosexuality using psychoanalysis as justification (APA, 2009). He was shamed for who he was, as were thousands of gay men before him (Global or Collective level). When he understood and accepted he would not change himself, he finally came out as gay (Self level). However, he internalised many homophobic assumptions and prejudices over the years, for example, "homosexuality is not a valid sexual identity", "homosexuality is a mental disorder", "gay men are not able to form long term loving relationships", "gay men spread HIV/AIDS", or "gay men are likely paedophiles". The current socio-political situation in the country does not help to get rid of these harmful messages. One of the most important Church officials coined a new queer-phobic insult – "the rainbow plague". The president of Poland named LGBTs+ ideology, not people. Moreover, social media are full of pictures of the latest attack on the Pride March in a big Polish city (Societal level). At the declarative level, the client would like to have a romantic relationship. Nonetheless, he rejects every man attracted to him not only sexually but also emotionally. Over the years, satisfying sex with other men became possible, although he has always been struggling with an emotional bond with a male partner. What had started with stereotypic gender expectations and homosexuality pathologisation (Societal and Global or Collective levels) finished with a wounded Self and insecure attachment adaptation.

It seems to be obvious that such prejudicial features of the socio-cultural domain as homo-, bi-, and transphobia are moderators of attachment. I would even risk a hypothesis that this moderation is unescapable for all of us, irrespective of gender and/or sexual identity, as homo-, bi-, and transphobic violence is sadly an integral part of the universal socialisation processes in so-called Western culture. Nevertheless, the most detrimental consequences should be expected in LGBT+ people. But, could the state with its socio-cultural and political context be considered not only the attachment moderating factor but also the attachment figure itself?

The state/society/culture as the attachment figure

The attachment behavioural system (Bowlby, 1969) enables three inborn, instinctual reactions to danger or insecurity: (1) looking for, monitoring, and staying close to the protective attachment figure, (2) perceiving and using the attachment figure as the secure base to explore unknown, and potentially dangerous places and experiences, and (3) resorting to the attachment figure perceived to be the safe haven when confronted with fear or threat.

For the LGBT+ citizens, legal protection guaranteed (or not) by a given country is central for their psychological well-being, the organisation of their daily lives (e.g., legally recognised partnership or marriage; parenthood), and sometimes – literally – for their survival. There are countries where homosexual people can still be sentenced to death because of their psychosexual needs. The central role of the state (the parliament, government, and president) is also apparent for the Polish LGBT+ citizenry. In particular, since the political transformation of 1989, the Polish state has not ensured any form of legally recognised same-gender partnership; a humanitarian legal procedure of gender recognition – trans people must sue their parents to make modifications in their birth certificates; adequate legal recognition and protection for children raised by same-gender parents; recognition of hate crimes motivated by homo-, bi, or transphobia (Gierdal et al., 2018). Among EU countries, contemporary Poland is a disturbing example of institutionalised heterosexism with institutionalised homo-, bi-, and transphobia being its tools. If you are an LGBT+ citizen living in Poland, your life, or your partner's, or your child's may dramatically change rather quickly. For instance, assume you live in a same-gender relationship with another woman, raising together a child conceived by an in vitro procedure. You were an egg donor and carried the child. What if you suddenly die, leaving your biological child with your partner – the social parent to your child for years? Your partnership could not have been registered in Poland, so now your partner is a legal stranger to the child, and your own parents (child's grandparents) want custody. Only a perspective of such a course of events, even without the actual court case, can be traumatising.

The legal system protective of gender and sexual diversity, the one being the emanation of the egalitarian and anti-discrimination state's politics could be the obvious rescue in circumstances similar to those described above. However, homo-, bi-, and transphobic countries like Poland do not give such protection to the LGBT+ citizenry. Especially in case of countries where LGBT+ emancipation processes are not advanced, the state constitutes a rather threatening institution. On the one hand, governing bodies have power over physical safety and psychological well-being of LGBT+ citizens. On the other, the state exercises this power to victimise the LGBT+ community. I claim the above description of the state is indeed reminiscent of the attachment figure as described by Bowlby (1969). I hypothesise it might not just be a resemblance or metaphor. If an LGBT+ person is reared in a homo-, bi-, and transphobic country, their sense of dependence from the state accumulates over time. This subjection to the state can be enforced through the domestic medical and psychological procedures, the country law, and courts. For an LGBT+ person, their relationship with the unsupportive state is almost visceral, as in case of LGBT+ citizens the state tends to regulate sexual anatomy and preferences, gender identity and expression, sexual orientation, family life, and reproduction. All of this must invoke shame instantly and challenge personal sense of dignity. In countries like Poland, the relationship between the state and the LGBT+ person seems to be the actual attachment, the insecure one: no safe haven provided.

Negative experiences of LGBT+ citizens with the attachment figure of the state may have the most profound consequences when they intersect with one's dominant attachment insecurity. Importantly, this distinction is useful, but – at least to some extent – artificial, as more general attachment adaptation is a synergistic effect of one's multiple attachment experiences. For the LGBT+ people, the relationship with the homo-, bi-, and transphobic state is just one of them. Nevertheless, from my clinical observations, it appears that the Polish LGBT+ clients living with inse-cure attachment adaptations in their romantic and/or sexual relationships present with two additional features when confronted with homo-, bi-, and transphobic hatred in Poland.

First, many of them react with a decision, or at least prolonged consideration, to leave Poland. Such a response was especially well marked among clients dem-onstrating high attachment anxiety. This association could be easily understood if we saw this "to-leave-Poland" impulse as a protest behaviour. By declaring "I am going to leave the country", clients mobilised their energy to signal to the environ-ment they were feeling endangered and demanded respect and dignity protection through sharing all civic rights with the heteronormative majority. Nevertheless, the state shaped by its political, cultural, societal, and institutional context is – by its nature – a rather dispersed and not easily accessible attachment figure. This inaccessibility is further bolstered in Poland by the fact that the currently ruling right-wing populists do not want to listen to the LGBT+ voices. The governing parties' politicians and the Catholic Church clergy mutually support each other in pathologising gender and sexual diversity.

The second type of reaction in clients with insecure attachment adaptations is withdrawal from: a/ LGBT+ social activism, b/ being an active part of the LGBT+ communities, or c/ living their gender and sexual identities openly. Frequently, those clients presented with high attachment avoidance. This seems to be compre-hensible as being an LGBT+ activist or an openly transgender person would mean staying in the constant dialogue with the state, culture, and society about discrim-ination, social exclusion, and pathologisation targeted at LGBT+ people. It would equal to the heated exchange with the socio-cultural environment, which people with the avoidant attachment adaptation try to refrain from.

In both cases the result is the same – decline in the sense of belonging. In the first situation it refers to the country, nation, or society. In the second – it is about the LGBT+ community. Belonging may give us psychological roots, thus facilitating identity processes, for instance, development of gay identity while being held by the local gay community. Belonging may also bring the sense of groundedness and feeling of the safe haven. Perceived similarities, common developmental tasks, shared history, same socio-cultural oppression confronted with, or acting together – all of them invite the spirit of protective togetherness. Oppression directed towards the LGBT+ citizenry deprives them of these essential supports. The sense of belonging seems to be an obvious antidote for attachment insecurity and other repercussions of the socio-cultural oppression. Nevertheless, it is important to notice that mentioned above strategies of protest behaviours and withdrawal may also be seen as entirely adaptive in confrontation with the violent and oppressive field.

Hope: the psychotherapist and client as psychosocial activists

"A psychosocial activist" is a term coined by Jack Aylward, a Gestalt psychotherapist (2018). It refers to a new role that could be ascribed to the therapist as well as client. Aylward (2018) proposes that therapists' interventions and clients' actions reaching the socio-cultural domain of the broader field create psychosocial activists. When the therapist and client interfere with the environmental sources of the client's psychological difficulties – societal, cultural, and political ones – they both strive for social change. A one-to-one meeting in a consultation room might be the beginning of a dialogue that fosters the individual change in the client, but this new development will affect the others' lives. It is a sign of hope that therapist's psychosocial activism can interact with apparently every level of Fern's (2020) model of attachment and trauma through interventions at the Self (individual therapy) and Relationships (couples and family therapy) levels. For instance, therapeutic work on internalised homophobia in a gay male client may bring a positive change in his self-acceptance as a homosexual person, body image, resilience when confronted with external homophobia, and sex life (Self level). Such personal advancement may in turn positively influence his partner/s (Relationship level). This new gay-affirmative thinking, feeling, and embodiment may change interpersonal dynamic in their family homes (Home level). They may decide to join the local LGBT+ organisation to receive further support from the community, but also engage in activist work (Local Communities and Culture level). Their efforts will help organisation visibility and LGBT+ emancipation movement (Societal level). Their standing for themselves with contemporary psychology, psychotherapy, and psychiatry developments at hand will be a win over the collective trauma of homosexuality persecution by the 20th-century psychiatry (Global or Collective level). However, there is one condition for implementing this scenario: enough respect and containment for diversity in the field.

I do need new healing relationship/s to rebuild what was destroyed or impaired by the past relationships. One of my crucial, lifelong attachments is Polish culture, society, and politics. As attachment figures sometimes change, giving a chance for more nurturing experiences, may I expect Poland to become a safe haven in the near future? Or should I leave?

References

APA Task Force on Appropriate Therapeutic Responses to Sexual Orientation. (2009). *Report of the Task Force on Appropriate Therapeutic Responses to Sexual Orientation*. American Psychological Association.

Ash, L. (2020, September 21). Inside Poland's "LGBT-free Zones." *BBC News*. www.bbc.com/news/stories-54191344

Aylward, J. (2018). *The Anarchy of Gestalt Therapy: A Proposal for Radical Practice.* Ravenwood Press.

Bowlby, J. (1969). *Attachment and Loss: Vol.1* Attachment. Hogarth Press and Institute of Psychoanalysis.

Bulska, D., Górska, P., Malinowska, K., Matera, J., Mulak, A., Poniat, R., Skowrońska, M., Soral, W., Świder, M., and Winiewski, M. (2021). *Sytuacja Społeczna Osób LGBTA w Polsce. Raport za Lata 2019–2020.* Kampania Przeciw Homofobii and Stowarzyszenie Lambda Warszawa.

De Groot, D. (2022, June). *Bans on Conversion "Therapies." The Situation in Selected EU Member States.* European Parliamentary Research Service. www.europarl.europa.eu/ RegData/etudes/BRIE/2022/733521/EPRS_BRI(2022)733521_EN.pdf

Fern, J. (2020). *Polysecure. Attachment, Trauma and Consensual Nonmonogamy.* Thorntree Press.

Galtung, J. (1969). Violence, Peace, and Peace Research. *Journal of Peace Research, 6*(3), 167–191.

Gierdal, K., Godzisz, P., Knut, P., and Więckiewicz, K. (2018). *Trzy Lata Złej Zmiany dla Osób LGBTI – Podsumowanie Rządów PiS.* Stowarzyszenie Lambda Warszawa and Kampania Przeciw Homofobii. https://kph.org.pl/wp-content/uploads/2018/11/Rap ort_podsumowanie_rzadow_pis.pdf

Górska, P. (2019). *Polaryzacja Polityczna w Polsce. Jak bardzo Jesteśmy Podzieleni?* Centrum Badań nad Uprzedzeniami. http://cbu.psychologia.pl/wp-content/uploads/sites/ 410/2021/02/Polaryzacja-polityczna-2.pdf

Grabski, B., Kasparek, K., Műldner-Nieckowski, Ł., and Iniewicz, G. (2019). Sexual Quality of Life in Homosexual and Bisexual Men: The Relative Role of Minority Stress. *The Journal of Sexual Medicine, 16*(6), 860–871. https://doi.org/10.1016/j.jsxm.2019.03.274

Lewin, K. (1953). *A Dynamic Theory of Personality.* McGraw-Hill.

Meyer, I.H. (1995). Minority Stress and Mental Health in Gay Men. *Journal of Health and Social Behavior, 36*(1), 38–56. https://doi.org/10.2307/2137286

Mijas, M., Blukacz, M., Koziara, K., Kasparek, K., Pliczko, M.P., Galbarczyk, A., and Jasieńska, G. (2021). Dysregulated by Stigma: Cortisol Responses to Repeated Psychosocial Stress in Gay and Heterosexual Men. *Psychoneuroendocrinology, 131*, 1–9. https://doi.org/10.1016/j.psyneuen.2021.105325

Perls, F., Hefferline, R.F., and Goodman, P. (1951/2006). *Gestalt Therapy: Excitement and Growth in the Human Personality.* Souvenir Press Ltd.

Punamäki, R.-L. (2021). Developmental Aspects of Political Violence: An Attachment Theoretical Approach. In C.W. Greenbaum, M.M. Haj-Yahia, and C. Hamilton (eds), *Handbook of Political Violence and Children: Psychosocial Effects, Intervention, and Prevention Policy (Development at Risk)* (pp. 33–69). Oxford University Press. https:// doi.org/10.1093/oso/9780190874551.003.0002

Soral, W. (2021). *Mowa Nienawiści Wobec Gejów i Lesbijek.* Centrum Badań nad Uprzedzeniami. http://cbu.psychologia.pl/wp-content/uploads/sites/410/2021/12/Raportl ast.pdf

Stawman, S. (2009). Relational Gestalt: Four Waves. In L. Jacobs and R. Hycner (eds), *Relational Approaches in Gestalt Therapy* (pp. 11–36). GestaltPress.

Tilles, D. (2020a, February 20). Polish Court Rules Campaign Linking LGBT and Paedophilia is "Informative and Educational." *Notes from Poland.* https://notesfrompoland.com/2020/ 02/20/polish-court-anti-lgbt-stop-paedophilia-campaign-is-informative-and-educational/

Tilles, D. (2020b, June 17). Poland's Anti-LGBT Campaign Explained: 10 Questions and Answers. *Notes from Poland.* https://notesfrompoland.com/2020/06/17/polands-anti-lgbt-campaign-explained-ten-questions-and-answers/

Tilles, D. (2020c, August 30). Polish Bishops Call for "Clinics to Help LGBT People Regain Natural Sexual Orientation". *Notes from Poland.* https://notesfrompoland.com/2020/08/30/polish-bishops-call-for-clinics-to-help-lgbt-people-regain-natural-sexual-orientation/

Tilles, D. (2021, June 23). LGBT "Deviants Don't Have Same Rights as Normal People", Says Polish Education Minister. *Notes from Poland.* https://notesfrompoland.com/2021/06/23/lgbt-deviants-dont-have-same-rights-as-normal-people-says-polish-education-minister/

Chapter 4

Living with climate change and environmental crisis

Between climate anxiety and new collective narratives

Magdalena Budziszewska

In human history, the moment when climate change became apparent is marked by a significant loss of safety (Kumar, Nagar, and Anand, 2021; Stollberg and Jonas, 2021). Never before has humanity been able to transform the planetary environment on such scale that it set geological processes in motion rather than only cultural ones. The invalided yet still persuasive argument of those denying climate change is premised on humility (Nagle, 2022): new environmental developments cannot be anthropogenic because humanity could never modify the basic life conditions on Earth. Certainly, the vision of humankind being as powerful as a geological force can be frightening. Beyond doubt, however, climate change is real and rapid, which has been ascertained by scientists who have reached unprecedented consensus on the matter (Lynas, Houlton, and Perry, 2021). At the same time, in psychological terms, climate change represents a whole new level of existential threat (Stollberg and Jonas, 2021; Weintrobe, 2022).

Climate as planetary life-support system

Earth's climate is more than the sum of local weather events. It comprises a dynamic physical system that allowed life to emerge and constitutes its planetary support. On a geological time scale, Earth's surface temperature is determined by the equilibrium between the amount of carbon stored in the ground and the amount in the atmosphere, where it has the form of carbon dioxide: a greenhouse gas that regulates the energy flow between the planet and outer space (IPCC, 2021). An alteration of this proportion could cause Earth to become frozen or, more likely, too hot for life. The planet's climate equilibrium is thus a rare wonder. The relative stability of the Earth's climate in the Holocene, a geological period going back eleven thousand years, enabled civilizations to develop and thrive (IPCC, 2021, Rockström et al., 2009). Humanity is indeed the child of a stable climate.

However, climate stability has been recently lost. Humanity has modified planetary conditions by burning fossil fuels and releasing a seemingly harmless byproduct to the atmosphere. We simply took carbon from the ground and pumped it into the atmosphere, thus reinforcing the natural greenhouse effect. Scientists

DOI: 10.4324/9781003308096-6

predicted this could happen as early as in the nineteenth century. In 1896, Swedish scholar Svante Arrhenius used common laws of physics to predict that fossil-fuel combustion could cause global warming. More recently, these processes have been studied in greater detail, with scientific models enabling to glean both past and future. Carbon dioxide – the Earth's thermostat – is currently at levels unseen in at least three million years (IPCC, 2021). Still, only few grasp what this actually means.

Explaining the unprecedented scale of human carbon dioxide emissions is beyond the scope of this chapter. However, these parameters are commonly misunderstood. To grasp the rate of change, anyone can estimate their personal carbon history online at parametric.press/issue-02/carbon-history/ (Bhatia, 2020), where it is possible to collate climate data with a personal lifetime. As for myself, I found it striking that around sixty percent of human-caused carbon dioxide emissions were made during my lifetime. I remember the fall of communism in Eastern Europe and the crumbling of the Berlin Wall. Atmospheric CO_2 was then at 353 parts per million. In 2022, however, it peaked at 421 parts per million. What we have collectively struggled to learn is that the change in the composition of the Earth's atmosphere will have much more profound consequences than any known historical event.

Contemporary civilization modifies planetary conditions to such a degree that humanity's planetary boundaries will soon be crossed, while various tipping points will be reached (IPCC, 2021; Rockström et al., 2009). Human population has nearly reached nine billion, massively altering the surface of the planet. The fate of these people thus becomes uncertain, raising the question whether they will be able to meet their needs and develop resilience in the face of habitat loss and resource scarcity.

Humanity's ability to subvert the systems that sustain it is the highest degree of scary and constitutes one of the gravest threats in history. There is plenty of reliable data and information on the subject (IPCC, 2021). Scientists keep track of the vital signs in the suddenly fragile-seeming biosphere: the concentration of atmospheric CO_2 and other greenhouse gases, temperature, sea ice coverage, and other parameters. Satellites are used to track the catastrophe around the clock and around the globe. The Intergovernmental Panel on Climate change (IPCC) has produced six rounds of state-of-the-art assessments of climate change progress, one more alarming than the other, the sixth published in several parts in 2021 and 2022 (IPCC, 2021, 2022).

For many people, climate change has the familiar air of an apocalyptic threat. However, this could make climate change even harder to grasp. After all, none of the previously expected millennial catastrophes happened, and apocalyptic Hollywood movies belong to the fantasy genre (Hoggett, 2018). However, this time the drama is real. As difficult as it is to acknowledge and fully comprehend, we are not a movie, but in a planetary crisis. At the same time in many places the gravity of crisis is still socially and politically unacknowledged.

Denial and disavowal around climate change

Social reactions to climate change involve many avoidances and silencing mechanisms. For example, Kari Norgaard (2011) studied everyday conversations about
climate change in the Norwegian town of Bydgaby. Using an anthropological perspective, she has brought to light multilayered means of denial. Notably, however,
this kind of rejection is not literal, negating climate change or arguing it be a secondary problem, but implicated as it consists in failing to translate environmental
awareness into adequate action. Cultural norms, accepted life goals, tendencies to
feel innocent, moral superiority and ignorance are some of the obstacles that preclude honest conversation about climate change (Norgaard, 2011).

Norgaard's study is indicative of blooming research on the denial-disavowal
spectrum of social reactions to climate change (Weintrobe, 2021). More recently,
focus largely shifted to discourses that deliberately hamper meaningful climate
action, even ones that do so in good faith. Consequently, two catastrophes in
fact loom ahead: the physical catastrophe of climate change and the social
catastrophe of political inaction. Lamb and co-authors (2020) described several persuasive discourses around climate change that have had the effect of
delaying climate action: surrender and fatalism, redirecting responsibility and
blame games, pushing non-transformative solutions, individualism policy per-
fectionism, and others.

Participating in climate change denial and more subtle pervasive distraction
strategies is a social and interpersonal phenomenon. Thus denial can also be understood in the light of modern attachment theory (Hautamäki, 2014) as an attachment
protective strategy. Attachments are crucial in deciding how people react to danger,
even if they can acknowledge them in the first place.

Climate change constitutes a hazard on both individual and collective level.
Still, this threat is unevenly distributed; some nations will be affected sooner than
others, which makes climate change also a question of social justice (IPCC, 2022).
Moreover, it causes reasonable fear and anxiety about the future of individuals,
especially children, entire social groups, nations, humanity, and the non-human
nature (Stollberg and Jonas, 2021).

Individual anxiety can motivate both climate denial and climate action (Stollberg
and Jonas, 2021). However, collective threats can elicit self-serving behavior,
fueling rivalry and violence between groups. Risk can be easily used as a pretext by
more potent agents to take advantage of the weaker, protecting their own group's
safety, even if only short-term. Water, fuel, food, and dominance wars are all possible consequences of the environmental crisis (Mach et al., 2019; Wohl, Squires,
and Caouette, 2012). From the Polish perspective, for example, the reality of war in
Ukraine shapes the discussion about possible outcomes of climate catastrophe. In
this conflict, the language used in reports is colored by awareness of climate change.
Constantly recurring themes include: fossil fuels, especially the weaponization of
gas supply, European energy crisis policies, discussions of energy transformation,
return to coal, vulnerable global supply chains, hunger in weaker economies, and

refugees. What is truly fearful about climate change is that it amplifies already existing problems.

Sally Weintrobe, a psychotherapist and writer, observes that one can be very fragile while emerging from denial of the climate crisis. The process can make everyone, including psychologists and psychotherapists, vulnerable, anxious, and disoriented. She describes disavowal as a dangerous mechanism that involves simultaneously knowing and not knowing something (Weintrobe, 2012):

> Climate awareness is not intellectual awareness alone, or a fleeting or sudden awareness, but a sustained effort to struggle to keep the issue in mind and to work through emotionally what that may bring up.
>
> (Sally Weintrobe, 22 April, 2001)

Emotional reactions to climate knowledge – anxiety and grief

Many qualitative studies explored difficult emotions that arise around climate change awareness. For example, in a large study conducted in Norway with participants from diverse groups and generations (Marczak et al., 2021), emotions of anxiety, even terror, fear, isolation, hopelessness, and sadness were reported by many participants. "It's like getting a diagnosis of terminal cancer" – one of the participants summarized it. Budziszewska and Jonsson (2021) explored similar feelings in Swedish participants seeking psychotherapy for climate-related anxiety and demonstrated that a sense of apocalyptic and existential threat is embedded into perceptions of climate change, often leading to guilt and isolation of those worried among the rest of the society. Verlie (2019) also explored similar feelings in an Australian undergraduate sustainability students sample. She shows that experiences of anxiety, frustration, disorientation, overwhelm, guilt, grief, and hope are characteristic of a learning process, which she terms "living with climate change" (see also, Verlie, 2022). These emotions mix, change, and attune as individuals confront the dire and realistic threat humanity is collectively experiencing. She summarizes her understanding:

> Collectively, these processes enroll people in practices of bearing worlds: enduring the pain of the end of the world they have known, and labouring to generate promising alternatives.
>
> (Verlie, 2019, p. 751)

Another facet of "bearing" climate change awareness is connected not to anxiety but to sadness, loss, and grief. Many people cherish a sense of connectedness with nature, which manifests in attachment to unique landscapes, including ones remembered from childhood: trees, forests, rivers, lakes, and so on. These attachments can be taxing as many people have to reconcile with the loss of these places later in life. One qualitative study on perceptions of climate crisis among senior

Polish citizens (Majchrowicz, 2021) has shown that many of them could remember natural areas such as forests, rivers and mountains, which they used to cherish. These local experiences serve as an embodied reminder of the global environmental crisis. Australian philosopher Glen Albrecht coined the term "solastalgia" (Albrecht, 2010) to describe feelings of having lost what would be considered an emotional home and connected with a specific unspoiled environment. Studies have confirmed that climate change is experienced through various "solastalgic" emotions (Cunsolo and Ellis, 2018; Lertzman, 2015). Loss of a local climate is an instance of this because people are accustomed to the rhythm of seasons, the character of clouds and winds, and countless other subtle details that characterize a specific microclimate. Valued and reassuring, these places are preserved in language and literature, contributing to the genius loci. This special aura is something that people mourn as local climates are destabilized. From the perspective of attachment psychology, it is striking what climate disruptions endanger. On a deeper level then, climate change involves the loss of comfort offered by nature as an emotional home.

Collective loss in unsettling but collective grief carries unique potential. Judith Butler (2004) explored how mourning inspires a sense of solidarity, revealing the need to recognize shared vulnerability. If such weakness could be recognized as shared with more-than-human nature, perhaps it could be also acknowledged as common to all human groups. After all, interdependence is a basic tenet of both ecological science and experiential psychology. It seems that a previously unrecognized grief for the more-than-human world is emerging as an important psychological factor these days (Head, 2016).

Climate crisis is fueling mental health crisis

According to APA reports on the intersection of psychology and climate change, the climate crisis also contributes to the mental health crisis (Clayton et al., 2017). Psychological consequences can be acute or gradual. The former concerns those who have already experienced disasters related to climate change, for example floods, fires, and loss of livelihood. The latter refers to the gradual worsening of living conditions in the warming world, entailing huge uncertainty about the future. The above-mentioned reports mention a range of vulnerabilities, which are not limited to ones directly connected with environmental factors, but include loss of social cohesion, economic stress, inequality, and, last but not least, war and conflict. These problems in turn cause others such as stress, anxiety, trauma, depression, substance abuse, helplessness, and fatalism, straining social relationships and complicating grief, even leading to loss of personal identity (Clayton et al., 2017; Pihkala, 2020; Verlie, 2022).

In this context, media coverage has made the term "climate anxiety" and "climate depression" hugely popular. However, professional use of these terms is much more moderated and critical. Professionals point out the danger of medicalizing normal and adaptive emotions and prefer to speak about "realistic" or "adaptive" anxiety (Pihkala, 2020; Budziszewska and Kałwak, 2022). As much as there is a proportion of the population that is experiencing significant impairment in everyday functioning due to macro-social worries and may benefit from psychotherapy (Budziszewska and Jonsson, 2021), sadness, grief, and anxiety are usually just a reasonable reaction to the drama of modern climate change. In climate change, strong emotional responses indicate a healthy relationship with reality and need not be medicalized (Horwitz and Wakefield, 2007; Pihkala, 2020).

The psychology of climate change distress seems to be caught in a paradox. It moves between socially sanctioned denial and avoidance on the one hand, and burdensome psychological effects among those who try to face the threat on the other. Perspectives of individual resilience are proposed (Clayton et al., 2017) and criticized (Kałwak and Weihgold, 2022). Individual resilience perspective seems not to be enough in the face of planetary catastrophe. Moreover, personal resilience comes bundled with the "resilience paradox" (Ogunbode et al., 2019); persons experiencing themselves as resilient are statistically less motivated to mitigate the collective threat.

Governmental betrayal and moral injury

Sense of betrayal by society, governments, and adults and moral injury for participating in harmful realties of modern life are just another facet of climate relevant emotions. Many studies on coping with climate change distress were carried out among children and adolescents, clearly a vulnerable group. Crandon and co-authors (2022) suggest that social support from parents, peers and institutions, as well as a sense of safety in relationships, may shield against climate anxiety by fostering safe attachment and trust. Ojala (2022), who studied Swedish adolescents coping with climate-related distress, found that social trust, especially confidence in institutions, state policies, and environmental organizations, helped to regulate climate concerns. As these results show, climate change is a collective problem, and can be only addressed with organized action, and only if powerful agents work together.

Today, however, the climate crisis entails the collapse of trust toward institutions and states. In a global-scale study carried out among young people living in ten countries and representing both the global North and South, the authors assessed dominant sentiments around climate change (Hickman et al., 2021). They found that alarming numbers of young people experience negative emotions and thoughts revolving around this question, with over half of participants arguing they felt anxiety, anger, and powerlessness. Many also reported negative thoughts, with 75 percent occasionally afraid of the future and 56 percent thinking humanity might be doomed. However, even more insight was obtained by the authors in relation to young people's perceptions of the government's response to the climate crisis. They discovered a deep-seated sense of betrayal, with the majority of participants reporting that the authorities are failing young people, dismissing people's distress and lying about the impact of their actions. In contrast, only around 30 percent study subjects trusted the government's response. Authors conclude that the upsetting feeling of having been abandoned or betrayed by authorities and institutions prevails in the experience of climate change.

Finally, confronting climate change can cause one to feel "moral injury" – term introduced by Sally Weintrobe (2020) – as the psychological effect of witnessing or participating in actions that violate basic ethical standards or fail to prevent unethical behavior. It is not only children and adolescents who feel betrayed, guilty, and helpless owing to the complex nature of responsibility for climate crisis, but also ordinary citizens, who share this sentiment as well as a sense of disempowerment. Agency seems to be the critical question in psychological responses to climate change (Fritsche and Masson, 2021). It remains unclear, however, whether agency can be retained in the face of processes occurring on such scale.

New narratives

It appears that many coping strategies helpful in facing unprecedented threat of climate change concern close relationships and social trust: the ability to make connections, build communities, and foster cooperation amid the crisis. In this regard collective agency offers more hope that individual one. The same is true for climate change adaptation, climate change mitigation, and climate change resilience.

In recent years, many authors have endorsed strategies that overcome individualism and alienation by prioritizing close relationships, community, and collective action (Budziszewska and Głód, 2021; Lertzman, 2015; Narin, 2019; Verlie, 2019, 2022; Weintrobe, 2020). Attachment and emotional connection – including a sense of participation in a more-than-human world – offer safe space for reflection on possible forms of resistance. Even in troubled times, people build relationships, form alliances, and create narratives that make living with climate change possible.

One of the sources of empowerment and connection is the deep concern about climate change and environmental loss – if socially shared. According to many qualitative studies (Budziszewska and Jonsson; 2021; Lertzman, 2015; Narin, 2019; Verlie, 2019, 2022; Weintrobe, 2020), citizens across the world, young and old, activists or not, tell emotional stories about their private experiences of climate change. Climate anxiety of grief can be re-storied as an awakening that facilitates deepened reflection and even personal transformation. Since people tend to focus on what is meaningful in life, this phenomenon can be described in psychological terms as meaning-focused coping (Ojala, 2022; Pihkala, 2017).

Climate distress is among the strongest predictors of climate action (Bouman, 2020). Anger at perceived injustice and nonfeasance significantly contributes to collective climate action (Stanley, 2021). Moral outrage at ethical injuries in destructive social systems can boost attempts to create and imagine new forms of social organization. Finally, loss and grief can help to build community by bringing together people who have been mourning for what is now lost, and motivating them to prevent further harm. Experiencing the above climate emotions (Weintrobe, 2021) seems to constitute the opposite of the denial-disavowal spectrum. In climate work, encountering, witnessing and storing experiences is in itself a form of political practice (Verlie, 2022). Storing power has also been traditionally the energy of the oppressed. All major social transformations – including the abolition of slavery and the emancipation of women and minority groups – were preceded by the emergence of intense, emotional, and morally-charged stories.

Ultimately, climate change is a collective problem that cannot be adequately addressed through one solution. Perhaps, as Verlie (2022) argues, there are "no solutions" at all for issues of this scale cannot be "solved" in the anthropocentric sense of the word. To some degree, global warming is already underway and "locked in." Moreover, given the current state of politics and technology, it may be already irreversible. However, there are still ways to limit the scope of the impending catastrophe and prevent even worse suffering, although some of it can no longer be avoided. How humanity will confront the crisis is crucial: whether the response will involve solidarity and sound action or hate and violence.

All reasonable pathways to limit global warming involve social cohesion and trust in caring for the common good. Therefore, the core of the climate issue concerns human psychology, especially the ability to trust, cooperate, and recognize shared vulnerability and interdependence, as well as the capacity to bond and build communities, also with the more-than-human world. In the end, if some sense of safety is to be reached in a volatile world, it is paramount to nurture relationships and act together.

References

Albrecht, G. (2010). Solastalgia and the creation of new ways of living. *Nature and Culture*, 235–252. Routledge.

Bhatia, A., Conlen, M., and Hohman, F. (2020). ParametricPress/02-carbon-history 1.0.2 (1.0.2). Zenodo. https://doi.org/10.5281/zenodo.4105533, https://parametric.press/issue-02/carbon-history/

Bouman, T., Verschoor, M., Albers, C. J., Böhm, G., Fisher, S. D., Poortinga, W., ... and Steg, L. (2020). When worry about climate change leads to climate action: How values, worry and personal responsibility relate to various climate actions. *Global Environmental Change*, *62*, 102061.

Budziszewska, M. and Głód, Z. (2021). "These are the very small things that lead us to that goal": Youth climate strike organizers talk about activism empowering and taxing experiences. *Sustainability*, *13*(19), 11119.

Budziszewska, M. and Jonsson, S. E. (2021). From climate anxiety to climate action: An existential perspective on climate change concerns within psychotherapy. *Journal of Humanistic Psychology*, https://journals.sagepub.com/doi/abs/10.1177/002216782 1993243

Budziszewska, M. and Kałwak W. (2022). Climate depression: Critical analysis of the concept. *Psychiatr. Pol 56*(1), 171–182.

Butler, J. (2004). *Precarious Life: The Powers of Mourning and Violence.* Verso.

Clayton, S., Manning, C., Krygsman, K, Speiser M. (2017). *Mental Health and Our Changing Climate: Impacts and Guidance.* American Psychological Association and ecoAmerica.

Crandon, T. J., Scott, J. G., Charlson, F. J., and Thomas, H. J. (2022). A social–ecological perspective on climate anxiety in children and adolescents. *Nature Climate Change, 12*(2), 123–131.

Cunsolo, A. and Ellis, N. R. (2018). Ecological grief as a mental health response to climate change-related loss. *Nature Climate Change, 8*(4), 275–281.

Fritsche, I. and Masson, T. (2021). Collective climate action: When do people turn into collective environmental agents? *Current Opinion in Psychology, 42*, 114–119.

Hautamäki, A. (2014). *The Dynamic-Maturational Model of Attachment and Adaptation–Theory and Practice.* Svenska social- och kommunalhögskolan vid Helsingfors universitet.

Head, L. (2016) *Hope and Grief in the Anthropocene: Re-conceptualising Human–nature Relations.* Routledge.

Hickman, C., Marks, E., Pihkala, P., Clayton, S., Lewandowski, R.E., Mayall, E.E., … van Susteren, L. (2021). Climate anxiety in children and young people and their beliefs about government responses to climate change: A global survey. *Lancet Planet Health, 5*(12), e863–e873. DOI: 10.1016/S2542-5196(21)00278-3. PMID: 34895496

Hoggett, P. (2018). Climate change and the apocalyptic imagination. In B. Halins (ed.), *Psychoanalytic Reflections on a Changing World.* Routledge, pp. 233–249.

Horwitz, A. and Wakefield, J. (2007). *The Loss of Sadness: How Psychiatry Transformed Normal Sorrow into Depressive Disorder.* Oxford University Press.

IPCC (2021). Climate Change 2021: *The Physical Science Basis. Contribution of Working Group I to the Sixth Assessment Report of the Intergovernmental Panel on Climate Change* [Masson-Delmotte, V., P. Zhai, A. Pirani, S.L. Connors, C. Péan, S. Berger, N. Caud, Y. Chen, L. Goldfarb, M.I. Gomis, M. Huang, K. Leitzell, E. Lonnoy, J.B.R. Matthews, T.K. Maycock, T. Waterfield, O. Yelekçi, R. Yu, and B. Zhou (eds.)]. Cambridge University Press, DOI:10.1017/9781009157896

IPCC (2022). Climate Change 2022: Impacts, Adaptation, and Vulnerability. Contribution of Working Group II to the Sixth Assessment Report of the Intergovernmental Panel on Climate Change [H.-O. Pörtner, D.C. Roberts, M. Tignor, E.S. Poloczanska, K. Mintenbeck, A. Alegría, M. Craig, S. Langsdorf, S. Löschke, V. Möller, A. Okem, B. Rama (eds.)]. Cambridge University Press.

Kałwak, W. and Weihgold, V. (2022). The relationality of ecological emotions: An interdisciplinary critique of individual resilience as psychology's response to the climate crisis. *Frontiers in Psychology, 13*, 823620–823620.

Kumar, A., Nagar, S., and Anand, S. (2021). Climate change and existential threats. In Singh, S., Singh, P., Rangabhashiyam, S., and Srivastava, K.K. (eds.), *Global Climate Change.* Elsevier, pp. 1–31.

Lamb, W. F., Mattioli, G., Levi, S., Roberts, J. T., Capstick, S., Creutzig, F., … and Steinberger, J. K. (2020). Discourses of climate delay. *Global Sustainability*, 3, e17, 1–5. https://doi.org/ 10.1017/sus.2020.13

Lertzman, R. (2015) *Environmental Melancholia: Psychoanalytic Dimensions of Engagement.* Routledge.

Lynas, M., Houlton, B. Z., and Perry, S. (2021). Greater than 99% consensus on human caused climate change in the peer-reviewed scientific literature. *Environmental Research Letters*, *16*(11), 114005.

Mach, K. J., Kraan, C. M., Adger, W. N., Buhaug, H., Burke, M., Fearon, J. D., ... and von Uexkull, N. (2019). Climate as a risk factor for armed conflict. *Nature*, *571*(7764), 193–197.

Majchrowicz M. (2021). Postrzeganie *zmiany klimatu z perspektywy osób po 65 roku życia Interpretacyjna Analiza Fenomenologiczna*. Climate change from the perspective of older 65+ adults. Interpretative phenomenological analysis. Unpublished master thesis, Faculty of Psychology, University of Warsaw.

Marczak, M., Winkowska, M., Chaton-Østlie, K., Rios, R. M., and Klöckner, C. (2021). "When I say I'm depressed, it's like anger." An Exploration of the Emotional Landscape of Climate Change Concern in Norway and Its Psychological, Social and Political Implications. Preprint. https://assets.researchsquare.com/files/rs-224032/v1/bbe12aa6-ee8d-4358-bc72-6f6d9160d91e.pdf?c=1631877163

Nagle, J. C. (2022). Humility, climate change, and the pursuit of scientific truth. *Notre Dame L. Rev. Reflection*, *97*, 125.

Nairn, K. (2019). Learning from young people engaged in climate activism: The potential of collectivizing despair and hope. *Young*, *27*, 435–450.

Norgaard, K. M. (2011). *Living in Denial: Climate Change, Emotions, and Everyday Life*. MIT Press.

Ogunbode, C. A., Böhm, G., Capstick, S. B., Demski, C., Spence, A., and Tausch, N. (2019). The resilience paradox: Flooding experience, coping and climate change mitigation intentions. *Climate Policy*, *19*(6), 703–715.

Ojala, M. (2022). How do children, adolescents, and young adults relate to climate change? Implications for developmental psychology. *European Journal of Developmental Psychology*, 1–15. DOI: 10.1080/17405629.2022.2108396

Pihkala, P. (2017). Environmental education after sustainability: Hope in the midst of tragedy. *Global Discourse*, *7*(1), 109–127.

Pihkala, P. (2020). Anxiety and the ecological crisis: An analysis of eco-anxiety and climate anxiety. *Sustainability*, *12*(19), 7836.

Rockström, J., Steffen, W., Noone, K., Persson, Å., Chapin III, F. S., Lambin, E., ... and Foley, J. (2009). Planetary boundaries: Exploring the safe operating space for humanity. *Ecology and Society*, *14*(2).

Stanley, S. K., Hogg, T. L., Leviston, Z., and Walker, I. (2021). From anger to action: Differential impacts of eco-anxiety, eco-depression, and eco-anger on climate action and wellbeing. *The Journal of Climate Change and Health*, *1*, 100003.

Stollberg, J. and Jonas, E. (2021). Existential threat as a challenge for individual and collective engagement: Climate change and the motivation to act. *Current Opinion in Psychology*, *42*, 145–150.

Verlie, B. (2019). Bearing worlds: Learning to live-with climate change. *Environmental Education Research*, *25*(5), 751–766.

Verlie, B. (2022). *Learning to Live with Climate Change: From Anxiety to Transformation*. Taylor & Francis, 140.

Weintrobe, S. (2012). The difficult problem of anxiety in thinking about climate change. In Weintrobe, S. (ed.), *Engaging with Climate Change*. Routledge, 33–47.

Weintrobe, S. (2020). Moral injury, the culture of uncare and the climate bubble. *Journal of Social Work Practice*, *34*(4), 351–362.

Weintrobe, S. (2021). *Psychological Roots of the Climate Crisis: Neoliberal Exceptionalism and the Culture of Uncare*. Bloomsbury Publishing USA.

Weintrobe, S. (2022). *Blog entry on 22 April, 2001.* www.sallyweintrobe.com/april-22-2021/.

Wohl, M. J., Squires, E. C., and Caouette, J. (2012) We were, we are, will we be? The social psychology of collective angst. *Social and Personality Psychology Compass*, 6(5): 379–391.

Chapter 5

Ecocultural context of attachment security, sense of safety, and trust

Katarzyna Lubiewska

The aim of this chapter aroused from reflections and my experiences of studying attachment and parenting across cultures differing in their Western or non-Western civilizational background (e.g., Nisbett, 2004; Wong and Cowden, 2022). Even though the perspective presented in this chapter may be found by some readers as underlying mainstream assumptions of attachment theory and practice, this approach is not novel or revolutionary (see references across this chapter). I start this chapter with my personal attachment theory-oriented considerations regarding terms of interest in this book related to safety, security, and trust. Then, in line with attachment theory, I will set the stage for Thesis 1 that most human beings have a propensity for trust associated with adaptive coping capacities. The other three theses will go beyond universal assumptions by addressing interactions between culture and safety-security-trust to answer the following questions: What level of distress is needed to activate attachment-related proximity seeking (distress threshold question)? To what extent does the nature of trust stem from the quality of the relationship with the trusted other and from his/her social role? What strategies are used by individuals to achieve a sense of security in times of distress?

Security, safety, and trust

Security term is derived from Latin *secures* and means freedom from anxiety. As proposed by Ainsworth and colleagues (1978/2015) anxiety, indicative for lack of security, is associated with behavioral avoidance in times of distress (anxious-avoidant attachment) or/and emotional preoccupation with past relational experiences and ambivalent behavioral and motivational tendencies (anxious-ambivalent attachment).

Can, however, security be equated to safety? Concepts of *secure base* and *safe haven*, core for attachment theory, seem to differentiate them. Both share the same basis of trust. Yet, security, but not necessarily safety, seems to demand an effort from the security provider. Parents provide secure environment to their children, so they can feel safe and flourish. Partners in intimate relationships reciprocate security provision in times of danger and distress. Security provision needs both: ability and willingness of its provider to succeed in making their own close other feel safe. Yet,

DOI: 10.4324/9781003308096-7

and importantly for this chapter, security can be acquired internally. Self-provision of security, whether conscious or not, rises another meaning of security defined not only as protection from but also *resilience* against potential harm (Bender and Ingram, 2018). The term *safety* can be, in this context, perceived as a feeling of calmness which is rather an outcome of security provision. In contrast to security provision from others, safety is the feeling that must be internally developed, achieved, and maintained.

Feelings of safety set a basis for generalized *trust* that the close other will be available and supportive when needed. General trust, described in attachment but also in Erikson's theory (1994), develops through experiences of security provision by close others and sets the basis for achieving feeling of safety. Research supports these relations, revealing that individuals with secure attachment have a higher sense of trust than insecure individuals (Mikulincer, 1998). Moreover, trust related to attachment security is also associated with interpersonal trust toward close others (Rotenberg, Wicks, and Bathew, 2021), social trust (Brulin, Lindholm, and Granqvist, 2022), or even trust in artificial intelligence (Gillath et al., 2021).

Focusing on person-centered feelings of safety (me feeling safe), relation-driven sense of security (other as security provider), and trust underlying both of them, I would like to discuss in this chapter their varying qualities in different cultural contexts in which assumptions about nature of security provision, feeling of safe, and thresholds of interpretation of events as threats may differ. To describe regulative function of culture to these psychological phenomena I will first shed light on the universal biological basis of human trust (secure base and safe haven) and then I will discuss the regulative function of culture.

Thesis 1: Universal basis of human trust

The capacity to develop trust toward self, others, and the world is rooted in our biological makeup. We are born equipped in various behavioral systems cooperating with each other, among which wariness/fear system and attachment system are interrelated (Stevenson-Hinde, and Shouldice, 1993). Threat in the environment activates our wariness system which in turn activates our attachment behavioral system. These processes shall lead to seeking proximity with an attachment figure to achieve comfort, safety provision, and protection (Bowlby, 1973; Cassidy, 2016; Cortina and Liotti, 2010). Attachment behaviors associated with proximity seeking are used in early stages of life mainly unconsciously to downregulate distress by reaching for close others who have more resources, skills, and knowledge to be effective in providing security in a given moment.

Securely attached individuals have expectations and experiences of being successfully protected by others. Thus, they develop a mindset characterized by trustworthiness that others are able, available and viable to provide security. This capacity developed in early childhood, becomes an important and powerful resource for optimal development through the life-span associated with resilience (Masten,

2015; Mesman, van IJzendoorn, and Sagi-Schwartz, 2016). As attachment security is an intra-psychic dyadic regulator of emotions, cognition, and behavior (Sroufe and Waters, 1977) it plays the core role in life-span development. Sroufe (2016) delinates five cornerstones which attachment security provides for personality. First, a *motivational basis* set by a sense of connectedness with others and positive expectations concerning relationships, that are implicitly assumed to be rewarding. The second, an *attitudinal base*, is associated with the sense of personal mastery, where one implicitly assumes that he/she may elicit responses that are needed from other people. Next, and similar, is the *instrumental base* which relates more to the object mastery than to the social world (exploration, a joy that comes with discovering and acting in the world, and positive problem-solving attitude). Fourth, the *emotional base* of attachment security is associated with dyadic emotional regulation. Secure individuals are capable of reaching for close others in times of distress and through proximity with an attachment figure to effectively downregulate their own distress. The last, fifth, is the *relational base* which is linked to the emotional base. Secure individuals not only use others to self-regulate, but are able and willing to reciprocate in this domain.

It is worth noting that even though approximately 65 percent of individuals have secure attachment orientation (Mesman, van IJzendoorn, and Sagi-Schwartz, 2016) being trustful is not always adaptive, or learned in childhood (Forslund et al., 2022; Hesse, 2008). Yet, in general the majority of the world's population (as indicated above) is expected to develop attachment security, thus feel safe in close relations and have general trust that close others will provide security if needed. This secure majority of world's population (as compared to their insecure counterparts) is also better off in most of ecological environments in meeting adaptational demands.

The attachment security fundaments, whether achieved in childhood or "earned" later in life (Saunders et al., 2011), add to individual capacity to bounce back after hardship, analyzed in psychology as resilience (Campbell-Sills and Stein, 2007). Resilience is a protective factor that buffers against adverse experiences people encounter in their lives. For example, research by Eloranta and colleagues (2017) revealed that securely attached children who had traumatic war experiences indeed bounced back and recovered from their mental health problems faster than their insecure counterparts. Importantly, however, they did it without therapy which in this study was found as not helpful in their recovery.

The fact that the majority of people is trustful should be therefore extended by an additional implication. These individuals who are trustful and secure in close relationships also have life-experiences-based fundamentals that make them resilient and more successful in bouncing back from hardships by positive expectations and view of relationships, mastery, and dyadic emotional regulation capacities. This attachment-oriented view on human nature as equipped with distress related defenses is in line with the concept of psychological immune system (Gilbert, 2006) which immunizes us against traumas and psychologically shocking information and events (see also Mischel, 2014).

Regulatory function of current culture on human trust

One critic of attachment theory refers to its Western nature and application in psychological science and practice as one-size-fits-all (Keller, 2018; Rothbaum et al., 2000). A part of this lies in the fact that attachment researchers discuss conditionality of attachment security almost exclusively in the context of qualities of previous and current relations with attachment figures. Nonetheless, there is evidence suggesting that ecocultural context may also condition differences in: (1) perceiving a threshold of events as threatening and calling the need for security provision; (2) the nature of trust in close relationships; and (3) individual strategies of security provision.

Only 12 per cent of the world's population lives in the Western, Educated, Industrialized, Rich, and Democratic (WEIRD) countries (Henrich, Heine, and Norenzayan, 2010; Wong and Codwen, 2022). Commonly referred to as Western cultures, WEIRD cultures are in majority individualistic, rather than collectivistic (e.g., Minkov et al., 2018) and oriented toward self-expression (versus survival) and science-based rational values (versus religiosity) (Inglehart, 2008; Inglehart and Beker, 2000; Richards, 2018). Even though this characteristic tends to be overgeneralizing and simplifying the nature of cross-cultural differences (e.g., Oyserman and Kemmetlmeier, 2002; Poortinga, 2015), it may shed a light on cultural variations in phenomena of interest in this chapter.

In WEIRD cultures socialization takes place in the nuclear family and is child-centered as well as distal (Greenfield et al., 2003; Keller, 2018) regarding prevalence of verbal contact over the physical mother-child proximity (e.g., co-sleeping). In highly WEIRD conditions in which people do not need to focus on survival, they are free to engage in self-actualization. Socialization parenting strategies also overlap with valuing self-expression as the leading gear of human behaviors. For the "WEIRD people" important existential issues are associated with answering the questions: What are my "true feelings"? How and to whom my own emotions should be expressed? Do I like myself? How happy (or depressed) I am in my life?

In non-WEIRD (majority) cultural contexts the individual need to survive (oftentimes economically) is of great importance, education is less popular, welfare systems are underdeveloped, and oftentimes natural threats present (like earthquicks). In these cultural contexts, group collaboration, especially close ties within extended family, becomes the basis for child socialization. Raising children is less child-centered, more physically proximal, less verbal, and based on expectations of obedience and compliance from family members (Greenfield et al., 2003; Keller, 2018; Rothbaum and Trommsdorf, 2007).

It should be added, though, that cultures are not stable and are undergoing social changes, along with an increase in education, wealth, and influences of other cultures or one bigger globalized (e.g., Western, American) culture. As studies reveal, these social changes taking place worldwide are based on the shift from traditional values toward secular-rational values and from survival values to self-expression values (Inglehart, 2008). Social changes also widely install Western-like characteristics of cultures to non-Western parts of the world.

Finally, it should be added and highlighted that with some exceptions the world, especially the WEIRD part of world, has never been so comfortable a place to live in the history of humankind (Fettweis, 2010; Pinker, 2018). National as well as individual wealth and longevity have increased, natural threats are largely controlled, and peace is more widespread than ever before. These conditions make human kind flourish with regard to creativity, technology, and adaptive problem solving in general. Yet, along with this widespread security some things have changed in our minds. Social changes triggered three trends observed nowadays: (1) smaller/ weaker stimuli perceived by individuals is needed today to interpret this stimuli as threat or distress they are less resilient today than before; (2) trust in others is easily destroyed; (3) security provision startegies have changed.

Thesis 2: Threshold of threat perception is culture-dependent

Resilience is a capacity to manage stress and adapt successfully in challenging and threatening circumstances (Leppin et al., 2014; Masten, 2015) and manage. Yet studies are likely to address adaptational strategies underlying resilience, rarely asking the question about the threshold at which circumstances are perceived (or not yet) as threatening, thus activating the need for other-related security provision or resilient-self-coping. This threshold may be ecologically and culturally dependent (Richards, 2018).

Such expectation may be driven from social learning and behavioral theories where the frequency of exposition to stimuli and the presence of models which can be observed regarding successful coping are the source of learning to cope and being successful in coping (Masten, 2015). Exposure to stress may immunize against it. In cozy, comfortable conditions people are relatively less often exposed to threats. If they live in a culture focused on self-expression of feelings and self-enhancement (like WEIRD cultures), they may have lower baseline readiness to face up to psychological disturbance and to acknowledge the emotional damage it caused (Richards, 2018). As an outcome a minor distress may be perceived as a major distress likely to lead to psychological damages defined as traumatic experiences. If this phenomenon refers to wider groups, social learning theory allows to expect that people will model from each other both the threshold for perception of a stimuli as stressful or traumatic and coping strategies undertaken to reduce discomfort. Individual-level mechanisms and capacities involved in resilience are the same as in more severely threatening conditions, however, the threshold of activation and particular coping strategies differ. One example comes from overprotective (intensive, overnurturing) parenting, described during recent decades in some of WEIRD, mostly Anglo-Saxon cultures (Ennis, 2014).

This type of parenting is child-centered and aim to protect the child against any distress, conflicts, or discomfort. Even though child-related outcomes of such overparenting are negative (Twenge, 2017), this overprotective caregiving strategy spilled out from nuclear family households and entered educational institutions. Overprotective parents put a pressure on schools and other child-care institutions to protect their children from distress of all kinds, including peer conflicts, unpleasant teaching materials, and broad range of topics recommended as to be avoided in school programs not to distress children (Sommers and Satel, 2005). Overprotection extended also to universities where students are coddled by teachers who avoid personally distressful topics and prevent them from effort providing teaching materials easily accessible online and creating a safety zone of student-directed programs. This caregiving strategy also brought a new phenomenon of cancel culture to universities, where students demand cancelation of lectures from university headmasters that might cause personal distress to students (Lukianoff and Haidt, 2019; Norris, 2021). The safety of children has become the main concern of socializing agents (security providers) pushing unpleasant challenging discussions and tasks out of the comfort zones.

Additionally, in current WEIRD cultures the world is presented as a place that is unsafe and dangerous for living. Daily news presented in mass media highlight crimes and topics showing the world and people in a negative light. Safety notifications sent to university students in the USA inform about suspected abuse, kidnap, assault, or the attempt of these. Even though people habituate and do not feel personally threatened to these alerts, the implicitly injected and unconsciously primed world-view is negative. Safety and security became a major concern that must be approached proactively in the world that is as peaceful as was never before.

In this context two socialization-related phenomena seem to be important to notice. First, various, considered as "unpleasant", activities are proactively avoided, thus cannot immunize developing individuals with small but not rarely occurring dosages of stress. These are needed to develop and strengthen resilience beyond the basis of attachment security which most of world's population have. Attachment security brings into resilience capacities of mastery and emotional regulation. However, these capacities cannot be trained, and, thus strengthened, in cozy comfort-like-organized circumstances where children are overprotected and parents smooth their developmental path leading to academic success (Milkie and Warner, 2014). Second, overprotective caregiving and lack of major threats is likely to result in lowering the threshold of interpreting previously considered events (previously considered as minor) as threatening. Lack of exposure to and immunization by various nontrivial life stressors make people not familiar with the wide range of stressors which, when encountered, are perceived as distressful or even traumatic. Furthermore, strategies managing these threats related to security provision have been professionalized in WEIRD cultures (Richards, 2018) leading to perceiving close others as non-professional agents of support provision.

Thesis 3: The nature of trust and security is culture-dependent

People living in more traditional non-WEIRD cultures, when encountered with distress, reach for strategies well known to anthropologists. First, they reach for their nuclear and extended family or community members for support. This phenomenon is known as *familiarism* and is used to describe usually more traditional cultures (Campos et al., 2014). Second, they reach, oftentimes collectively, for their supportive groups and rituals to support their coping capacities. For example, people in indigenous Nahua groups in Mexico deal with major problems or extremly distressful and distressful experiences by gathering together in extended families, including godparents, to collectively look for possible solutions and support, whether instrumental or psychological. The institution of a godparent is taken seriously in Mexican culture as this social role is linked to responsibility for a godchild to which instrumental or psychological security must be provided when it is needed.[1] The social role of godparent in this traditional culture is associated with responsibility of security provision. That has an important implication – trust is embodied in the social role and not necessarily in the attachment of a long-lasting relationship between a child and his/her godparent. An individual in need of security provision turns to those whose role, as assigned by society, is to provide security. The sense of security is based on assurance of support provision that is embedded in social role of spouse, godparent, sibling, or a parent (Jing et al., 2020; Keller, 2018; Trommsdorff, 2006).

This notion of trust seems to be contrasted with perception of trust in the WEIRD part of the world. Trust, sense of security, is described as constructed over the life-time-experiences that provide (or not) the basis for internal construction of trust regarding availability and willingness of a particular close other to provide security when needed. This process of constructing trust is not linked to social or the biological role of the security provider but results from long-lasting experiences in a particular relationship. Additionally, this individual and relation-specific long-lasting development of trust in majority takes place in the WEIRD cultures where relational mobility (Kito, Yuki, and Thomson, 2017) is likely to be high. In high relational mobility cultures society, through developed social norms, is not restrictive about choosing and changing relational partners in family (divorces are widely accepted) or in work-networks. When one feels dissatisfaction about one's own relational partner is free or even encouraged to look for another, more satisfying partner. (Kito et al., 2017). Even parental responsibility as security provider may be volitionally rejected by a parent or a child (when close to adulthood) and terminated if dissatisfaction is explicitly felt.

In this context the basis of trust on which a secure base and safe haven are constructed differs across ecocultural settings. A sense of safety may be culture-dependent. As such security provision may be expected because it is assured in the social role of security provider or because it is constructed based on relational experiences with a close other (Jing et al., 2020; Keller, 2018; Trommsdorff, 2006). Furthermore, trust in both cultural contexts has a different nature. It is solid in more traditional non-WEIRD cultural settings as social roles are generally stable (as well as related trust), or it is fragile, easy to destruct and difficult to rebuild later on, as in WEIRD cultural contexts (Taleb, 2012).

Thesis 4: Strategies of achieving sense of safety vary across cultures

Changes in our mindset are also related to strategies of reaching for security provision in WEIRD cultural contexts. First, individualism, focus on self-expression, and "own true feelings" as the decision compass, as well as shift from extended to nuclear family living patterns characterizing WEIRD cultures, may be discouraging many individuals in their own struggles of bouncing back from hardship by self-effort-based coping and reaching for family members and community-like circles for potential support provision. In contrast, today's tendency to seek professional mental health care is more visible (Richards, 2018; Sommers and Satel, 2005).

From the evolutionary perspective, human beings need other humans to adapt and feel well (Coan and Sbarra, 2015). Even though the effectiveness of close others in support-giving, is comparable to professional interventions (Olowokere and Okanlawon, 2018), only the last adds to strengthening of the social relationships one has and one's dyadic regulation capacities. Yet, wealthy people in WEIRD cultures seem to be less likely to reach out for family help. Not only are family members oftentimes physically distant (by living arrangements) but they are also preoccupied with their own individual problems (not rarely geared by self-actualization goals). Additionally, trust in science found as increasingly important in WEIRD countries (Inglehart, 2008) seems to make us unwilling to reach for close others, but also rituals and other unscientific and unprofessional means in achieving and maintaining sense of safety. Furthermore, along with social revolution in the 1960s of the 20th century psychology entered into humanism through the revolutionary concepts of Maslow and Rogers shifting (through popular culture) social focus toward self, including happiness and self-actualization as a golden standard for all (Sommers and Satel, 2005). As the outcome in this WEIRD, oftentimes considered as dangerous world, people may be left to their individual self, with always a quest for happiness, self-acceptance, and self-actualization. We may add to this picture a lowered threshold of distress perception fostered by the WEIRD cultural norms, and a negative view of the world as a source of danger. Having such broader perspective in result we may ask whether our culture is not at the point where pills, psychological counselors, and therapists are widely needed to heel a large portion of the wealthy part of society form numerous traumas and stressors considered decades ago as barely distressing and managed individually or collectively in their proximate social environments.

Conclusion

The problems of medicalization and "therapism" (Richards, 2018; Sommers and Satel, 2005) are nontrivial in the WEIRD part of the world where people can economically afford and are socially welcome to analyze their own insecurities with the assistance of pills or therapists. This need may be seen as likely to be aroused from vulnerability of WEIRD people, who are less willing to address it collectively in their proximate social environment. This may not be easy as relationships are fragile, security provision uncertain, and the WEIRD culture itself is focused on importance of individual's own "true feelings and emotions". Access to and progress in medicine and psychological diagnostic and therapeutic methods may be another source of therapism and medicalization. In traditional non-WEIRD cultures many individuals with mental health problems were and still are left without proper diagnosis and treatment. Yet, keeping that in mind, the reasons gearing individuals from WEIRD cultural contexts to reach for medicalization and therapism are worth noting.

If one's coping resources are considered not sufficient (including insecure attachment) we, as therapists and psychologists, feel responsible for intervention based on education and security provision by supporting the resilience-related capacities one displays or by becoming a temporary attachment figure who provides a secure base for recovery. Even though therapy and medicalization may be helpful in this process, it is worth asking to what extent and how both medicalization and therapism add to the resilience capacities of individuals undergoing therapy. Resilience, as each skill, needs training to be effective. Yet, this training should be self-worked-out. Its provision and stimulation in safety zones may be ineffective by definition. It is done mainly through learning coping strategies from parents in childhood but these coping strategies must become habitual to the child. This is possible by their use in practice in non-cozy situations in which a child experiences distress and has to use them to self-regulate.

Yet, in the external world where minor events are perceived as threatening, reaching for therapy or medicine may be the easy way to go, more easy than self-coping and self-training. People might be motivated to attend therapy just because they can afford it, or are socially welcome to do so, and do not want to invest their own effort in self-coping, even regarding minor problems. Additionally, the trust in therapy, medicine, and science noticed in the WEIRD cultures might also discredit close others (e.g., parents) as security providers who might be perceived as not professional in their support provision. All of these phenomena narrow the range of security providers to those who have professional skills discrediting family members (like parents or grandparents) as traditionally available supporters in coping and providers of a secure base and safe haven.

The world is as it is. What is our role in times of social changes where individuals are likely to have a low threshold of threat, invest in long-lasting development of fragile trust toward a close other, and expect the rapid need for non-familial, professional security provision aid? Should we, as professionals, accept it and respond to societal needs with security provision and therapism whenever it is individually requested? One way is to respond with the provision of support and security to everyone who considers their own coping capacities as not sufficient or their own family members as not professional enough for security provision. Then, however, we also become responsible for characterizing the human psyche as fragile in the world in which the majority of people have successfully managed to develop attachment security that is viable in the evolutionary sense, to buffer against threats based on mastery and emotion regulation capacities allowing them to bounce back after hardships with the help of others. What may be another way to go? Maybe the problem is more global and relates to our expectation that the world, especially the one of children, must be a safe, cozy place with safety zones in which resilience capacities have no arena to be worked out and, if they appear, are coddled with therapeutic professional care. Even though the theses presented in this chapter may be perceived as extreme, certainly formulated, the aim of this chapter was to reflect on social changes that have taken place in the Western part of the world.

Note

1 Description based on the interview-based experience of the author of this chapter in Nahua sample in Mexico in 2022. RISE COLING Minority Languages, Major Opportunities. Collaborative Research, Community Engagement and Innovative Educational Tools – COLING" This project has received funding from the European Union's Horizon 2020 research and innovation programme under the Marie Skłodowska-Curie grant agreement No 778384.

References

Ainsworth, M. D. S., Blehar, M., Waters, E., and Wall, S. (1978/2015). *Patterns of Attachment.* Hillsdale, NJ: Erlbaum.

Bender, A. and Ingram, R. (2018). Connecting attachment style to resilience: Contributions of self-care and self-efficacy. *Personality and Individual Differences, 130,* 18–20.

Bowlby, J. (1973). *Attachment and Loss. Vol. 2: Separation.* New York: Basic Books.

Brulin, J. G., Lindholm, T., and Granqvist, P. (2022). In the state we trust? Attachment-related avoidance is related to lower trust, both in other people and in welfare state institutions. *Journal of Social and Political Psychology, 10*(1), 158–172, https://doi.org/ 10.5964/jspp.8381

Campbell-Sills, L. and Stein, M. B. (2007). Psychometric analysis and refinement of the Connor–Davidson resilience scale (CD-RISC): Validation of a 10-item measure of resilience. *Journal of Traumatic Stress: Official Publication of the International Society for Traumatic Stress Studies, 20*(6), 1019–1028.

Campos, B., Ullman, J. B., Aguilera, A., and Dunkel Schetter, C. (2014). Familism and psychological health: The intervening role of closeness and social support. *Cultural Diversity and Ethnic Minority Psychology, 20*(2), 191–201. https://doi.org/10.1037/a0034094

Cassidy, J. (2016). The nature of the child's ties. In W. J. Cassidy and P. R. Shaver (eds.), *Handbook of Attachment: Theory, Research, and Clinical Applications* (s. 3–24). New York: Guilford Press.

Coan, J. A. and Sbarra, D. A. (2015). Social baseline theory: The social regulation of risk and effort. *Current Opinion in Psychology, 1,* 87–91.

Cortina, M. and Liotti, G. (2010). Attachment is about safety and protection, intersubjectivity is about sharing and social understanding: The relationships between attachment and intersubjectivity. *Psychoanalytic Psychology, 27*(4), 410.

Eloranta, S. J., Peltonen, K., Palosaari, E., Qouta, S. R., and Punamäki, R. L. (2017). The role of attachment and emotion regulation in the psychosocial intervention among war-affected children. *Journal of Child and Adolescent Trauma, 10*(4), 301–314. https://doi.org/10.1007/s40653-016-0115-y

Ennis, L. R. (ed.) (2014). *Intensive Mothering: The Cultural Contradictions of Mother Motherhood*. Bradford: Demeter Press.

Erikson, E. H. (1994). *Identity and the Life Cycle*. New York: WW Norton & Company.

Fettweis, C. J. (2010). *Dangerous Times? The International Politics of Great Power Peace*. Washington: Georgetown University Press.

Forslund, T., Granqvist, P., van IJzendoorn, M. H., Sagi-Schwartz, A., Glaser, D., Steele, M., Hammarlund, M., Schuengel, C., Bakermans-Kranenburg, M. J., Steele, H., Shaver, P. R., Lux, U., Simmonds, J., Jacobvitz, D., Groh, A. M., Bernard, K., Cyr, C., Hazen, N. L., Foster, S., ... Duschinsky, R. (2022). Attachment goes to court: Child protection and custody issues. *Attachment and Human Development, 24*(1), 1–52.

Gillath, O., Ai, T., Branicky, M. S., Keshmiri, S., Davison, R. B., and Spaulding, R. (2021). Attachment and trust in artificial intelligence. *Computers in Human Behavior, 115*, 106607.

Gilbert, D. (2006). *Stumbling on Happiness*. New York: Alfred A. Knopf.

Greenfield, P. M., Keller, H., Fuligni, A., and Maynard, A. (2003). Cultural pathways through universal development. *Annual Review of Psychology, 54*(1), 461–490.

Henrich, J., Heine, S. J., and Norenzayan, A. (2010). The weirdest people in the world? *Behavioral and Brain Sciences, 33*, 61–135.

Hesse, E. (2008). The adult attachment interview: Protocol, method of analysis, and empirical studies. In W. J. Cassidy and P. R. Shaver (eds.), *Handbook of Attachment: Theory, Research, and Clinical Applications* (s. 552–599). New York: Guilford Press.

Inglehart, R. F. (2008). Changing values among Western publics from 1970 to 2006. *West European Politics, 31*(1–2), 130–146. doi: 10.1080/01402380701834747

Inglehart, R. and Baker, W. E. (2000). Modernization, cultural change, and the persistence of traditional values. *American Sociological Review, 65*(1), 19–51.

Jing, Y., Cai, H., Bond, M. H., Li, Y., Stivers, A. W., and Tan, Q. (2020). Levels of interpersonal trust across different types of environment: The micro-macro interplay between relational distance and human ecology. *Journal of Experimental Psychology: General*. Advance online publication. http://dx.doi.org/10.1037/xge0000997

Keller, H. (2018). Universality claim of attachment theory: Children's socioemotional development across cultures. *Proceedings of the National Academy of Sciences, 115*(45), 11414–11419.

Kito, M., Yuki, M., and Thomson, R. (2017). Relational mobility and close relationships: A socioecological approach to explain cross-cultural differences. *Personal Relationships, 24*(1), 114–130.

Leppin, A. L., Gionfriddo, M. R., Sood, A., Montori, V. M., Erwin, P. J., Zeballos-Palacios, C., ... and Tilburt, J. C. (2014). The efficacy of resilience training programs: a systematic review protocol. *Systematic Reviews, 3*, 1–5.

Lubiewska, K. (2018). Attachment ambivalence: The concept, psychological importance, and measurement issues. In W. I. Albert, E. Abbey, and J. Valsiner (eds.), *Cultural Psychology of Transgenerational Family Relations: Investigating Ambivalence*. Charlotte, NC: Information Age Publishing.

Lukianoff, G. and Haidt, J. (2019). *The Coddling of the American Mind: How Good Intentions and Bad Ideas Are Setting Up a Generation for Failure*. New York: Penguin.

Masten, A. S. (2015). Pathways to integrated resilience science. *Psychological Inquiry, 26*(2), 187–196.

Mesman, J., van IJzendoorn, M. H., and Sagi-Schwartz, A. (2016). Cross-cultural patterns of attachment: Universal and contextual dimensions. In W. J. Cassidy and P. R. Shaver (eds.), *Handbook of Attachment: Theory, Research, and Clinical Applications* (s. 852–877). New York: Guilford Press.

Mikulincer, M. (1998). Attachment working models and the sense of trust: An exploration of interaction goals and affect regulation. *Journal of Personality and Social Psychology*, *74*(5), 1209.

Milkie, M. A.. and Warner, C. H. (2014). Status safeguarding: Mothers' work to secure children's place in the social hierarchy. In L. R. Ennis (ed.), *Intensive Mothering: The Cultural Contradictions of Mother Motherhood* (pp. 66–Bradford: Demeter Press.

Minkov, M., Dutt, P., Schachner, M., Jandosova, J., Khassenbekov, Y., Morales, O., ... and Mudd, B. (2018). What values and traits do parents teach to their children? New data from 54 countries. *Comparative Sociology*, *17*(2), 221–252.

Mischel, W. (2014). *The Marshmallow Test: Understanding Self-control and How to Master It*. London: Random House.

Nisbett, R. (2004). *The Geography of Thought: How Asians and Westerners Think Differently ... and Why*. New York: Simon and Schuster.

Norris, P. (2021). Cancel culture: Myth or reality? *Political Studies*, *17*(1), 145–174.

Olowokere, A. and Okanlawon, F. (2018). Improving vulnerable school children's psycho-social health outcomes through resilience-based training and peer-support activities: a comparative prospective study. *Vulnerable Children and Youth Studies*, *13*(4), 291–304.

Oyserman, D., Coon, H. M., and Kemmelmeier, M. (2002). Rethinking individualism and collectivism: Evaluation of theoretical assumptions and meta-analyses. *Psychological Bulletin*, *128*(1), 3.

Pinker, S. (2018). *Enlightenment Now: The Case for Reason, Science, Humanism, and Progress*. London: Penguin.

Poortinga, Y. (2015). Is "culture" a workable concept for (cross-) cultural psychology. *Online Readings in Psychology and Culture*, *2*(1), 1–21.

Richards, B. (2018). *What Holds Us Together*. New York: Routledge.

Rotenberg, K. J., Wicks, C., and Bathew, R. (2021). Security of attachment and trust beliefs in close others during middle childhood. *Infant and Child Development*, *30*(5), e2252.

Rothbaum, F. and Trommsdorff, G. (2007). *Do Roots and Wings Complement or Oppose One Another? The Socialization of Relatedness and Autonomy in Cultural Context*. New York: Guilford Press.

Rothbaum, F., Weisz, J., Pott, M., Miyake, K., and Morelli, G. (2000). Attachment and culture: Security in the United States and Japan. *American Psychologist*, *55*(10), 1093.

Saunders, R., Jacobvitz, D., Zaccagnino., M, Beverung, L. M, and Hazan, N. (2011). Pathways to earned-security: The role of alternative support figures. *Attachment & Human Development*, *13*, 403–420. https://doi.org/10.1080/14616734.2011.584405

Sommers, C. H. and Satel, S. (2005). One Nation under Therapy: How the Helping Culture Is Eroding Self-Reliance. *Review-Institute of Public Affairs*, *57*(2), 47.

Sroufe, L. A. (2016). Attachment theory: A humanistic approach for research and practice across cultures. In W. S. Gojman-de-Millan, C. Herreman, and L. A. Sroufe (eds.), *Attachment Across Clinical and Cultural Perspectives. A Relational Psychoanalytic Approach* (s. 3–29). New York: Routledge/Taylor & Francis Group.

Sroufe, L. A. and Waters, E. (1977). Attachment as an organizational construct. *Child Development*, *48*, 1184–1199.

Stevenson-Hinde, J. and Shouldice, A. (1993). Wariness to strangers: A behavior systems perspective revisited. In K. H. Rubin and J. B. Asendorpf (eds.), *Social Withdrawal,*

Inhibition, and Shyness in Childhood (pp. 101–116). New York: Lawrence Erlbaum Associates, Inc.

Taleb, N. N. (2012). *Antifragile: Things that Gain from Disorder* (Vol. 3). London: Random House.

Trommsdorff, G. (2006). Parent-child relations over the life-span. A cross-cultural perspective. In K. H. Rubin and O. B. Chung (eds.), *Parenting Beliefs, Behaviors, and Parent-child Relations: A Cross-cultural Perspective*, Psychology Press, 143–183.

Twenge, J. M. (2017). *iGen: Why Today's Super-connected Kids Are Growing Up Less Rebellious, More Tolerant, Less Happy--And Completely Unprepared for Adulthood--And What That Means for the Rest of Us*. New York: Simon and Schuster.

Wong, P. T. and Cowden, R. G. (2022). Accelerating the science and practice of psychology beyond WEIRD biases: Enriching the landscape through Asian psychology. *Frontiers in Psychology, 13,* 1–7.

Part II

Safety and security in the community context

Chapter 6

"I am still scattered"

Attachment security and belonging after forced migration

Lydia Guthrie

Introduction

This chapter will consider how attachment relationships within families may develop within the context of forced transnational migration, brought about by war. Attachment theory has long been used as a framework to consider the impact of conflict; for example, Bowlby was commissioned by the World Health Organization to investigate the impact of the Second World War upon children (Bowlby,1952). Systemic thinking can help to elaborate the complex both/and processes involved in migration – the advantages and possibilities of establishing a life in a new country, co-existing alongside the multiple losses brought about by the uprooting of physical, social, cultural, and religious contexts. The impact of both the losses and possibilities extend far into future generations, as the children of transnational migrants are raised by adults who are themselves negotiating how to balance the old with the new, and how to create a sense of safety within new social contexts.

The first relationships experienced by an infant are usually with their primary caregivers, and across the lifespan the relational context expands to include extended family members, peers, and in adulthood, possibly partners and children. The development of attachment strategies is situated within multiple levels of context; we can zoom in to the level of a neuron connecting with other neurons within the brain, and zoom out to the levels of families, communities, and wider social networks. Each level of context influences and is influenced by others. Cozolino and Walker (2008) describe this as the "social synapse" – the medium through which we are linked together into larger organisms, such as communities, tribes, societies, nations, and ultimately species.

Wider contexts, including social and cultural institutions, can support or threaten the development of safe attachment bonds. Writing about the impact of war, Leaning (2008) elaborates the concept of human security, defined as "the essential social expression of human attachment" (2008, p.125). Human security involves a sense of home, a link to community, and a positive sense of future possibilities. The concept of home is connected to having a place to belong, to feel safe, and to develop a sense of personal identity. Community participation supports the development of

DOI: 10.4324/9781003308096-9

a wider network of social contacts, many based upon the daily activities of living, such as buying food, participating in education or work, and knowing where to obtain help and support when needed. A positive sense of the future can support individuals to make decisions for their families based on long-term goals or hopes. This chapter will consider how forced transnational migration impacts upon human security, safety, and the development of attachment bonds.

The context for refugees

A refugee is defined as:

> someone who is unable or unwilling to return to their country of origin owing to a well-founded fear of being persecuted for reasons of race, religion, nationality, membership of a particular social group, or political opinion.
>
> (1951 Refugee Convention)

The United Nations High Commissioner for Refugees estimates that at the end of 2017, there were 79.5 million displaced people, including 25 million registered refugees (UNHCR, 2020). The experiences of refugees are situated within a suite of global stories characterised by injustice and oppression in relation to race, ethnicity, culture and religion, and the legacies of colonialism (Papadopoulos, 2002).

This chapter will draw upon research which I conducted as part of an MSc in Systemic Family Therapy. With the support of an Arabic interpreter, Nala, I interviewed three families who had settled in the UK under the Syrian Vulnerable Persons Resettlement Scheme (SVPRS). I reflected upon their experiences using the Multidimensional Ecosystemic Comparative approach (Falicov, 2017) as a frame. The participants gave their informed consent for their experiences and words to be described in this chapter, and each person chose their own pseudonym. Demographic details of the participants are outlined in Table 6.1. This is a small sample, within a particular and limited context, and there is no intention to imply that the ideas or themes can be generalised to other contexts.

Working with an interpreter

I arranged for an independent Arabic/English interpreter to be present, as I do not speak Arabic. Nala is an Arabic speaking woman who moved to the UK ten years ago and works as a self-employed interpreter. Lee (2017) describes the generative potential of fluid relational positioning when working with interpreters and asylum seekers. During the conversations, I noticed moments where Nala's gestures, facial expressions, and the tone and rhythm of her voice suggested to me that she was engaged on an emotional level – as more than simply a translator of words. I also acted as meaningful witness to moments where she and the participants connected through aspects of their shared identities.

Table 6.1 Demographic details of participants

Names and ages	Mother:
	  Hiba (36)
	Father:
	  Juan (38)
	Daughter:
	  Sarah (9)
	Son:
	  Ahmed (5)
		Father:
		  Adnan (35)
		Mother:
		  Hannan (30)
		Son:
		  Karim (5)
		Son:
		  Omran (4)
		Daughter:
		  Rawan (1)
			Mother:
			  Hasnah (44)
			Daughter:
			  Nadine (26)
			Daughter:
			  Jasmine (24)

Where did they go after leaving Syria	Egypt for 5.5 years	Jordan for 6 years	Jordan for 4 years
Length of time in UK	1.5 years	1.5 years	3 years
Work/education situation	Both looking for work	Father works full time Mother is caring for under 5s	Mother does not work; daughters are studying at university and working in part time jobs

I experienced fluid positioning while Hiba was describing her dilemma about her daughters being taught sex education in a mixed-sex class, which was not in accordance with her religious and cultural beliefs. Nala began to nod emphatically, and I had the sense that she was connecting with this experience as a Muslim, a mother, and a transnational immigrant. Nala and Hiba then began to speak together in Arabic. After a few moments, Nala looked over to me, and smiled, and explained, in English, that she had felt an urge to share her experiences with Hiba, as she had faced similar dilemmas navigating the education system when her daughters were younger. I asked Nala to ask Hiba, in Arabic, if she would be willing to say a few words about what it had been like for her to have the conversation with Nala. Hiba smiled, and said, in Arabic, that she had welcomed the conversation because she didn't know any other Muslim women with older daughters who had also faced these issues. I was struck by the warm, emotional tone of this conversation – two women engaged in mutual collaboration to support the safety and wellbeing of their children within an unfamiliar social, cultural, and religious context.

Following a moment where Hannan recalled feeling vulnerable in a shopping centre after being mocked by a group of boys, Nala and Hannan shared a spontaneous conversation in Arabic about the different ways in which they prefer to wear their hijab. After a few moments, Nala looked up at me with an expression which I interpreted as reflecting her realisation that, as a White British woman who does not wear a hijab, I could not join in the conversation. I responded with an open-handed gesture to both Nala and Hannan, which I intended as an invitation to continue. My inability to speak Arabic, and my outsider witness position, caused me to focus upon the gestures, facial expressions, shared emotional content, and rhythm of this interaction. These moments of Nala, Hannan, and Hiba co-constructing safe relational connections based upon gender, migration status, religion, language, and culture seemed like precious examples of building a shared sense of human security to navigate new contexts.

Multidimensional Ecosystemic Comparative Approach (MECA)

This framework elaborates upon the experiences of transnational migrants, drawing on social constructionist and systemic epistemologies. It is underpinned by ethical positions of respecting subjugated cultures, and promoting social justice. The MECA (Falicov, 2012) is rooted in the position that the emerging identities and relational worlds of people who have made transnational migration journeys are influenced by multiple cultural and contextual resources, within a wider context of global inequalities.

The MECA focuses upon four domains:

1 Migration and Acculturation – the family's reasons for migrating, the nature of the migration journey, and the extent to which they resettle in the host country.
2 Ecological context – how the family live within the broader socio-cultural climate of the host country, including the impact of their marginalised status, their experiences of racism, and access to resources.
3 Family organisation – including diversity in family arrangements, and the relational and intergenerational stresses which can be evoked by changing socio-cultural contexts and relational patterns.
4 Family life cycle – the ways in which developmental stages and transitions are navigated and constructed by the family in the context of their culture and beliefs.

Migration and acculturation

The families each left Syria due to the impact of the war, which led them to fear for their safety. They each spent between five and seven years in either Egypt or Jordan, which they chose due to its geographical and socio-cultural proximity to Syria. Each family chose to apply from the intermediary country to the UNHCR scheme, seeking supported resettlement in a safe Western country. The families did not choose the UK as their final destination, and they had between four and six weeks' notice of their flights to the UK.

Each person described a deep ambivalence inherent in their migration journey, as they simultaneously looked backwards towards their Syrian home, and forwards towards an unknown future for them and their children in a new country. Adnan offered a powerful description of his emotional experience of boarding the aeroplane to the UK:

Adnan: I was devastated. I was in a wreck. Especially when I was in the aero-plane. I felt like my soul was out of my body. I felt that I was dead. But, obviously, I was living … just a living corpse.

Adnan's wife, Hannan, offered a different perspective. She was seven months pregnant with her third child during the flight to the UK, and smiled at her youngest child while telling me that she had been excited to board the plane:

Hannan: I was happy going out of the country, and flying to another country. I had learned about the UK, and I loved to come to the UK. I thought that life would be better here, and it is.

Adnan explained that he had wanted to remain in Jordan, because he had found work, and was proud of his ability to provide a good standard of living for his family. Hannan spoke movingly about wanting a future for her children where they could access education as equal citizens. These conversations may have illustrated their different priorities in how they understood safety and protection for their children – Adnan was prioritising financial security in the here and now, and Hannan was valuing citizenship and access to education for her children. I was curious about how much this might be influenced by their constructions of gender roles (Burck and Daniel, 1995) and about how they might construct a narrative for their children which made space for the different emotional experiences of their journey to the UK and, in turn, how their children might come to understand and to tell the story of their migration.

UK social context

The social context into which the families are adapting is itself influenced by narratives of perceptions of safety and danger within the host country. Within the UK, the dominant portrayal of immigrants is often negative; they can be positioned as representing a threat by competing with British families for scarce resources such as houses, jobs and school places (Allen and Blinder, 2013). Some newspaper headlines describe migrants as "flooding" into the country, and it is the express policy of the current UK government to create a "hostile environment" for migrants.

Support services

As part of the SVPRS, local organisations were commissioned to offer support with finding housing, school places and with accessing language lessons. The families appreciated this support, but also offered multiple examples of a lack of fit between dominant social norms in the UK, and their values and aspirations.

Hiba described feeling infantilised by support services, perceiving that they held fixed ideas of the ways in which they should be adapting to dominant cultures, and weren't holding in mind that they were accomplished people who had been forced to leave behind their homes and businesses due to war.

Hiba complained that it took several attempts to convince her doctor to refer her for physical tests for chest pain, as the doctor seemed convinced that her physical symptoms were related to traumatic experiences. Hiba urged her doctor to accept that her health could be affected both by her experiences of trauma and migration, and by physical health conditions, rather than all symptoms being indicative of the somatic expression of trauma.

Ecological context

This domain considers the interaction between the family's values, norms, and behaviours and the dominant cultural norms of the new country. Parental behaviours which support healthy development in Syria may not secure safety in the UK. The stress of normative family transitions, such as a child starting school, or an older adult retiring from paid employment, may be exacerbated by social and cultural dissonance.

Learning the new rules

Many psychotherapy traditions recognise the importance of a sense of belonging and competence for psychological wellbeing. Writing about identity and belonging from a social constructionist and systemic perspective, Shotter (1993) describes how we become who we are only in relation to others. To feel at home within a community, one must feel able to contribute to it, and to do that, a person needs access to what he describes as a "living tradition":

> A hierarchically structured organised, unitary system of already accepted knowledge that is supposed to provide members with ready-made solutions to the problem of how to be proper members of their group.
>
> (p. 3)

Through this lens, the families can be understood as describing the dissonance they experience when their "ready-made solutions" cease to be effective, in the context of a transformed socio-cultural context. This presents many parenting dilemmas – how do you keep your family fed and housed when you can't find work? If you have lost your sense of routine and structure, how do you support your children to feel that the world is predictable? How do you raise a child to feel safe in their environmental context if there are aspects of that context which you as an adult are not yet able to navigate?

Each person described their developing ability to negotiate from a marginalised position within their transformed socio-cultural world. For example, Adnan spoke of an argument with his neighbour on Christmas Day. Adnan had not appreciated that his neighbour would find it unacceptable for him to undertake noisy home improvements on Christmas Day. In the context of his Muslim faith, Christmas Day was just a day off work, which offered an opportunity to catch up on household tasks. However, when his neighbour came to the door and chastised him angrily, Adnan quickly appreciated that he had broken a rule which had been invisible to him, and apologised. Later in the day, the neighbour brought some Christmas foods to Adnan and his family, and they have been on very friendly terms since.

This episode of rupture and repair with his neighbour offers an example of skillful navigation of new contexts. This appears to be an example of the flexibility of mind, capacity to reflect, and the social skills which have supported Adnan in developing a bi-cultural transnational identity, based upon fluid both/and positions.

Language

In each family, the children were more fluent in English than their parents. Hannan was unable to understand her children, aged 4 and 5, when they used English to communicate with each other at home. Hannan did not describe this as a problem – she framed it as a story about how quickly her children were learning English, which seemed to be a source of pride.

Focusing on the issue of language, Hasnah and Jasmine both aspire to become fluent, which Hasnah explicitly frames as her duty to the country which has offered her citizenship. Hiba and Hannan expressed ambivalence about learning English. Hiba stated that on the one hand she wishes to learn English, but on the other she resents feeling pressurised to learn it, and felt that support agencies were telling her that she needed to improve her English in order to progress. Hiba has chosen not to speak English at home with her husband or children, as she wants her children to be fluent in Arabic and Kurdish.

This can be thought of as a Strange Loop (Pearce, 2007) – when mutually exclusive meanings exist at different levels of context, resulting in oscillating patterns of behaviour. A dominant cultural story is that migrants owe a reciprocal duty to integrate, especially by learning English, and a subjugated family story is that they did not choose to come to the UK and would prefer to communicate in Arabic.

A useful way forward may be to adopt a third position outside of these binaries, which both recognises the potential economic and cultural benefits of learning English and holds onto the important contribution which speaking Arabic (and also Kurdish for Hiba's family) makes to their sense of cultural identity. Falicov (2007) suggests that families which operate in multiple languages can draw strength and flexibility from their linguistic skills. Burck (2004) describes language as a source of connection between individuals, society, and culture, and that multiple languages can offer a source of strength and resilience. Burck (2004) describes language as "culture-soaked" and draws attention to different aspects of self-identity which are expressed in different language systems. Hannan began our conversation speaking in English, and spoke Arabic when she was describing her family's life in Damascus. She explained to me that she thought about her early life in Arabic, and she could express her emotions more freely in the language of her childhood.

Family organisation

This domain is concerned with the ways in which family relationships within and between generations may be influenced by the impact of migration, and how differences may be negotiated.

Intergenerational differences

Hasnah and her daughter Jasmine expressed different views about whether the UK could ever feel like home for them. Hasnah described Syria as home, and stated that she would never feel "at home" in the UK:

Hasnah: So, often, I think whether I'm going to go back or not. And I think that here I have rights and I'm much stronger here, but still the feeling that this is not my home still is inside me. I am still scattered, moving from one place to another, and then from one place to another. I have complex feelings, but here, I feel safe and the girls obviously are settled.

Although Hasnah feels that she and her children are physically safe in the UK, she is unsure whether she can ever feel psychologically at home outside Syria – for her, a feeling of being at home is more than being physically safe. In contrast to her mother, Jasmine reflected that the UK is now her home, because it is where her family is, although she regrets the interruptions to her life plans necessitated by her migration:

Jasmine: So, basically home of course, it's here, we're settled, we have mum and my siblings. When I think about Syria, who is there? No-one. Some are in Egypt, some are in Jordan, and some are other places in the world. So, this is home.

Jasmine takes a pragmatic view – if ideas of home are linked to being with people who are close, and the people are no longer where they were, then perhaps a new place can become home?

This can be understood as an example of "intergenerational acculturational conflict" (Falicov, 2017). Young people may experience the losses of the home country with a different emotional intensity from their parents. However, they are also exposed to the loss through their parent's experiences of disconnection from their home, and their sense of "ambiguous loss" (Falicov, 2017). Children can play an important role in co-constructing continuity and change with their parents in the context of the new society and culture. For example, Hasnah speaks with delight about her daughter's graduation from a UK university after many years of disrupted academic studies, and this achievement supports Hasnah to feel more connected to social structures in the UK. The tension between preserving a sense of connection to the home country while building a sense of belonging in a new country goes to the heart of the challenges of transnational migration.

Gender roles within relationships

Hiba and Hannan both explained that they would not routinely expect women in Syria to work outside the home, especially if they are caring for children. Hannan framed this as a question of trust between men and women:

Hannan: Well, it's very restrictive back home, women are not allowed to work, so they just stay at home, look after the house and look after the family. And the man would just go out and bring the money and everything for the house. Whereas here in the UK, there is a lot of trust between men and women.

Hannan viewed this as a positive development, and she appreciated what she perceived as newfound freedoms:

Hannan: From my point of view, women here are treated fairly, not like Syrian women.

Hiba explained that she had not needed to work outside the home in Syria, as her husband was able to earn enough money for the family. However, in the UK, her family's rent is higher than her husband's earnings, so she is also looking for work, with her husband's support.

This suggests that the ways in which gender is constructed within relationships can be flexible in relation to the wider needs of the family, and individual views. Hiba and Hannan were both engaged in developing a new construction of gender roles, particularly in relation to work, which fitted with their new social and economic environment, in order to build a sense of financial security and safety for their family.

Family life cycle

This domain is concerned with how families experience anticipated and unanticipated transitions within the context of their community's culture. For migrant families, how to navigate life cycle stages in an unfamiliar cultural context where they are positioned as "other" can be a particular challenge.

Preserving a link to Syria

All of the families recognised the tension between wanting to raise their children to be able to stay safe and navigate danger within their new country of the UK, while also wanting them to feel a meaningful connection to their Syrian homeland.

Hiba explicitly framed keeping her Syrian culture alive as a challenge:

Hiba: We want to implement and have our culture and for it to remain, and to help them to live our own culture. And obviously the UK culture is completely different. This is the challenge there is going to be.

None of the families in the study is able to return to Syria at present, and contact with extended family is negotiated through video calls and messages. Hiba speaks of how difficult she finds it to share her cultural heritage with her children without being able to visit her extended family there. She stated that everything the children learn about Syria they will have to learn from her, and she experiences this as a heavy responsibility. She emphasised that she and her husband do not speak English at home, so that her children learn to speak Arabic fluently.

Each family left behind family members and community ties when they boarded the plane to the UK. Adnan spoke of a family party at his father's house, the night before he and his family flew to the UK, attended by over a hundred family members and friends:

Adnan: Here I am lonely. Back home, you will find people who will help you, your cousins, other relatives, will help you if you face some problems. But here I am lonely.

Being separated from wider family networks has a considerable impact upon the resources available to parents to support them in raising their children, and in turn upon the parents' ability to seek comfort and safety from their own parents and loved ones.

School transitions

Two of the families had children who attended local primary school, and were learning to navigate different social and cultural expectations about education. Hiba identified two issues which highlighted these tensions – teaching sex education to a mixed gender class, and expecting boys and girls to get changed for PE in the same changing area. Hiba had spoken with school staff about making exceptions for her daughters, but had not been successful. Her way of navigating these complex contexts was to discuss with her daughters the family's preferred way of organising themselves, and to contrast that with the school's preferred ways. She then supported her children to adopt a both/and position, where they did not feel that they needed to choose between home and school. Hiba described this as adopting an open-minded approach:

Hiba: As Muslims, we have certain restrictions. Here in the UK, it is quite open to different things. And we don't want to be forcing the children into certain things. We want to be open minded and balance things.

Adnan's son was due to start school later that year. He was already anticipating some challenges ahead:

Adnan: Other families have told me that they will pick up things that I will not approve of. But you can obviously change their understanding.

Adnan was learning from other Muslim families that the local school was able to support their children to maintain a Halal diet, and to pray and fast in accordance with their religious needs. This seemed to be another example of Adnan's developing skill set of negotiating with community organisations to enable his children to participate in wider social structures while protecting important aspects of their cultural and religious identity. Falicov (2005) notes that a challenge for migrants is to learn how to navigate life cycle transitions where the dominant norms differ from those of the home country. I found myself wondering how the transitional stage of a child starting school might be experienced differently in Oxford as compared to Syria – what family parties or celebrations might have been possible?

Rituals of connection

Falicov (2012) describes "re-creation rituals"; a form of psychological return to keep cultural memories alive and evoke continuity amidst change. An embodied example of Hasnah's attempts to settle into life in the UK while preserving her ties to Syria is that she has filled their home with beautiful textiles which she brought with her from Syria. She described this as an attempt to recreate aspects Syria in her new home in the UK:

Hasnah: Yes, you can combine the two cultures or the two countries, and you can never isolate yourself from your culture. In a way, you will always come back to it. For example, here, this house, it's almost like you are in Syria. There is a way that you will always come back, regardless of the country that you are in, you will always come back to your roots.

When Hasnah showed me the fabrics, her posture seemed to soften, and her eyes shone, and I felt an urge to show my appreciation for them as a means of conveying respect. These items seemed to represent a physical manifestation of her ties to the country and culture where her heart feels at home, with their threads weaving together the past, present, and future. I had the sense that they might embody continuity and connection for her, in a way which provides physical, psychological, and emotional comfort as she negotiates multiple positions across multiple contexts.

Conclusion

This chapter has applied the Multidimensional Ecosystemic Comparative Approach (Falicov, 2012) to explore the ways in which the migrant families construct multiple identities across multiple contexts. These processes are located within a social context characterised by dominant social stories in the UK which often position them as vulnerable and "other". They vividly described their experiences of ambiguous losses, of their home and extended social networks, and also their hopes for a safer future for their children. They are seeking safety and security for their families by developing ways of preserving essential themes of faith, culture and language, while learning to adopt new practices and to negotiate across social difference. Returning to the concept of human security, each participant was striving to create safety for their families by building a sense of home through repeated patterns of negotiations across multiple levels of social contexts in their families and wider communities. Each person spoke of ways in which they held home in their hearts (Lee, 2013) while collaborating to build new connections while holding on to what was precious. There were many examples of the power and value of hope – Adnan repairing a rupture with his neighbour, Hiba and Nala speaking about how to negotiate a respectful way forward with school and Jasmine completing her degree and beginning to build her career in the UK. Hannan's metaphor of weaving together the past, present, and future in the threads of her beautiful fabrics offers a useful frame to think about the process of joining together the old and the new to create a meaningful new identities to support psychological safety.

References

Allen, W. and Blinder, S. (2013). Migration in the news: Portrayals of immigrants, migrants, asylum seekers and refugees in national British newspapers, 2010 to 2012, *Migration Observatory Report*. Oxford: COMPAS, University of Oxford.

Bowlby, J. (1952). *Maternal Care and Mental Health: A Report Prepared on Behalf of the World Health Organization as a Contribution to the United Nations Programme for the Welfare of Homeless Children*. World Health Organization.

Burck, C. (2004). Living in several languages: Implications for therapy. *Journal of Family Therapy* 26, 314–339.

Burck, C. and Daniel, G. (1995). *Gender and Family Therapy*. Routledge.

Cozolino, L. and Walker, M. D. (2008). The social construction of the human brain. In M. Green (ed.) *Risking Human Security: Attachment and Public Life* (pp. 3–18). Karnak.

Combs, G. (2019). White privilege: What's a family therapist to do? *Journal of Marital and Family Therapy*, 45(1), 61–75.

Falicov, C. J. (2005). Emotional transnationalism and family identities. *Family Process*, 44(4), 399–406.

Falicov, C. J. (2007). Working with transnational immigrants: Expanding meanings of family, community, and culture, *Family Process*, 46(2), 157–171.

Falicov, C. J. (2012). Immigrant family processes: A multidimensional framework. In F. Walsh (ed.) *Normal Family Processes: Growing Diversity and Complexity* (pp. 297–323). Guilford Press.

Falicov, C. J. (2016). Migration and the family life cycle. In M. McGoldrick, N. Garcia-Preto, and B. Carter (eds) *The Expanded Family Life Cycle: Individual, Family and Social Perspectives* (pp. 222–239). Allyn & Bacon.

Falicov, C. J. (2017). Multidimensional Ecosystemic Comparative Approach (MECA). In
J. Lebow, A. Chambers, and D. Breunlin (eds) *Encyclopaedia of Couple and Family
Therapy* (pp. 1–5). Springer.

Leaning, J. (2008). Human security and conflict In M. Green (ed.) *Risking Human
Security: Attachment and Public Life* (pp. 125–150). Karnak.

Lee, P. L. (2013). Making now precious: Working with survivors of torture and asylum
seekers. *The International Journal of Narrative Therapy and Community Work*, (1), 1–10.

Lee, P. L (2017). Narrative conversations alongside interpreters: A locally-grown outsider-
witnessing practice. *International Journal of Narrative Therapy & Community Work*,
(4),18–27.

Papadopoulos, R. K. (2002). Refugees, home and trauma. In R. K. Papadopoulos (ed.)
Therapeutic Care for Refugees. No Place Like Home. Tavistock Clinic Series Migration
review, 37(3), 812–846. Karnak.

Pearce, W. B. (2007). *Making Social Worlds: A Communication Perspective.* Blackwell
Publishing.

Shotter, J. (1993). Becoming someone: Identity and belonging. In N. Coupland and J.
Nussbaum (eds) *Discourse and Lifespan Development.* (pp. 5–27). Sage.

UN General Assembly, *Convention Relating to the Status of Refugees*, 28 July 1951, United
Nations, Treaty Series, 189, p. 137. available at: www.refworld.org/docid/3be01b964.
html [accessed 27 November 2022].

UNHCR (2020) *Global Trends: Forced Displacement in 2019.* United Nations High
Commissioner for Refugees.

Chapter 7

'We will keep you safe'

Reflections on caring relationships in children's residential homes

Olivia Polisano, Andy Glossop and Laura Ogi

'We will keep you safe'

The concepts of safety, security, danger and protection are at the heart of children's social care (CSC) services in the UK. These terms orient social workers and care providers towards 'child protection' and providing 'safeguarding' from harm. The sad reality is that these aims can never fully be realised. Children who live in residential homes have been confronted much sooner than we would hope for any child, with the devastating knowledge that the world is not always safe.

Carers of these children face a complex challenge of integrating the possibility of future dangers with a desire for the future of children to be a happy one. The practice of promising protection from harm appears to resolve discomfort and makes us all feel safer in the short term. However, our experiences have taught us that these promises are sadly impossible to keep. Parents and carers might identify with the desire to 'wrap our children in cotton wool' and prevent any harm coming to them. Yet we know this can never be realised without compromising essential aspects of the caregiving relationship and developmental opportunities. Danger does exist and, in some cases, cannot be avoided. Learning to navigate the dangers of life is key to becoming a well-functioning adult.

This chapter will discuss how issues of danger and protection exist in caring relationships within children's residential homes. We'll reflect on our experiences of these relationships, considering what forms of safety are possible for those living and working across these settings. We end with the intention of cultivating realistic hope, suggesting more possible promises that we hope might direct practitioners towards greater opportunities for interpersonal connection and feelings of security.

Andy, Laura and Olivia's experiences

We work in a team of psychologists, teachers, psychiatrists and family practitioners within a Local Authority CSC service in England. Our roles involve providing psychological consultation and reflective practice sessions for staff working in residential homes and their managers, as well as working directly with children and their families.

DOI: 10.4324/9781003308096-10

In the time we have spent working together across residential homes we have been inspired by the children we have met (directly and indirectly). We have been left with a deep respect for these children and come to challenge the dominant narrative upheld that predicts a life defined by loss, of ongoing hardship and exclusion from society. We do not mean to dismiss the presence of the very darkest of traumas unjustly experienced by these children but to acknowledge the presence of hope alongside such difficulties. The pedagogical concept of the 'rich child' (Malaguzzi, 1993; Moss, Dillon and Statham, 2000) has helped us to make room for hope where we may otherwise have despaired. Malaguzzi's invitation to notice the resources, strength and potential held within the child has transformed feelings of helplessness and hopelessness.

The work has at times been uncomfortable, challenging our own feelings of security. We have found our practice of Clinical Psychology within social care has offered a unique (and at times challenging) lens. Our relationships as a team have also developed amongst personal and professional dangers and we have invested in building security with each other. Though we have been on a journey of learning, it may disappoint our readers to learn that we do not profess to have the answers! In fact, in this relational world, we are not sure they exist. Instead, we offer an account of our experiences that we hope can open opportunities for others & inspire curiosity. This is our 'possible promise' to you.

Think of a child who lives in a residential home – what do you see?

The narrative that society upholds about children who live in residential care appears centred around experiences of danger, vulnerability and a need for care (Berridge, Biehal and Henry, 2012). This group of children have usually survived multiple physical, psychological and interpersonal dangers (Department for Education, 2016). They have profound experience with feelings of rejection and loss. These losses could have been caused by abuse, death or illness of a parent, or by community-based dangers such as exploitation (Anda et al, 2006). For unaccompanied asylum-seeking children, their lives may have been marked by war or by long journeys to the UK. Children have often been moved between various care placements, whether these are within family arrangements, placements with foster carers or residential homes. Often their families have experienced abuses across multiple generations and learnt 'how to parent' in these contexts (Greenwood, 2016). These and other experiences mean their exposure to Adverse Childhood Experiences (ACEs) is significantly higher than children in the general population (Perry, 2014). As such, they are more likely to receive a mental health diagnosis, achieve poorer educational outcomes and enter the criminal justice system (NICE, 2010).

Sadly, when children arrive in residential care, intrusions upon their sense of safety do not stop. The experience of separation from family and the daily legacy of trauma continues. They must develop new relationships with a number of people, establish new routines and experience unfamiliar ways of being cared for. Their daily lives are marked by uncertainty – am I safe? How long will I be staying? Where am I going next? Who will look after me?

The rich child

And yet, the concept of the rich child invites us to look again. What resources, skills and talents might these children who have indeed suffered, hold? What are these children's hopes and aspirations? Who do they look up to? What have they taught us? Through these questions we have found new respect both for the person this child is now and for the future they will grow into. New possibilities begin to emerge for how we view these children and for how we relate to them.

The experience of the carer

We have observed that caring adults exposed to such great suffering in children naturally want to take that pain away. Humans are biologically predisposed to protecting children, and keeping them safe from harm (Bowlby, 2005). For those who have chosen to enter professionally caring roles, this urge is likely to be amplified (McFadden, Campbell and Taylor, 2014). Yet, in acknowledging the existence of this suffering we are also exposed to the existence of danger. The intolerable knowledge that children experience abuse, poverty, deprivation and loss may be considered an existential threat (Waterhouse and McGhee, 2009). In our experience, daily exposure to this threat can come with significant emotional implications, such as anxiety, grief, anger and more.

Understanding the residential childcare workforce and their experience is a particular research gap (Parry, Williams and Oldfield, 2022). However, in our experience the discomfort staff experience through daily exposure to existential threat and the urge to reduce the suffering of children they care for can impact on them in many ways. Practically, it is evidenced in the dedication that people in residential roles bring to their work. This dedication is often highly valued, labelled as 'going above and beyond' and described as serving a 'duty of care'. This sense of duty may be personal as well as professional, perhaps giving meaning to complex personal histories by 'giving something back' (Beckler, 2014; Moses, 2000). Within the workforce, we have observed and connected with staff who have experienced difficulties in their own childhood that range from having grown up in care, to difficulties in relationships with their parents, amongst peers or at school.

The challenges faced by the sector are also likely to impact on the experience of the workforce. The issues we have described here point towards a need for high rates of supervision, reflective spaces and focus on staff wellbeing (resources we as psychologists have ready access to), but sadly these can be hard to come by for care staff (Happ, Glossop and Ogi, 2018). Further challenges include a paucity of training, restricted salaries, as well as a 'broken' market and profiteering from private providers (MacAlister, 2022). The independent review of Children's Social Care (MacAlister, 2022) also notes the impact of serious case reviews and high profile 'failures' of CSC, as well as consistent reporting of underfunding on staff morale. The setting is beleaguered by high rates of staff turnover and burnout (Seti, 2008). Such contextual issues can provoke feelings of helplessness and hopelessness.

Seeking safety 'for now': impossible promise-making

Elevated exposure to existential threat and the anxieties this generates, alongside the natural urge to take away suffering and a context of a highly stressed system, understandably impacts on the ways that people within it relate. One of the clearest ways we have seen this discomfort resolved is through the act of promise-making. Promises of reduced danger, increased safety and protection are likely made with the intention of helping both child and carer feel safe in the present.

Some of the impossible promises we have witnessed being made to children include:

- We will always be here for you, no matter what.
- We will never leave you. We won't serve notice on your placement.
- We will always protect you. We will always keep you safe.
- We will make it better. We know how best to help you.
- We know what you've been through. We understand.
- We can help you to leave the past behind. This is a new chapter.

Breaking impossible promises

The act of promise-making is a well-intentioned attempt to build relational security in a context where time is limited and resources precious. However, all children experience dangers in their day to day lives – at school, at home, in the community, in relationships with peers, carers and family. Thus, the promises made to children in residential care usually reveal themselves to be impossible to keep. When promises of safety or protection are inevitably broken, a child is left with further evidence of rejection and instability. Thus, the intention to create safety inadvertently leads to further harm.

The risk of invisible harm

Barry Mason's quadrants of 'safe uncertainty', 'safe certainty', 'unsafe certainty' and 'unsafe uncertainty' (Mason, 1993) can be a helpful tool in understanding the impact caused by impossible promise-making. When we strive for positions of safe certainty (as often appears the case throughout CSC (Williams, 2019)) we sign up to a fantasy that we can remove all risks.

In the context of a child's development, attempts to protect children from the dangers of the world can cause invisible harm. Risk taking is in fact considered to be a vital aspect of adolescent development (Steinberg, 2008). This raises important questions for caregivers: how can we support safe risk taking? How can we help children to make sense of times when risk taking leads to negative outcomes? How can they be best supported to learn? Providing safe and connected opportunities to explore is likely to deliver the unspoken message 'I have confidence in you that you can learn to do this'.

The residential childcare environment is often marked by a greater number of rules and regulations than in the family home. For example, the 'sleepover' rite of passage experienced by many children (a relatively safe and supported opportunity to explore new aspects of social relationships) is exceptionally hard to facilitate. This small but significant example highlights how the environment of residential childcare can in some cases overprotect children, removing freedoms and opportunities to develop and prepare them for adulthood.

The tension between the developmental and evolutionary need for adolescents to take risks and the caregiver's intention to protect children from danger is ever-present in the residential context (Narey, 2016). For example, when a child stays out beyond a curfew or experiments with alcohol, children in care are reported missing and are often picked up by the police. Over time, these experiences are more likely to reinforce feelings of shame rather than opportunities for relational repair between the child and caregiver. It is possible to see how such experiences may increase shame and lead to even more extreme risk-taking behaviour. Alternatively, children who are over-protected from life's dangers may develop anxiety around their ability to function in the social world. Our task as caregivers of adolescent children is not to remove all risks, but to support children in their safer navigation of these risks.

When I encounter danger, will you be there?

The residential context can also introduce challenges to the ways that caregivers are able to be present with children when they do face dangers. Following significant incidents residential staff can encounter conflict between their emotional drive to care for or protect a child and legal obligations presented by their role as an employed member of staff. For example, they may be required to avoid talking in a way that could hinder investigations. The child's experience of this may be one of confusion, invalidation, misunderstanding and rejection. Thus, in a moment of extreme developmental challenge caregivers are hampered in their availability to provide connected opportunities that promote learning in a timely manner leading to the relationships being more prone to disconnection. This not only has consequences for a child's learning about the incident itself, but also for their beliefs about a caring adult's support for them. The world is instantly a scarier place where dangerous things do happen and where they must face them on their own. It is easy to see how these children might question their sense of belonging, worthiness of love and faith in safe others.

Developing safe and connected relationships

When reviewing the literature surrounding children who have experienced relational or developmental trauma it is clear that most theories and therapeutic models place the caring relationship at the fore (Golding, 2010; Hughes, 2009; Perry, 2014). This makes sense in the context of attachment theory, which describes how the survival of all human babies is dependent on their relationship with their primary caregivers, and that the nature of these relationships has implications for their emotional, social and physiological regulation systems (Bowlby, 2005; Crittenden, 2006). It is therefore just as important to identify the potential for growth offered by relationships these children experience within the context of residential caregivers as it is to present the different challenges that these relationships face or may perpetuate. This is our task for the remainder of this chapter.

We believe that whilst the many challenges associated with working in these settings might sometimes lead us to veer off course, keeping the compass pointing in the direction of 'safe and connected relationships' (NSPCC, 2014) allows workers to keep returning to the relational needs of the child and the caregiving relationship as the means by which these needs can be met.

Recognising reciprocity: Helping staff feel safe so children can too

The reciprocal nature of relationships is widely recognised as a key underlying concept of relational approaches to working with children who have suffered relational trauma (NSPCC, 2014). Despite this, recognition of the experience of the carer and the reciprocal nature of these 'parent'-child relationships is noticeably absent from discussions of the needs of children in residential settings (e.g. MacAlister, 2022[1]). Whilst the key concern of CSC must of course be the needs of children, failing to acknowledge the experience of those in caring roles means the reciprocal nature of these relationships is overlooked. If the relational needs of children are to be met, we need first to attend to the needs of people who provide these relationships. As we might consider each child to be 'rich', we might consider what makes those who care for them 'rich' too.

Our discussions above have highlighted the need for children to feel safe in relationships with care givers, and the reciprocal nature of caregiving relationships indicates that this requires caregivers to feel safe too. This premise has multiple implications including recruitment, pay, shift patterns, training, the environment, the make-up of teams, team process, working relationships and more. Supervision is key. We recognise that standards of care and appropriate management of risk must have a place in supervisory processes, supervision should also attend to the experience of staff as *people*. How do they feel today? About this child? What's on their mind? What are their needs? What are they bringing to caring today? It is clear that there is a real possibility of staff experiencing 'blocked care' (Hughes and Baylin, 2012) in the same way that parents might, and that they might even be at a heightened risk of doing so given the complexity of the task of caring for highly traumatised children living in residential settings (Casswell et al., 2014). Furthermore, reciprocity exists beyond caregiving relationships and must be acknowledged throughout the multiple levels of the system: in relationships between managers and staff, directors and managers and so on.

The relationship as a vehicle for growth

Once the relationship between caregiver and child is placed front and centre of how care is organised, this has vast implications for how care is delivered. A focus on the relationship between caregiver and child highlights the possibilities for learning from experiences of rupture and repair, inevitable in any parenting relationship. Relational rupture is considered an important part of parent-child interactions, with the experience of repair in childhood suggested to be the foundation for attachment security, and hence adult resilience (Hughes, 2009).

Dan Hughes (2009) describes how caregiving relationships with a greater level of security also tend to feature a greater degree of Playfulness, Acceptance, Curiosity and Empathy (PACE) towards the child's lived experience. We have found the concept of a 'PACE'-full attitude, 'a way of thinking, feeling, communicating and behaving that aims to make the child feel safe', a simple and transformative approach (Hughes, 2009). Caregiving utilising a more PACEful approach helps to facilitate more opportunities for attunement between the caregiver and child, providing connected moments for the co-creation of meaning related to the child's lived experiences.

For those children whose life experiences have shown them how dangerous caring adults can be, this can be a new experience that over time allows them to start to develop trust. Casswell and colleagues (2014) propose that incorporating PACE (drawn from Dyadic Developmental Psychotherapy principles) into residential care can help teams to work with a new understanding of what might underlie behaviour and enables children to experience a more secure base from which they can continue to develop and grow.

Non-violent resistance (NVR; Jakob, 2018) has become integral to our approach to working with children who use violence as a means of communicating their needs. We have used NVR to help staff to tune into the unmet needs underlying a violent act in order to work towards prevention, de-escalate children in distress and develop relational responses after violence has occurred.

The challenges of the residential context can also be navigated with a developmental and relational frame in mind. The Neurosequential Model is a developmentally informed, biologically respectful approach to working with at-risk children (Perry, 2014). It highlights the various ways that trauma can impact on a child's emotional, social and biological development. Assessing the effect of trauma across these developmental domains can inform how caregivers, educators, therapists and related professionals, can best meet the needs of the child as they grow (Perry, 2014). This approach points both to the long-term needs of a child as well as what is needed in the present moment. This has taught us about the value in each interaction between caregiver and child. We have found this particularly useful in restoring hope in the context of short-term placements and a fast-moving system which can sometimes generate feelings of helplessness and hopelessness amongst ourselves and staff. Perry highlights the value in maximising the opportunity for moments of safe experience, to increase relational and attachment security and provide the foundations for child specific development.

Family

The ways in which we conceptualise the place of a child's family in their life once they have moved into a residential home are also implicated once we place relationships at the fore of how we care for children. These relationships are likely to continue to be a source of challenge for both carer and child, whether a child has been 'given up', 'removed' from the care of their parents or experienced bereavement. It is deeply distressing to witness a child continue to be rejected by their parent. We have often heard workers say 'I would take them home if I could' when talking about these kinds of encounters. It is easy to see how these situations activate that innate biological drive to remove suffering and lead to promise-making.

We have come to consider in our practice how we might have conversations with children we care for about their families, knowing they are often limited in how they can care. What would it look like to make space for the imperfect care that their family can provide, knowing that they will always be the child's mother or father, brother, or sister? If we were to help this child to build a positive sense of self and of their place in the world, how might they relate to their family?

The place of love in corporate parenting

The residential childcare sector, and beyond it the corporate parenting system, seems to experience a dilemma in regard to the emotional experiences evoked by caring for children. This is evident in the oxymoronic term, 'corporate' 'parenting' which joins a word usually used to describe emotion-less business settings with a relational verb which is necessarily emotion-full. The question of love and its place in residential childcare is particularly challenging. Despite the widely accepted idea that children need love, indeed that they have a right to be loved, 'love' is a word that the sector is not always comfortable in using. Yet, logic suggests these children would benefit from more rather than less love.

Positively, there does seem to be a building recognition of the role that love plays in the lives of children who enter care. A recent review of CSC in the UK names 'loving relationships' (MacAlister, 2022, p. 6) as the first of five priorities for improving the lives of care-experienced young people, pointing to the wealth of evidence for the protective role these relationships can play in biopsychosocial development.

Recognising the presence of emotions in care-as-work invites the opportunity to consider what leads to love feeling more possible and less possible. Naturally, there will be times when love is easy for people to access and times when it feels beyond us. However, by acknowledging this, by welcoming the emotional experience of care, we can provide a space for safe processing and incorporate emotions into our planning. This might be done by simply bringing curiosity to the emotional experience of the carer. How do you feel about this child? When you think of them, what emotions are present? Once we have acknowledged the presence and influence of emotions, we are in a better position to work out how best they can be communicated through care.

Possible promises

We bring this chapter to a close by leaving our readers with a series of what we believe are possible promises that can be made for any child, including those who live in residential homes.

- I am here now and I'm glad you are here right now
- I want to care for you
- I will get it wrong sometimes
- We want to hear what you have experienced and try to understand this with you
- We will do our best to equip you to face the challenges that life might bring
- We both know you will leave here one day, and we will think about this together

These promises are contextual and relational, based on feelings and brought with respectful authenticity. They are intended to be considered in the context of each caring relationship and may mean something different in each set of circumstances. They may open up more questions. How can we learn together? When our relationship hits the rocks, what do I want you to learn about how we can repair and reconnect? What do you need now that will help you build the life you want as an adult? What do I think my role is in supporting you to get there?

Concluding reflections

In deconstructing safety, protection and danger in caring relationships of residential childcare we hope that we have presented enough small, do-able actions that can have a profound impact on the rest of a child's life. Recognising relationships are the primary lens through which we can understand a child's needs, and through which these needs can be met, may feel drastically different (and it will for children too!) but it is not a paradigm shift. Relationships have always been there – they are there now. It is how we use them that is key.

We believe the sector would benefit from defining a philosophy of care. We wonder, is the apparently sought-for state of 'corporate parenting' possible to achieve at all? What do we mean by 'professional caregiving'? What do we hope children in our care to feel? How do we use our relationships to prepare them for adulthood? We have introduced how developing a perspective of children as 'rich' and recognising the richness within caregivers across residential care settings can form the foundation for the relationships needed to support children's growth and development. We hope that in bringing awareness to the act of impossible promise-making we have opened up room to consider the possible promises and the ways these can be navigated with children living in residential care.

These ideas take us beyond concepts of safety, security, protection and danger, contextualising them in the relationships in children's lives, past, present and future. We have acknowledged the ways that safety has been betrayed in the past, the existence of danger in the future, our desires to protect and a child's need for security and how we might build it together. These acts are necessarily personal. They require us to think, feel and act. We bring our whole being into the care of each child and acknowledging this brings up new and transformational ideas for the roles we can play in a child's life and the adults they will become. We must open ourselves up to growing with children and learning together. We hope this is a possible promise that we can all keep.

Note

1 Whilst the recent review of CSC recognises the workforce's need for reflective super-vision in order to provide high standards of care, as well as the needs of children within relationships with social workers it does not go so far as to recognise the needs or lived experience of the people who provide care.

References

Anda, R. F., Felitti, V. J., Bremner, J. D., Walker, J. D., Whitfield, C. H., Perry, B. D., Dube, S.R. and Giles, W. H. (2006). The enduring effects of abuse and related adverse experi-ences in childhood. A convergence of evidence from neurobiology and epidemiology. *European Archives of Psychiatry and Clinical Neuroscience*, 3, 174–186. doi: 10.1007/ s00406-005-0624-4

Beckler, L. E. (2014). *Who Would Be a Residential Child Care Worker?* Prof Doc Thesis University of east London Tavistock and Portman NHS Foundation Trust. https://doi.org/ 10.15123/PUB.4586

Berridge, D., Biehal, N. and Henry, L. (2012). *Living in Children's Residential Homes.* http://eprints.whiterose.ac.uk/74283/

Bowlby, J. (2005). *A Secure Base*. Routledge.

Casswell, G., Golding, K. S., Grant, E., Hudson, J. and Tower, P. (2014). Dyadic devel-opmental practice (DDP): A framework for therapeutic intervention and parenting. *The Child and Family Clinical Psychology* Review, 2, 19–27.

Crittenden, P. (2006). A dynamic-maturational model of attachment. *Australian and New Zealand Journal of Family Therapy*, 27(2), 105–115. https://doi.org/10.1002/j.1467-8438.2006.tb00704.x

Department for Education (2016). *Residential Care in England: Report of Sir Martin Narey's Independent Review of Children's Residential Care*. Retrieved from www.gov. uk/government/uploads/system/uploads/attachment_data/file/534560/Residential-Care-in-England-Sir-Martin-Narey-July-2016.pdf

Golding, K. S. (2010). Multi-agency and specialist working to meet the mental health needs of children in care and adopted. *Clinical Child Psychology and Psychiatry*, 15, 573–587. doi: 10.1177/1359104510375933

Greenwood, J. (2016). Influencing systems. In L. Smith (ed.), *Clinical Practice at the Edge of Care: Deveopments in Working with At-risk Children and Their Families* (pp. 29–48). Springer.

Happ, M., Glossop, A. and Ogi, L. (2018). Initial reflections and learning from the development and delivery of staff consultations in an innovative residential childcare pathway. *Journal of Social Work Practice*, 32, 433–446. https://doi.org/10.1080/02650 533.2018.1503165

Hughes, D. (2009). *Principles of Attachment Focused Parenting: Effective Strategies to Care for Children*. W.W. Norton & Company.

Hughes, D. A. and Baylin, J. (2012). *Brain-based Parenting: The Neuroscience of Caregiving for Healthy Attachment*. Norton.

Jakob, P. (2018). Multi-stressed families, child violence and the larger system: an adaptation of the nonviolent model. *Journal of Family Therapy*, 40 (1), 25–44. https://doi.org/ 10.1111/1467-6427.12133

MacAlister, J. (2022). The independent review of children's social care. https://childrenssoc ialcare.independent-review.uk/final-report/

Malaguzzi, L. (1993). For an education based on relationships, *Young Children*, 49, 9–13.

Mason, B. (1993). Towards positions of safe uncertainty. *Human Systems: The Journal of Systemic Consultation and Management*, 4, 189–200.

McFadden, P., Campbell, A. and Taylor, B. (2014). Resilience and burnout in child protection social work: Individual and organisational themes from a systematic literature review. *The British Journal of Social Work*, 45, 1546–1563. https://doi.org/10.1093/bjsw/ bct210

Moses, T. (2000). Why people choose to be residential child care workers. *Child and Youth Care Forum*, 29 (2), 113–126.

Moss, P., Dillon, J. and Statham, J. (2000). The 'child in need' and 'the rich child': Discourses, constructions and practice, *Critical Social Policy*, 20, 233–254. doi: 10.1177/ 026101830002000203

Narey, M. (2016). *Residential Care in England*. https://assets.publishing.service.gov.uk/gov ernment/uploads/system/uploads/attachment_data/file/534560/Residential-Care-in-Engl and-Sir-Martin-Narey-July-2016.pdf

NCPCC (2014). *Promoting the Wellbeing of Children in Care: Messages from Research*. National Society for the Protection of Cruelty to Children https://letterfromsanta.nspcc. org.uk/globalassets/documents/research-reports/promoting-wellbeing-children-in-care-messages-from-research.pdf

National Institute for Health and Clinical Excellence and Social Care Institute for Excellence. (2010). *Looked-after Children and Young People*. Retrieved from www.nice.org.uk/guida nce/ng205/resources/lookedafter-children-and-young-people-pdf-66143716414405

Parry, S., Williams, T. and Oldfield, J. (2022). Reflections from the forgotten frontline: 'The reality for children and staff in residential care' during COVID-19. *Health & Social Care in the Community*, 30 (1), 212–224. doi: 10.1111/hsc.13394

Perry, B. D. (2014). The neurosequential model of therapeutics in young children. In Kristie Brandt, Bruce D. Perry, Stephen Seligman and Edward Tronick (eds) *Infant and Early Childhood Mental Health*, pp. 21–47, American Psychiatric Press.

Seti, C. L. (2008). Causes and treatment of burnout in residential child care workers: A review of the research. *Residential Treatment for Children & Youth, 24*, 197–229. https://doi.org/10.1080/08865710802111972

Steinberg, L. (2017). A social neuroscience perspective on adolescent risk-taking. *Developmental Review, 28* (1) 78–106. doi: 10.1016/j.dr.2007.08.002

Waterhouse, L. and McGhee, J. (2009). Anxiety and child protection – Implications for practitioners – Parent relations. *Child & Family Social Work*, 14 (4), 481–490. https://doi.org/10.1111/j.1365-2206.2009.00631.x

Williams, J. (2019). PSDP – Resources and tools: Safe uncertainty. https://practice-supervisors.rip.org.uk/wp-content/uploads/2019/11/Safe-uncertainty.pdf

Chapter 8

Safety and danger in an intensive care context

Psychological and systemic approaches to staff support during the COVID-19 pandemic (and beyond)

Jennifer Wallis

Introduction and context

In a general hospital context in the UK, peaks of successive COVID-19 infections led to wards dedicated to patients with COVID-19 continually expanding. This led to a sense of COVID 'taking over the hospital'. Outside of work, COVID-19 seemed to overshadow our lives. Personal and professional resonances intertwined, presenting unique challenges. With my family living in southern Africa and the global threat of the pandemic evolving, I found myself in dialogue between the southern and northern hemispheres, reflecting on the differences between resources, constraints, and injustices.

Concerns within the hospital were rightly raised about the effects of the pandemic on the mental health of staff. These concerns were underlined by studies reporting high levels of probable common mental health problems and post-traumatic stress disorder among healthcare workers (Bates 2020; Lamb et al., 2021). It was notable that those reporting higher levels of moral injury, that is, the 'distress resulting from violation of one's moral code or values' (Lamb et al., 2021, p. 802), were also at higher risk.

These concerns about workplace stressors led many hospitals to develop or extend staff support services. This opened up an opportunity for me to work within a staff well-being and psychology team. The work was primarily focused on staff working in or deployed to intensive care. Meetings with staff included informal encounters during ward visits, formal individual meetings, consultations with leads and managers and organised reflective spaces during a shift or on team days. The staff who engaged with me may represent those more troubled by their experiences as well as those who may have had good experiences with seeking help previously.

In my discussions with staff, I was interested in what was important to them, how they made sense of their experiences and what had helped them to cope/survive and even thrive. For some staff, the trauma response to COVID meant that resonating past experiences re-emerged, contributing to a heightened sense of threat. For others the relational context of work contributed to a sense of both safety and threat. I elaborate on different contexts and meanings of 'safety' and 'threat' and how this relates to aspects of staff experiences.

DOI: 10.4324/9781003308096-11

Contexts and meanings of safety, threat and resilience

Healthcare has been described as a 'safety-critical industry'. Research has revealed links between the way stress is experienced and the 'psychological safety climate' (Afsharian et al., 2017; Casey et al., 2017). The 'safety climate' refers to *what* happens in the organisation that individuals can see, for example, policies, procedures and practices. This includes management commitment to implementing policies and supporting staff to prevent psychological injury (Afsharian et al., 2017).

A related concept, the 'safety culture', helps us understand *why* things happen in organisations (Tear and Reader, 2023). A 'safety culture' refers to shared attitudes, values and perceptions of safety. In addition, an organisation's capacities in social relationships, such as team work and leadership (or 'social capital'), contribute to a safety culture (Casey et al., 2017).

Both the concepts of a safety climate and safety culture are important to organisational safety. In response to threats, organisations may differ according to the strategies used to control risk, for example, defensive or adaptive strategies (Casey et al., 2017). When risk and uncertainty is high, reactive defensive strategies aimed at reducing uncertainty, may be activated. However, if adaptive strategies are activated, responses are quick and flexible and learning from mistakes is promoted. Adaptive strategies are thought to promote a positive psychological safety climate (Casey et al., 2017).

Edmundson's (2019) research into errors in organisations led her to describe psychological safety as a 'factor ... that helps explain differences in performance in workplaces' (p. xiv). She described a psychologically safe workplace as a climate in which people are 'not hindered by interpersonal fear but are comfortable expressing and being themselves, raising concerns and mistakes without fear of embarrassment or blame' (p. xv). In organisations, therefore, the qualities of relationships as well as processes, policies and the ethical demands of the task impact on safety and threat.

Relationships are thus essential to the safety culture in hospitals. This is especially important if we consider hospitals to be 'care-giving organisations', as patient care is accomplished through relationships (Kahn, 2005). Relational theories, such as attachment and systemic theory, can enhance our understanding of safety. Linington (2012) asserts that when we have experiences that connect to our hurt in our relationships with managers, colleagues and peers, parts of our attachment or care-giving and care-receiving histories are activated. When this occurs, leaders and colleagues then also have the potential to provide comfort, security and social support (Linington, 2012). Thus, organisations can therefore be viewed as 'attachment spaces' (Linington, 2012).

Attachment security may be the foundation for care-giving organisations. Johnson's (2008) Emotion-focused Couple therapy (EFT) approach, based on Bowlby (1969) proposes that our primary need is for 'felt security with the other; a safe haven to go to ... a secure base to go out from'. According to Johnson (2008), the following are the key questions we ask of our important relationships: 'Do

I matter? Can I depend on you? Are you engaged with me?' From this perspective, emotional presence is the solution. This is a profound disjuncture from our common tendency to want to 'fix' or 'get rid of' problems. An attachment injury or threat occurs when we are abandoned in a crucial moment of need, and this can be considered a form of relational trauma (Johnson, 2008). When speaking with healthcare staff, experiences of relational threats or trauma were present. These were, however, interwoven with examples of actions that promoted security in relationships, teams, and units.

Resilience in healthcare

Multi-level approaches to the threats posed by COVID-19 were necessary to enable resilience in healthcare systems (Corbaz-Kurth et al., 2022). Organisational resilience is defined as the capacity to anticipate, adapt, resist, transform and recover (Corbath-Kurth et al., 2022). From this perspective, the cornerstones of safety are: anticipating (being proactive); monitoring (listening, attending); responding (acting, adjusting); and learning (examining experience and integrating this into future action). While governments were responsible for macro-level responses, Corbaz-Kurth et al. (2022) argue that meso- and micro-level adaptations by institutions, teams and individual workers, have been overlooked. Macro-level responses, although beyond the scope of this chapter, cannot be ignored as they provide the context for stressors at the other levels.

Staff experiences during the COVID pandemic were widely documented, such as in newspapers as well as in research (Firouzkouhi et al., 2022; White, 2021). In reflecting on staff experiences in intensive care during COVID-19, I consider the moments that might be overlooked and stories that may be marginalised. I am interested in exploring the adaptability of individuals, teams and units that might contribute to the organisation's resilience and promote a safety culture.

Reflections on staff experience

My reflections on staff experiences enabled me to consider layers of meaning in our interactions. This is not research and the expressions of experiences are not direct quotations but amalgamations of discussions over time. Thus, the experiences reflected may relate to more than one individual and care has been taken to protect confidentiality. These conversations have influenced my work and teaching, and I am hopeful that the experiences described will benefit others. Experiences of working in COVID-19 wards impacted on the physical care of staff, their experience of relationships with their managers (as authority figures), teams/peers as well as layers of their identity (for example, personal, professional and cultural identities).

Physical safety/care

An aspect of the 'dread' of working in COVID-19 wards related to difficulties in addressing physical needs, particularly in the first wave:

The door (to the ward) was closed; you can't leave; you are isolated and alone. You couldn't get loo breaks or pop out to eat as there was no cover.

The failure to have basic physical needs attended to can be described as neglectful (or worse). Attention was given to breaks through successive waves, however, seniors then prioritised breaks for their junior staff rather than their own. One example of a challenge to this has been the development of a 'Well-Being Charter', naming the 'right to breaks' as a principle of well-being. However, questions about the policies and procedures required to meet the basic physical needs of staff remain.

'No safety net'

Despite the knowledge of COVID-19 coming ... people had a 'heads up'; there were no plans ...

There is no safety net, no structure. If the Seniors just planned ahead and told us what the plans were, it would help.

The precariousness of the work environment and sense of feeling 'let down' by attachment figures is conveyed here. Communicating plans as well as uncertainties could help prepare staff and contribute to creating a safety climate. This could avert the additional relational distress associated with little discussion of preparations.

'Not being seen': invisibility

You were not seen ... you became *a number on a spreadsheet* ... it hurt ... and a category (for example, of a professional group). You had a label rather than a name. The label showed hierarchies and capabilities ... It showed there was not time for you as a person ... Every day you didn't know where you were going and who would be with – you just lined up.

De-personalisation of staff is highlighted through the sense of being 'a number' or a 'label'. Staff are referred to by their salary scales (bands), emphasising hierarchies and status. The challenge of staffing shifts with the right skill mix no doubt influenced attempts to simplify the task of staff allocation. However, this led to unintended emotional and relational distress. The time and space created in the unit to reflect on and process these experiences showed care and contributed to repair of this type of rupture.

'There was no feedback'

The sense of staff being unappreciated or acknowledged was voiced during the pandemic and continues to be a theme in staff surveys.

There was no feedback ... Senior staff could have given re-assurance, just say you are doing it right.

It would have been good just to hear 'thank you'.

I got no acknowledgement; no feedback. (As a Senior) I compensate for others now – in giving feedback. But I haven't had any feedback.

Creating a culture where people are able to voice appreciation in relationship with each other, is likely to make a qualitative difference. For this to be meaningful to staff, it would be most helpful if appreciation or acknowledgement the emotional experiences depicted here, namely: being seen and valued.

Lack of presence of leaders

Striking themes discussed included a sense of *abandonment* of frontline staff by their seniors. This disconnection is painfully felt, for example:

From the start the {Seniors} were managing from the office. This instantly *drove a wedge* between them and the rest of the staff. Like 'Upstairs downstairs' (a television drama about class); it created a hierarchy.

Senior staff were undoubtedly overwhelmed by the pressures emanating from their job roles. However, the sense of seniors not being present and 'shutting the door' seemed to create a *disconnect* and highlight positions of unequal power.

Some areas of work were more isolating than others. A staff member spoke of recurring nightmares of being isolated and alone in a side room. Initially, it took time for 'help to come' as medics or seniors had to don PPE. These powerful emotional experiences often resonated with earlier attachment experiences of 'being alone/abandoned' and unimportant.

Experience of death

So many died.

I see faces and faces of people who I think probably died.

Staff did not always know the outcome of what happened to patients after their shift ended. Death has different meanings for different team members. In making sense of the cumulative grief, loss and trauma, Papadatou (2000) contends that professionals manage by fluctuating between two positions; that is, experiencing grief and avoiding or repressing grief. Professionals adapt to the reality of their situation by disconnecting at times and also re-connecting. This process is multi-layered and informed by individual beliefs, histories and values interacting with workplace goals, values, assumptions, rules and the meaning people give to this.

There were staff teams in the hospital to support with experiences of death. The Spiritual Care team assisted staff in containing and processing their sadness and grief by facilitating rituals. Staff psychologists led reflective group discussions in which people said it helped to realise they were not alone.

Threats to identity

The stigma associated with experiencing anxiety and mental health problems was evident in a number of ways. The sense of a loss of identity was expressed:

> I (used to be) the 'go to person' for cheerfulness. I am sad as this is 'not me'. I wanted {something terrible to happen to me} so I had a valid reason for not coming to work … Valid because then no-one would judge me.

Emotional or mental health problems were not seen as a 'valid' difficulty and disclosure risked judgement. How emotional distress is responded to, is of course important as ignorance could be experienced as invalidating and discomfort as rejection. An unintended consequence of the focus on mental health may be that the social and contextual issues contributing to distress remain unaddressed. Problems then become located within the individual and the 'solution' is focused on the individual, rather than organisational change. A relational focus could have identified where conflict within teams, bullying, discrimination or other hurtful interactions were causing stress and distress. These could then be the focus of intervention, resulting in improved team and unit functioning while also reducing individual suffering.

COVID-19 has allowed mental health/illness to become more visible and more possible to be talked about. Responses included the funding of primary care level Talking Therapies interventions. This possibly contributes to individualised conceptualisations of distress. Based on bio-psycho-social understandings of distress, our approach to staff psychology/support focussed on addressing work related (contextual) presentations of difficulties. Staff psychology and organisational development teams, if aligned, could contribute different perspectives in working towards organisational resilience.

Threat of blame for mistakes

Staff expressed fear about the ability to do their work adequately and the impact on their mental health:

> I was in charge and short staffed … 'all eyes were on you'
> I went off sick. I couldn't sleep; I was recalling the sound of the monitors.

Reflection, or rumination after a shift seemed to be of self-scrutiny:

> What didn't I do; what did I miss.

The threat of making mistakes was heightened during COVID-19 especially during the first waves when there was so much that was unknown about the illness. Nurses and medics, working in a climate of uncertainty and complexity, seemed to maintain their expectations of certainty. Cultural myths of control seemed to prevail despite complex and ambiguous environments (Pidgeon, 1988). Staff discussed their fears of expressing uncertainty, which could lead to criticism. The challenge in this environment appeared to be the desire to feel certain rather than 'safe enough'.

When leaders and seniors acknowledged ambiguity, it was extremely affirming for staff. The way leaders and seniors dealt with uncertainty may have influenced the 'safety climate', as it may have invited feedback and discussion. This potentially created more learning within team as well as having an impact on staff's experience with mental health symptoms.

'Sparkling moments'

Conversations creating hope and safety

Identifying leaders' experiences with 'moral distress' and 'moral injury' opened up conversations about 'circumstances in which people work' (Murray, 2022, p. 100), such as a lack of resources. Recognising the ethical dilemmas posed by not being able to work to a recognised standard of care and having a term to describe this, can be validating (Murray, 2022).

Relational restoration

Staff had the opportunity to talk about what was important to them in group reflective spaces. Many expressed the value of talking together as 'knowing that you were not alone in what you were experiencing'. The shame and stigma associated with mental health had the potential to silence, and these group forums facilitated a recognition of shared human experiences and vulnerabilities. It seemed important to question the binary distinction between 'safe and unsafe' and rather to think about how we are moving towards 'safe-er' relationships (Reynolds, 2012).

In reflective group spaces, team members responded compassionately to those expressing a lack of belonging or an 'outsider position'. This solidarity meant that the groups seemed to provide an important forum for connection.

Where managers were present (for example, on team days) and able to voice vulnerabilities and uncertainties, group discussions were particularly powerful. Both staff and leads were able to give and receive feedback, listening and adjusting their views. This process enabled an integration of experiences and facilitated some of the necessary healing of tensions resulting from hierarchical roles and responsibilities.

Growth through adversity

Staff talked about surprising, positive developments during the pandemic: some found that they were given responsibility, able to take up challenges and to advance their careers quickly. They felt a sense of 'being able to cope with anything' after enduring the extreme hardships of working through the pandemic.

Leaders spoke of 'really not knowing' what the best course of action was and being more reliant on the perspectives of staff. Staff in turn valued being included in decision-making and thought this was an important step change in relationships between managers and staff in some units. These experiences demonstrate the adaptive strategies that some were able to employ, contributing to organisational resilience.

'Making sense'

In my conversations with staff, I was inspired by the creative adaptations many were making and how energising this was. Leaders who were able to voice their uncertainties and vulnerabilities, inspired engagement. This seemed to address some of the hierarchical splits experienced.

The importance of working as teams was addressed through 'staff huddles' (that is, meetings for those working together at the start of their shift). In this way, some of the issues raised, such as invisibility and feelings of insignificance, may have begun to be resolved.

Work during COVID-19 provided an opportunity to connect with colleagues when we faced isolation from many friends and family. Staff experiences had strong resonances with attachment themes, such as abandonment, not being seen or valued, powerlessness and rejection. This was also a time of heightened uncertainty when professional risks were high and the demands of work raised ethical dilemmas. We were challenged by experiencing overwhelming emotions at times as well as avoiding emotions by withdrawing or shutting down. It seemed that these avoidant or mobilising fight or flight strategies could become identified with individuals or job roles. Thus, some staff were very appreciative of space to talk and think and others seemed dismissive. Compassionate relationships require an acceptance of differences in responses to the emotional nature of the work.

My emotional experience of the work at times felt like a roller-coaster of ups and downs. Influenced by Dana's (2020) application of polyvagal theory (Porges, 2009), I depicted this through drawing a figure of eight with a calm, connected state at the centre, helped to ground me (see Figure 8.1). This enabled me to reflect on where I was on the figure of eight and how I might find my way back to connection. This movement between disconnecting from one's experience and allowing it to be experienced is important not only for our individual well-being but also for team and manager-staff relationships. In my view, this ability to manage ourselves and support each other to do the same contributes to 'social capital' and a culture of safety in organisations. The challenge of both experiencing and avoiding emotion emphasises the importance of reflective spaces for staff:

It was more helpful than anticipated to share experiences and created a bit of a bond.

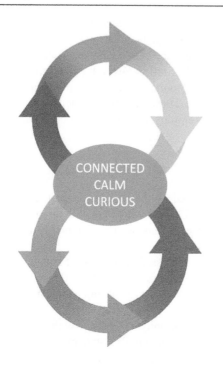

Mobilised: fight or flight
• 'Experiencing' emotional states

Immobilised: shut down
• 'Avoiding' emotional states

Figure 8.1 From threat to connection.

Reflective groups have provided important spaces for connection, reducing hierarchical splits, sharing and normalising distress, and creating a sense of belonging. Leaders and managers can support the practical requirements of reflective spaces. However, given the levels of cumulative stress caused by the pandemic's successive waves and the subsequent healthcare pressures, relationships will inevitably be strained. Relational repair processes could provide a 'safety net' that allows us to engage with one another, take risks and restore our relationships.

Restorative organisational practices

In the post-COVID-19 UK context, conversations that enable those impacted by relational trauma and also the unintentional harm by those in authority, may enable people's experiences to be acknowledged and dignity restored. Without hearing different experiences of the pandemic and its' effects, 'our memories will be partial' (Truth and Reconciliation Commission, TRC/Report, n.d.). This will therefore limit learning possibilities and undermine the capacity of the organisation to adapt.

Restorative justice is an established process with the potential to repair harm in challenging situations and address the legacy of trauma. It is described as most powerful as 'a systemic response with the capacity for re-setting, reclaiming and recovering resources where they are most needed' (Moore, 2022).

The following are the principles of restorative justice:

- Restoration (addressing and repairing harm)
- Voluntary (participation at one's own free will and accessible)
- Trauma-informed (not compounding social injury; that is, one injury on top of another) and
- Respectful (maintaining the dignity for all parties) (Moore, 2022)

These principles are challenging to apply in situations where people may be avoiding emotions and conversations and may therefore not engage in the process. Where people are in states of high arousal or 'experiencing' emotions, maintaining respect for all involved may be a challenge. To enter restorative justice conversations, people may need to be supported to be calm, curious and grounded (see Figure 8.1).

The specific format of restorative justice conversations used in youth justice settings, may aid in relational repair:

What happened? (Storytelling)
Who has been affected by this? (Impact)
What needs to happen now? (Action oriented, solution-focus).

Telling the story of an incident that had a negative impact enables both parties to engage rather than avoid the relational rupture. The person who may be overwhelmed by the impact of their actions that have caused distress, can remain connected by identifying actions to repair the rupture.

These conversations encourage connectedness as well as justice, laying the groundwork for future relationships and our ability to recover from the stress of relational ruptures. Importantly, this would contribute to just practices within organisations.

Summary and learning points

The crisis of COVID-19 has challenged some of the norms, practices and processes in hospital-based healthcare. If organisations are to be resilient, creating a safety climate or culture of psychological safety is required. Our understanding of mental health/distress has needed to broaden from an individual symptom orientation to an understanding of how relationships and ethics impact on distress. Staff expressed what can be described as attachment ruptures, for example, a lack of attention to basic care needs, a lack of a 'safety net', not being seen or acknowledged and a lack of presence of authority figures. Threats included threats to identity.

In contrast, creating attachment security requires an awareness of our emotional strategies when faced with threat and our ability to move between positions of avoiding and experiencing. Where leads and managers have found ways to adapt, for example, by engaging staff in decision-making and/or enabling staff to attend reflective sessions, then creative problem solving and 'making sense' has been evident. These adaptive and learning capacities are likely to support organisational resilience.

Safety or effective care for staff, therefore, needs more than an individual focus but also a focus on teams, culture and leadership (Highfield and Neal, 2022). The central task is about *connecting, maintaining and repairing connections*:

- Connecting with our own emotional experiencing, attachment triggers and being aware of these in interaction with others
- Both experiencing and 'letting go' of our emotional responses to maintain balance
- Leaders, teams and organisations that value and promote relational safety

Importantly, we need *processes for re-connecting* when things go wrong so that we do not become stuck in positions of experiencing or avoiding. Restorative justice provides a useful framework for these conversations.

References

Afsharian, A., Zadow, A., Dollard, M. F., Dormann, C. and Ziaian, T. (2017). Should psychosocial safety climate theory be extended to include climate strength? *Journal of Occupational Health Psychology, 23*(4), 496–507.

Bates, A., Ottaway, J., Moyses, H., Perrow, M., Rushbrook, S., and Cusack, R. (2020). Psychological impact of caring for critically ill patients during the Covid-19 pandemic and recommendations for staff support. *Journal of the Intensive Care Society, 0*(0), 1–7. https://doi.org/10.1177/1751143720965109

Bateson, G. (1972). *Steps to an Ecology of Mind*. University of Chicago Press.

Bowlby, J. (1969). *Attachment and Loss, Vol 1. Attachment*. Hogarth Press and the Institute of Psycho-Analysis.

Casey, T., Griffin, M. A., Harrison, H. F. and Neal, A. (2017). Social climate and culture: Integrating psychological and systems perspectives. *Journal of Occupational Health Psychology at 20, 22*(3), 341–353.

Corbaz-Kurth, S., Juvet, T. M., Benzakour, L., Cereghetti, S., Fournier, C.-A., Moullec, G., Nguyen, A., Suard, J.-C., Vieux, L., Wozniak, H., Pralong, J. A., Weissbrodt, R. and Roos, P. (2022). How things changed during the COVID-19 pandemic's first year: A longitudinal, mixed-methods study of organisational resilience processes among healthcare workers. *Safety Science, 155*(105879), 1–11.

Dana, D. (2020). *Polyvagal Exercises for Safety and Connection: 50 Client Centered Practices*. W.W. Norton & Company.

Edmundson, A. (2019). *The Fearless Organisation: Creating Psychological Safety in the Workplace for Learning, Innovation and Growth*. Wiley.

Firouzkouhi, M., Abdollahimohammad, A., Rezaie-Kheikhaie, K., Mortazavi, H., Farzi, J., Masinaienezhad, N. and Hashemi-Bonjar, Z. (2022). Nurses' caring experiences in COVID-19 pandemic: A systematic review of qualitative research. *Health Science Review*, (Oxf), June (3:100030). https://doi.org/10.1016/j.hsr.2022.10030.

Hennekam, S., Ladge, J. and Shymko, Y. (2020). From zero to hero: An exploratory study examining sudden hero status among nonphysician health care workers during the COVID-19 pandemic. *Journal of Applied Psychology, 105*(10), 1088–1100.

Highfield, J. and Neal, A. (2022). Strategic working and supporting leadership within a healthcare context. In H. Conniff and A. Kurtz (eds), *Psychological Staff Support in Healthcare* (pp. 301–316). Sequoia Books.

Johnson, S. (2008). *Hold Me Tight*. Piatkus.

Justice.gov.za (n.d.). *Truth and Reconciliation Commission TRC/Report*. [online] Available at: www.justice.gov.za/trc/ [Accessed September 2022].

Kahn, W. A. (2005). *Holding Fast: The Struggle to Create Resilient Caregiving Organisations*. Routledge.

Lamb, D., Gnanapragasam, S., Greenberg, N., Bhundia, R., Carr, E., Hotopf, M., Razavi, R., Raine, R., Cross, S., Dewar, A., Docherty, M., Dorrington, S., Hatch, S., Wilson-Jones, C., Leightly, D., Madan, I., Marlow, S., McMullen, I., Rafferty, A.-M., …Wessely, S. (2021). Psychosocial impact of the COVID-19 pandemic on 4378 UK healthcare workers and ancillary staff: Initial baseline data from a cohort study collected during the first wave of the pandemic. *Occupational Environmental Medicine, 78*, 801–808.

Linington, M. (2012). Attachment, trauma and organisations. *Attachment: New Directions in Relational Psychoanalysis and Psychotherapy, 6*(3), 232–248.

Luke, M. A., Carnelley, K. B. and Sedikides, C. (2019). Attachments in the workplace: How attachment security in the workplace benefits the organisation. *European Journal of Social Psychology, 50*, 1046–1064. https://doi.org/10.1002/ejsp.2652

Moore, E. (2022). Trauma and restorative justice. In P. Willmot and L. Jones (eds), *Trauma-informed Forensic Practice* (pp. 396–412). Routledge. https://doi.org/10.4324/978100 3120766-29

Murray, E. (2022). Moral injury: Why exploring novel terms makes space for talking in staff support. In H. Conniff and A. Kurtz (eds.), *Psychological Staff Support in Healthcare: Thinking and Practice*. Sequoia Books.

Neal, A. and Highfield, J. (2022). A relational guide to establish and maintain a psychologically healthier workplace. In H. Conniff and A. Kurtz (eds), *Psychological Staff Support in Healthcare: Thinking and Practice*. Sequoia Books.

Papadatou, D. (2000). A proposed model of health professionals' grieving process. *OMEGA, 4*(1), 59–77.

Pidgeon, N. (1998). Safety culture: Key theoretical issues. *Work & Stress, 12*(3), 202–216. https://doi.org/10.1080/02678379808256862

Porges, S. W. (2009). Reciprocal influences between body and brain in the perception and expression of affect: A polyvagal perspective. In D. Frosha, D. J. Siegal and M. F. Solomon (eds), *The Healing Power of Emotion: Affective Neuroscience, Development, Clinical Practice* (pp. 27–54). Norton.

Reynolds, V. (2012). An ethical stance for justice-doing in community work and therapy. *Journal of Systemic therapies, 31*(4), 18–33.

Tear, M. J. and Reader, T. W. (2023). Understanding safety culture and safety citizenship through the lens of social identity theory. *Safety Science, 158*, 1–14.

White, J. H. (2021). 'It was never enough': The meaning of nurses' experiences caring for patients during the COVID-19 pandemic. *Issues in Mental Health Nursing, 42*(12), 1084–1094. https://doi.org/10.1080/01612840.2021.1931586

Chapter 9

Safety and security in psychotherapy practice and supervision

Arlene Vetere

Introduction to the secure base

This chapter is about the feeling of safety. What is it? How can we recognise it? How can we describe it, especially for someone who tells us they do not know what safety feels like? In particular, we shall explore how we can feel 'felt' in our relationships with therapists and supervisors, and similarly, and perhaps less well recognised, with our clients and supervisees. Relational mutuality in our therapeutic work can bridge different roles, responsibilities and power dynamics in ways that support the growth of self-esteem, relational esteem and resilient responding (Vetere, 2021). Systemically speaking, if we address how therapists and supervisors can be helpful and effective in their practice, we realise their responsibilities are nested within wider professional, familial and community supports. If we ask how communities can be supportive of effective practice, we see immediately how these roles are nested within wider social, economic and political norms and realities that shape such community support. Culture in this wider sense influences the development of a range of coping responses and in therapy and supervision we focus on creating the secure base so that we can all better respond to what our culture requires of us.

Attachment theory helps explain how a supportive secure base for both practice and personal development is created, either through the sensitive management of attachment dynamics in therapy and supervision, or in the development of an attachment bond. For example, in post-qualification supervision practice we may enjoy very long-lasting relationships, and if interpersonal trust develops we have the potential to access deeper recesses of experience for both supervisor and supervisee. In meeting with a supervisee or therapy client we always ask 'How are you?'. This is not a polite question as such, it is a serious question, and a request to explore their current state of mind and embodied experience. Our supervisees and clients come to expect this enquiry and may well turn it over in their minds prior to meeting with us. Occasionally someone will enter our meeting and say, 'I know what you will ask me, and I don't know how I am feeling ....' And therein lies our invitation to proceed – 'What is happening with you right now?'. Our awareness of the

DOI: 10.4324/9781003308096-12

importance of well-being, listening to our bodies as they speak through movement and breath, noticing our moments of stumbling and hesitation as we talk together all inform the development of trust in a mutually rewarding experience over time.

In my experience it is not uncommon to bring key life decisions to supervision, such as job or role changes, much as we might bring them to therapy. Bowlby (1988) observed that personal autonomy and interpersonal dependency are different sides of the same attachment experience, that is, we do better and make better life decisions with the help and support of at least one other trusted person, and this person could well be our supervisor and/or our therapist. Bowlby's attachment theory is an integrative, developmental theory of the social regulation of emotions in family systems. Attachment is understood to be both a relationship with a specific person and also what we learn in that relationship about how to keep ourselves safe; for example, how we make sense of information about relational safety and danger, and in particular information that is ambiguous. How we have learned to protect ourselves during childhood influences how we then protect those we love and care for, at home and at work. It would seem that it is not so much what happened to us, but more how we are supported, and have been supported to make sense of those experiences that predicts, for example, the safety of the future child (Siegel, 2018; Sroufe et al., 2005). And, importantly, we can be assisted to make sense of our memories no matter how old we are. In the words of Mikulincer and Shaver (2007): 'What began as a theory of child development is now used to conceptualise and study adult and couple relationships, work relationships and relations between larger social groups and societies'. This chapter will both explore and speculate on how this major body of theories and research can illuminate experiences of safety in both therapy and supervision relationships for all concerned.

Attachment and supervision

Watkins and Riggs (2012) have written of the supervisor's role in the training of novice psychotherapists to be that of providing protection and security, encouraging exploration in the work and awe in both being and becoming a therapist, for example, knowing we are not alone in our work and that we can turn to our supervisor for advice, guidance, comfort and support when we are in need. However much less has been written on the supervisor's attachment strategies (and similarly of the therapist) and how they might be activated during tense and/ or difficult moments both in the supervision relationship and in the therapeutic work itself.

Fitch, Pistole and Gunn (2010) were amongst the first to bring attachment related affect regulation strategies into supervisory focus. If someone, such as a client, supervisee or supervisor, has developed a more avoidant/dismissing strategy for affect regulation/self-protection when under threat or anxious, these relationships of trust and acceptance can create the context for personal growth, specific learning and relational risk-taking. Threat can manifest as a fear of criticism or rejection, or of being a disappointment to others. However, the sensitivity to threat could mean that in some professional contexts we avoid rather than learn, remaining caught up in negative strategies of self-defence. One detrimental consequence of avoidance and over reliance on the self could be for the emergent quality of the professional/practice relationship with a resultant lack of safety. On the other hand, for a person who has developed a more preoccupied, self-absorbed strategy that activates when under threat, these relationships of trust and support can foster the development of confidence and a more outward looking focus. The risk would be that the use of hyper-activating strategies might lead to the exaggeration of distress and excessive approval seeking from the supervisor. This may be more of a risk for novice psychotherapists and supervisors in training? Clearly both extremes of self-protection as described above can interact with the supervisor's own sensitivity to attachment cues and their preferred strategies in circumstances of risk, for example, when supervising therapeutic work with domestic violence, threat of suicide and unanticipated and adverse consequences of actions taken with the best of intentions.

Hill, in 1992, was probably the first to note that illuminating and understanding the attachment strategies of the client, therapist and supervisor triangle would offer useful information for working in the therapeutic context. A systemic analysis would consider this triangle as the basic building block for understanding and illuminating relationship dynamics in this professional context. A triangular understanding is underdeveloped in the literature and offers much potential for exploring what goes well in therapeutic work, and how we might navigate and untangle unexpected difficulties in the work. Bowlby suggested we start with dyads, and then build more complex understandings of relationships. A stable triangle for practice can provide a more reliable and secure base for practice, that is, a supportive relationship between supervisor and supervisee can assist the client-therapist relationship to stabilise when the client may be traumatised and/or the therapist has experienced an unexpected and painful resonance in the work (see Sammut Scerri et al., 2017 and Vetere and Dallos, 2009 for further examples of working therapeutically with stable triangles). For example, the supervisor can encourage the supervisee to slow down in the therapeutic work, and have the courage to stay with the process when the supervisee fears stuckness and failure. This is often the signal to explore the process and go deeper into understandings rather than avoiding them. In the stable triangle, the supervisee comes to understand themselves and how a context of safety makes this possible, such that the supervisee in turn can then support the client/s in their exploration and acknowledgement of dilemmas and distress.

During the recent COVID-19 world pandemic and the lockdown requirements, work teams of colleagues in health and social care, education and the corporate world all reported missing the daily back and forth of social interaction with responsive and interested colleagues. These daily social rituals of everyday life loomed in importance in our collective consciousness as we realised how and why they are so very supportive. We experienced, in varying degrees, the loss of feeling 'felt' by others. We thrive through our wish to connect and being met in that wish.

Stress in our work: supervision and therapy

The experience of stress is to be expected in life and can be a useful activator for coping but in excess can interfere with effective functioning. Tolerable stress can be buffered by supportive relationships that help us regulate ourselves. However, when we are exposed to toxic and/or prolonged stress, we can manage much better with warm, responsive, caring and predictable relationships. In the absence of these protective and comforting relationships we remain hyper-vigilant or dissociated with the risks of distractibility and loneliness. At the heart of responsive and accessible close relationships is the felt experience of interpersonal trust (Gottman, 2011). Such trust is developed through the soothing and calming nature of listening – being seen and heard, and knowing the other understands what matters to us and what we are feeling. Both the therapeutic and supervision relationships have the potential to help with the development of earned security. Security is a measure of the relationship, that is, the 'mind' is both within us and between us. Irving Yalom (2003), working within an existential perspective, writes of the importance of being open and vulnerable in our work as therapists, and for me, by implication, in our work as supervisors. In his view we are required to creatively engage with our clients' lives to help establish a strong and deep alliance. Yalom has long advocated for focused therapist self-disclosure (rather than self-exposure) as a way of modelling how we as clients (or supervisees?) might take emotional risks. He argues that the more emotional risks we take as a client, the better work we shall do in the therapy process, that is, it is in the discussion of the process of risk-taking, such as 'did you take a risk?', 'can we go back and look at it?', that self-awareness and focused attention develops. We need a focus of attention as an aspect of being well and healthy. Davidson (2010) writes of the four pillars of mental wellbeing: the development of awareness and reflective functioning for self and others, a sense of purpose and belonging, and insight into behaviour in context. We can see this as an expression of a form of safety because to feel safe, the experience also needs to be embodied and sensory and integrated with our cognitive understandings and capacities. The experience of giving, seeking and offering comfort and protection are neither disembodied nor disconnected from what we know. But therein lies the paradox – we may know we want to feel safe and be safe, but without a mental representation based in past experience we may struggle to turn cognition into action. Thus in our practice as therapists and supervisors we need to take account of our capacity to have multiple attachments and our different past and present experiences of safety, trust and intimacy within them.

Van der Kolk (2014) writes of trusting our bodies to know what we need. Our brain, body and mind are inextricably connected. In his work he translates the neuroscientific knowledge for us as therapists/supervisors to help us heal the body – providing insight into disconnections within the brain, for example, warded off experiences of fear or shame, and processes not under voluntary control, for example, trauma response 'triggers' such as sights, smells or sounds. In the example below, I wish to show how trauma triggers can function out of conscious awareness but can become conscious through a process of discovery grounded in trust. This is the story of Pete.

Pete assaulted his 13-year-old stepson when he thought his stepson had physically attacked his 3-year-old half-brother, Pete's birth son. Pete acknowledged his responsibility for the assault and was sent to prison. Upon release, he and his wife asked their social worker if there was any possibility for them all to live together again as a family. Pete told the social worker that whilst in prison he met this helpful prison psychologist who offered him cognitive behaviour therapy. This apparently helped Pete understand his 'background' anger, but he said the assault on his stepson was 'explosive' anger, and hand on his heart he said he did not understand it, and thus could not promise it would never happen again. The social worker approached us, asking if we would conduct a risk assessment with Pete and advise on how safety could be achieved for the family. Upon meeting with Pete, we warned him that talking with us about his recent behaviour and experiences, and in particular, talking about his past history might 'stir the pot' and bring to memory surprises or fragments of recall. Pete was keen to work with us and we began exploring and illuminating his account of recent events, and his understanding of safety in relationships as thought, intention, action and feeling. We knew that Pete's birth parents had separated when he was three years old and that he had not seen his birth father since. Family members had told Pete that his birth father had behaved with extreme physical violence to his birth mother. Pete had no conscious memories of this. Some weeks into the work, Pete telephoned us one Saturday morning, sobbing and choking. The only thing he could say was 'it is the smell of the sawdust, it is the smell of the sawdust'. Pete is a carpenter and had been working in the wood shed that Saturday morning. Subsequently we learned that his birth father had been a carpenter, and we speculated that Pete had been exposed to fear as an infant, his own and/or his mother's fear, and had formed an association with the smell of sawdust. This association was likely held in implicit memory and the work with us had begun to make this explicit and thus accessible to processing. In this example we can see why recovery from unprotected danger as a young child might need a longer time frame (Vetere and Sheehan, 2020).

Polyvagal theory: safety and danger

In our relationships with family members and significant others, relational danger may not always be visible. For example, physical assault can be threatened by a raised eyebrow, and forms of emotional neglect and psychological abuse can leave a child confused, frightened and fearful of looking at faces for fear of doing the wrong thing – thus they might learn not to read faces at all, or not under conditions of anxiety and threat, such as fear of abandonment and/or rejection.

Neuroception is the brain's ability to detect danger without conscious awareness, that is, responding to cues of safety and relational danger without involving the thinking systems of the brain. The danger can originate from three sources: inside the body (embodied); outside our bodies (environmental); and between people (relational). The therapeutic task is to help bring neuroception to perception, and then to encourage reflection and curiosity. For example, we might ask, in this moment, does your neuroception see me as a resource or a threat? In supervision and therapy we can bring forth the capacity for discrimination and add discernment, using curiosity about what was activated in that particular difficult moment. We can build trust and offer validation for a person's safety strategies that have kept them safe in the face of uncomforted and unprotected danger. For example, withdrawal may be how we have learned to keep ourselves safe for fear of making matters worse, but now withdrawal becomes an impediment to the development of felt intimacy. According to van der Kolk, self-observation and reflection, whilst staying calm, is the only known pathway to reintegrate the perceptual systems of our brains.

Polyvagal theory explores the state of our central nervous system (CNS) and helps us understand from a neurological perspective why our choices might feel limited in our pursuit of connection with others, and/or in our self-protective retreat (Dana, 2021; Porges, 2022). Being safer in therapy or in supervision with the assistance of our therapist/supervisor does not necessarily bring a neuroception of safety, that is, make us feel safer. When planning for safety we may find a person's narration of harm is not coherent, that is, they might blame others, or their narration of healing might be to blame themselves. We can see a systemic feedback process between how we have learned to narrate our experience and how we experience our close relationships. If our past experience has taught us not to trust others because they hurt, harm and disappoint us, we need time and repeated practice to come into regulation. It is repeated exposure to features of safety that slowly develops resilience. The active, regular experiencing of safety is needed more than the reduction or removal of the cues of relational danger. Our trauma responses and stories are carried in the sympathetic and dorsal vagal ANS states, and in those states we have limited access to ventral vagal resources. In the ventral vagal state we can revisit experience and reflect, as we saw in the example with Pete above once he had established trusting relationships with us. Van der Kolk writes that the best predictor of what happens after exposure to danger is whether we can seek and take comfort, rather than the trauma history itself. When the cues of safety are greater than the cues of danger we are open to explore connection with others. When it is the other way round, we remain stuck in a story, that we risk both rehearsing and embedding.

Shame

Working with the emotion of shame in therapy and supervision is demanding. As children we may have lived with the tension of being told who we are versus who we feel ourselves to be. We are most vulnerable to feeling shame in our close relationships with those we love. Our protest may have been silenced, we may have learned it is unsafe to read faces and their expressions, we may not have known what we were thinking and feeling at certain times, all leading to the development of false affect and in more extreme circumstances, a false self, as this confusion interacts with the child's development of causal understandings. This makes it harder to know what we need to be safe and to feel safe. We may not feel entitled to our needs for comfort and protection. Thus we live out the double bind of trying to maintain authentic awareness in the face of possible disapproval (from clients, supervisors and therapists perhaps), with the risk of losing important support, or trying to be what we think others want, with the concomitant loss of autonomy. For example, whilst the supervision relationship may not be an attachment relationship as such, it has the potential to elicit attachment dynamics, for example, self-protective strategies, in demanding and challenging moments in the work. The feeling of shame may have emerged through childhood as a self-protective response and it is important that we can validate a shamed response as a form of protection. But herein lies the conundrum – we need a felt sense of safety in order to broach talking about shame, and feelings of shame can block our accessibility to others, who may 'give up' on us in these circumstances. However, as therapists and supervisors, we travel hopefully and with persistence in mind. We realise that confusing, ambivalent and ambiguous interactions with supervisees, supervisors and clients may signal the presence of unspoken shame, and if it is present, it will interfere with our readiness to learn, to embrace new experience and to be playful. Developing the quality of our social connections both through and within a safe experience of therapy and supervision is an antidote to the loneliness of shame and predicts improved health and satisfaction in all relationships (Vaillant, 2012).

Safety and responsibility – is this a moral imperative?

Safety also brings with it a sense of responsibility. This is a responsibility to understand our own states of mind and to tune in to what is happening for others. If we have experienced not being believed, listened to or taken seriously it can erode our sense of personal power. In my experience the development of a shared explanation for what has been confusing and distressing can lead to the helpfulness of recognition, naming of feelings and relief. The Boston Change Process Study Group (2010) suggest that co-regulation is the key to recovery, found in those small 'moments of meeting', as they call them. As Haraway (2004) notes, being responsible is also about being response-able – able to listen to others in a responsive and accessible way. Both polyvagal theory and attachment theory see connection as a biological imperative. If someone feels trapped by limited choices, or cannot access enough contextual information to make choices, we need to ask how connection is being challenged and find ways to explore other means of connecting. As therapists and supervisors our abilities to regulate our arousal patterns are key, and may at times be assisted with the help of our supervisors and colleagues. This is how we remain present and focused in the face of the storm, for example, when exposed to clients' and supervisees' feelings of rage, grief, sadness, shame and anger. Trauma-informed therapy and supervision processes contribute to the support of equity, inclusivity and empowerment in our work and more widely in life.

Action-based methods

Some therapeutic and supervision practice can at times be at risk of overly relying on narration, and by implication, semantic understanding of experience. And, for someone who has relied on semantic understandings and the dismissing of physiological feedback for survival in the face of relational danger, this may well be the safest place to start the therapeutic journey, and possibly the supervision journey, also. However, there are times when we know what is required of us and what we seek in others, but we struggle to turn cognition into action. It is at these times that we can recruit both implicit and explicit representational memory systems, using our whole brain resources. Action-based systemic interventions, such as button sculpting, empty chair work, visual tracking of problematic cycles of interaction and genogram work are predicated on helping to integrate both right and left brain processing, using action and vision, such that disconnected experiences (held implicitly in memory) can be made conscious, illuminated, understood and processed in thoughtful, reflective ways.

For example, internalised other interviewing (IOI) (Tomm, 1988) was developed to deepen empathic understanding between couples in therapy. It can be adapted and used in supervision to assist a therapist who feels, stuck, disconnected and/or less empathically attuned with their client/s. We negotiate permission to explore the therapist's representation or working model of their client/s, trying to imagine how their client/s might think, feel and act. The supervisor carries out the IOI with the supervisee's 'internal other'. Thus the supervisor addresses the supervisee by their client's name, and explores their imagined thoughts, intentions, feelings and actions, perhaps asking questions, such as: 'How do you feel and think about working with your therapist?' 'What is helpful, and not helpful? … and perhaps why?' The IOI can continue to explore possible resonance and/or attachment significance for the client/s and/or supervisee, with possible questions, such as: 'Does your therapist remind you of any members of your family, or other attachment figures in your life?' 'What is the effect of this resonance in the therapy relationship/process?' Or we might explore the goals and tasks of therapy: 'What problems do you most/least want to focus on?'. 'How do you understand your challenges/difficulties/hopes and fears?'. 'How do you think your therapist understands them?'. 'How do you think your therapist sees you?'. 'How do you think your relationships impact on these dilemmas?'. 'And vice versa?'. And so on …

The IOI process can be lengthy, taking one or two meetings and thoroughly exploring and hypothesising about what might be happening in the therapy and for the therapeutic relationship. However, and also, some of the above questions can be more routinely and briefly thought about in the process of supervision with client work that for whatever reason is experienced as more challenging for the therapist.

Similarly, and importantly, the IOI process can be used in the supervision of supervision where the supervisor is challenged and/or struggles to assist a supervisee. In this way, we can layer our understandings, building richer pictures. Pausing and reflecting back allows processing to take place. Rhythmic movement and the pacing and tone of the therapist and supervisor can slow down the work, for example, with a careful systemic tracking of an event. We can encourage clients and supervisees to experiment and play with these ideas. Sometimes, when we take action it alters how we perceive our situation.

Conclusion

Supervision and therapy practice can be seen as an attachment context that provides both the secure base and the safe haven for optimal learning and the development of trusting relationships. There is an interaction between supervisor and supervisee affection regulation strategies that are activated under conditions of interpersonal threat, such as the fear of shame, of being seen to make a mistake, and in similar ways for therapist and client relationships. When the therapist and/or supervisor invites an attachment related risk, the client and supervisee are likely to remember all the reasons why they should not trust. Adjustments and adaptations are needed when insecurity is felt and it is very important not to underestimate the courage needed to address directly and straightforwardly what is needed and would be helpful.

Peter Levine (2015), in his somatic experiencing therapy, suggests we pay attention to the physical and non-verbal cues our clients (and supervisees) give us, before we dive into the therapeutic conversation. In the therapeutic and supervision relationships we have powerful and reciprocal resources at our disposal to help build flexible, resilient systems that carry the possibility for narratives of healing and repair. For example, offering full, present and focused listening – deep listening as it is sometimes called – remaining curious about what the other needs, and acknowledging and repairing ruptures if they occur. If ruptures are not repaired, distrust and distancing can develop. Any resulting emotional isolation can be traumatising since our basic need is for a felt sense of security. This is what makes stress manageable because connection is a source of strength, helping to regulate our CNS so that we do not need to remain vigilant all the time. If we bring our awareness to any ruptures in our close working relationships, and notice when we become defensive, or when we stop breathing, we can explore the meaning, apologise when needed, and try again. The attachment implications of felt safety for our practice as therapists and supervisors are clear – developing our shared capacities for reflection and our intellectual potential, achieving some balance under stress and regulating unhelpful arousal, and creating meaningful and intimate relationships. As Diana Fosha (2009) writes: 'The roots of resilience … are to be found in the sense of being understood by and existing in the mind and heart of a loving, attuned, and self-possessed other'.

References

Boston Change Process Study Group (2010) Change in Psychotherapy: A Unifying Paradigm. New York: Norton.

Bowlby, J (1988) A Secure Base. New York: Basic Books.

Dana, D (2021) Anchored: How to Befriend Your Nervous System Using Polyvagal Theory. Louisville, CO: Sounds True Inc.

Davidson, R (2010) Empirical explorations of mindfulness: Conceptual and methodological conundrums. Emotion, 10, 8–11.

Fitch, JC, Pistole, C and Gunn JE (2010) The bonds of development: An attachment-caregiving model of supervision. The Clinical Supervisor, 29, 20–34.

Fosha, D (2009) The Healing Power of Emotion: Affective Neuroscience, Development and Clinical Practice. New York: Norton.

Gottman, J. (2011) The Science of Trust. New York: Norton.

Haraway, D (2004) The Haraway Reader. New York: Routledge.

Hill, E W (1992) Marital and family therapy supervision: A relational-attachment model. Contemporary Family Therapy, 14, 115–125.

Levine, P (2015) Trauma and Memory: Brain and Body in a Search for the Living Past. Berkeley, CA: North Atlantic Books.

Mikulincer, M and Shaver, P (2007) Attachment in Adulthood: Structure, Dynamics and Change. New York: Guilford Press.

Porges, S (2022) Polyvagal Theory: A science of safety. Frontiers in Integrative Neuroscience, 16, 871227. https://doi.org/10.3389/fnint2022.871227

Sammut Scerri, C, Vetere, A, Abela, A and Cooper, J (2017) Intervening After Violence: Therapy with Couples and Families. New York: Springer.

Siegel, D (2018) Aware: The Science and Practice of Presence. New York: Tarcher-Perigee.

Sroufe, A, Egeland, B, Carlson, E and Collins, W (2005) The Development of the Person. New York: Guilford Press.

Tomm, K (1988) Interventive interviewing: Part 3. Intending to ask circular, strategic or reflexive questions. Family Process, 27, 1–17.

Vaillant, G (2012) Triumphs of Experience: The Men of the Harvard Grant Study. Harvard University: Belknap Press.

Van der Kolk, B. (2014) The Body Keeps the Score. New York: Penguin.

Vetere, A and Dallos, R (2009) Family Mirrors: Reflective practice in systemic therapies. In J Stedmon and R Dallos (eds) Reflective Practice in Psychotherapy and Counselling. Maidenhead: McGraw Hill.

Vetere, A (2021) Safety and Self-care of the Supervisor. In O. Ness, S. McNamee and O. Kvello (eds) Relational Processes in Counselling and Psychotherapy Supervision. Cham, Switzerland: Palgrave.

Vetere, A and Sheehan, J (2020) Long Term Systemic Therapy. Cham: Palgrave Macmillan

Watkins, CE and Riggs, S (2012) Psychotherapy supervision and attachment theory: Review, reflections and recommendations. The Clinical Supervisor, 31, 256–289.

Yalom, I (2003) The Gift of Therapy: An Open Letter to a New Generation of Therapists and Their Patients. New York: Piatkus.

Chapter 10

Spirituality

A meaningful philosophy of life and a "lifeline" in times of crises

Åse Holmberg and Per Jensen

Introduction

As human beings, we are affected by not only our immediate family but also by what happens in our relationships, surroundings and society at large. We live in a time with great global challenges, and the pandemics, wars, hunger, suffering and environmental disturbances can make people uncertain about life and the future. Even if any of those factors do not affect someone directly, we are all reminded of these things through the media and conversations with others. However, we all face death, and crises are a part of life. We are all vulnerable to a greater or lesser degree. As family therapists, we work with people in different life situations, whether major or minor crises. Safety and security for family members are important perspectives, from cradle to grave, but family life can be a danger rather than protection, and a lack of these perspectives can create insecurity, anxiety, and a different set of problems.

In this chapter, we will draw attention to a perspective that has too often been forgotten or under-communicated – clients' spirituality. Our spirituality can be a help and support, a lifeline in the middle of storms and a way to find direction from a source of strength and growth. We will give some examples from practice and research and present a model from a PhD study (Holmberg, 2018) for how therapists can better encounter spiritual clients.

As family therapists, we meet people who each come with their unique experiences and problems from their lives, and they each have their own understanding of life. As therapists, it is our task to embrace and be open to what clients bring to the therapy room and to also be receptive to whatever is on their minds.

What does it mean to feel safe and secure? The words have different explanations, but as systemic family therapists, we are concerned about the client's understanding of reality. Yes, we intend to work in line with the law and human rights, but beyond that, we do not push our ideas on our clients, and we do not diagnose. We explore human life and the challenges between people in dialogue and from a systemic perspective. When we say systemic perspective, we include all aspects of human life, including the spiritual part. This, in turn, can make clients feel safe when dealing with the professional. As one of our informants who was very satisfied with family therapy said:

DOI: 10.4324/9781003308096-13

You know humans are much more than the physical body, much more than their psychology. I felt I was met at every level. Of course, the practical things, how to live life with a violent husband and two children, it was the main emphasis, but the spiritual dimension or the spiritual openness was always there, so I became completely relaxed and completely natural with myself.

What is spirituality?

Spirituality is a word that includes many perspectives. It can be called philosophy of life, religion, faith, meaning, existential perspective, view of reality, soul, the sacred or ethics.

In Hebrew, the word *Nefesh* means soul and breeding. We find the same root in English where *spirituality* comes from the word *spirit*, which means "breath". To breathe means that you are alive and are a living soul. This power of life is closely connected to existential perspectives like meaning, values, hope and faith, and it helps people find connection and direction in life. It is also about transcendence – our relationship to the non-material, which we do not fully understand. We are part of something bigger. This is not a static condition, but a process that changes and develops throughout life. The spirituality of humans has different sources, depending on the various views of life. Everyone has their unique spiritual journey that develops throughout life, from birth to death. The spirituality of humans can give a sense of wholeness, harmony and connection with others, nature and the universe. Therefore, eco-thinking, peace, justice and solidarity can be deeply spiritual questions (Canda and Furman, 2010).

To be spiritual is a universal human dimension, but people can reflect on this to varying degrees throughout life. In some periods, the spiritual life will probably be stronger, perhaps when one is at a crossroads, in crisis, during transitions or in cases of illness and death. The spirituality of life is connected to culture, history and relations, and each one of us shapes our spirituality from this.

The spirituality of humans is bodily and closely connected to emotions and feelings. The body holds meaning, rationality and tradition, and there exists a close relationship between the mind and the body. People experience their world through the body, and the body also has a social influence on our surroundings (Bourdieu, 1990). Spiritual experiences often exist partly in the language but are felt fully in the body, and the spiritual body can be an important source of knowledge. Therefore, recognition of clients' bodily experiences is important.

Religion

Humans have different spiritual sources, with religion an important source for many people. The term "religion" comes from the Latin word *religion*, which means a bond between humanity or a power greater than human beings. Religion often refers to formal systems of belief that typically encompass a concept of God or a higher power. It also often includes belonging to a particular group or community (Swinton, 2001).

Humanistic spirituality

In this chapter, we embrace a humanistic spirituality that goes beyond religion, which means we are concerned not with what separates us, but rather with what unites us. We prefer a more cosmic "we", where we look through a cosmic lens and the driving force is love for oneself and others. We support Elkins (1999) who said that spirituality is an experience-based belief that there is a transcendent dimension to life, natural or supernatural, and that life is deeply meaningful and one's existence has a purpose. Life is sacred, and social justice and altruistic love and action are important values. Research says that generativity gives a strong sense of meaning and a commitment to the betterment of the world (Schnell, 2011).

We often find limited constructions of spirituality and religion as created by our cultures, traditions and experiences, and we acknowledge that spiritual wisdom is far greater than we can comprehend. Spiritual wisdom is more of a synthesis than an analysis, more paradoxical than linear, and more dance than march. We prefer non-dualistic thinking, embracing the ability to read the moment without judgemental or exclusionary attitudes. If there are parts we do not understand, we will live with openness – and we will let them speak to us (Rohr, 2019).

Two levels of communication

Spirituality and religion are both communicated on multiple levels. Gregory Bateson (2000) suggested that human communication can be understood as happening simultaneously on more than one level, and digital and analogue communications are presented as two such levels. In communication, the digital level is used to share content, understandings and definitions. In spirituality and religion, the digital level of communication is connected to explanations, dogma and discussions of belief systems and faith.

In contrast, the analogue level works relationally and is concerned with ambiguity and interpretations. It seeks to determine how the relationship is to be understood. This is about the relationships with other people and the relationships between people and their environments – including spirituality, faith or religion. In some religious contexts, people begin to behave in a particular manner when they enter, for example, a church, synagogue or mosque. During services, the congregation may act together as part of a fixed ritual. In these cases, the body is mainly used to express a shared language, and the language is part of a common ritual.

Our spiritual lens

We were both born in Norway and have lived and worked there for most of our lives. We know that the world is big, and there are many different spiritual and religious perspectives, but we deal with the context in which we work and do research. As are 78 per cent of the Norwegian population, we are part of the Protestant Church (only 2.8 per cent of the population of Norway is part of the Catholic

Church). However, our experience is that there can be a lack of space in the church, which can make it difficult to be touched and find nourishment for the soul. Our systemic professional grounding is also part of our belief system. We believe that we all are connected and that reality is much bigger than we can understand. The spiritual part of life is a mystery, and we believe there is more to discover. We have surrendered a dualistic image of God and instead hold that God loves their creation and wants contact with us. Life is deeply meaningful, and one's existence has a purpose. Our most important task in the world is to carry on the love of God. The only thing we know is now – and now matters. The spirituality of humans can make a difference in self, others, nature and life in general.

Spirituality as security and protection: Clients' experiences

The study "Making room for spirituality? Family therapists' and clients' experiences about spirituality in family therapy" (Holmberg, 2018) encompassed interviews with fifteen therapists and twelve clients. Most of the clients came from a Christian tradition. Some were also agnostic or had abandoned their faith but still had a spiritual life. There was a little more variety among the therapists: Christians, agnostics, atheists and an ex-Muslim.

The client, Betty, said that in getting strength and support for handling life, it is important to explore how the client's spirituality can help. She said that, deep within herself, she finds the power that, for her, is God, a power that is much greater than herself. This power has carried her through years of difficulties. She had no management without God, and said she is impressed with her therapists when they say things like "Do you grow spiritually from this? Does it break you down spiritually?" She felt it was a strength that she could come with all of herself.

We find it interesting to see that a lot of the clients in the study lean on God. Although many were not regular churchgoers, and some have even rejected their religion, God was still a very important foundation in their lives. In difficult periods, God was a source of power. For Diana, spiritual life was connected to breathing. God was in her breath, which gave her peace. God was part of her all the time: "I just say, God, I breathe out my powerlessness and breathe in your peace … so easy, banal and basic, maybe, if you can call it that."

Brian was another client who talked about his God relationship:

> Life has some ups and downs. And when you get your downs and have nothing to hold you, to use that kind of expression, I think not having something outside myself, only trusting entirely to my existence, no, it wouldn't work out.

The therapists also said that spirituality was a resource in times of crisis. The therapist Adam said something deep emerges in humans when they are out of the limits of their existence, on the border of madness or collapse. In the middle of chaos, it can be good to find your values and sail through the values as the compass. His experience is that clients with faith seem to endure great pain with patience and perseverance and see possibilities through the darkness. "I relate to faith because it gives access to resources like friends in 'higher places' … and, for some, truths to keep them in the middle of the storm."

Other therapists find it interesting to listen to what spiritual aspects are helpful for clients. If you lose contact with your spirituality, you lose a part of yourself. Having contact with your spirituality can offer new openings for change. It can have a healing effect.

The therapist, Tomas, who works with refugees, often asks them how they manage to come through crises and he explores who was there for them. He says almost everyone says God/Allah is an important guide in life. It is a helper, a protector, and a way to handle adversity and pain. "It (God/Allah) is there when I have no other way to go, like an anchor, a lighthouse." Asking them what their spirituality means helps them find their resources in life.

"I never walk alone" – a story from a client

Many of our stories from research and practice are taken from a Christian context, but we believe they can transfer value to other traditions as well.

As therapists, we listen to the various stories from clients' lives, including stories from spiritual perspectives. We want to share a story from Louise, who had been in therapy for several months when one day she said that despite her strained relationship with the church and the faith of her childhood, it was a chapter in the Bible that had been a great help for her through crises in her life. We obtained permission from her to use the story in this chapter:

I'm not good enough. I have felt different all my life. My upbringing was limiting. They defined what was inside. It was all about right and wrong – and about sin. If I asked WHY I was not the daddy's girl. He didn't know what to say – and pushed me away. I have felt different all my life. I have felt that I do not belong. I thought I was adopted until I was over 18 years old.

There is a chapter in the Bible that has followed me through difficult times in life, Isaiah 54. In the early 2000s, I was married to another man, and I had trouble getting pregnant. I had several test tube attempts, but nothing worked. I asked God why this had to happen to me. What had I done wrong? I opened the Bible and read Isaiah 54: "For the children of the desolate one will be more than the children of her who is married." For me, it was a consolation, a verse I read again and again. I felt it was to me. I was going to have children …

But the years passed, the children did not come, and I was divorced. However, I met a new man, and some years later, we became foster parents for two kids. I went back to the chapter: "Enlarge the place of your tent and let the curtains of your habitations be stretched out."

There have been some ups and downs, but the chapter has followed me: "Fear not, for you will not be ashamed; be not confounded, for you will not be disgraced." Or: "In righteousness, you shall be established; you shall be far from oppression, for you shall not fear; and from terror, for it shall not come near you."

For me, this is greetings from God. God is with me, I'm not alone. It comforts me, I do not feel alone. My father thinks I'm lapsed and have nothing to do with God. But God is greater than my father. I can meet God in different ways. The spiritual life is a part of me. The spiritual life gives me security and belonging.

Before we go back to Louise's story, let's take a closer look at how therapists can give resonance and develop literacy in therapy, which includes spiritual aspects.

Resonance

When listening to a client, there are a number of meanings or perspectives in any one story. From an experience-based viewpoint, it is easy to overlook spiritual perspectives, particularly if it is not important in our own lives, or we do not know how to deal with that aspect in therapy. From a client's point of view, they may be unsure if they are allowed to address their spiritual life or if the therapist can manage it. The spiritual can be a vulnerable topic, and clients may need to be met by an appreciative therapist. So how does the therapist get resonance with the spirituality of the client?

The concept of resonance was developed to understand what occurs when a client or a family communicates and presents narratives that remind the therapist of their own personal and private experiences (Jensen, 2008). This awareness is not only intellectual, and possibly even outside conscious awareness, but is also embodied.

Resonance in this context means that something happens when people and stories meet each other. The therapists' personal and private context adds meaning to their therapeutic practice. Our starting point is Bateson's (2000) idea that context is our mental or psychological frame of understanding about our own life and experience. The context that is of interest here is that when resonance between the therapists' personal/private life and their therapeutic practice, it forms a meaningful whole in the therapeutic process. Or sometimes, the resonance that occurs makes it difficult to go on in a common process.

Elkaïm (1997) helps us understand the dynamics of how one part of life may influence another. He said, "*Resonance* occurs when the same rule or feeling appears to be present in different but related systems" (p. xxvii). What occurs then is a kind of symmetry that invites the person to relate in certain or similar ways to what is going on. Resonance is a concept for giving meaning to the circularity that occurs between the therapists' personal and private lives and the clients' narratives.

Psychotherapy research demonstrates that the therapeutic relationship is of central significance as a contribution to change in psychotherapy. Thus, it is important to understand how this factor provides meaning to therapeutic practice (Wampold and Imel, 2015).

The resonance between our private values and experiences and what we experience in meetings with clients may take different dimensions. In some situations, our entire way of thinking and our attitude towards the current situation or the client can be within a framework of specific personal presumptions or our own local culture. This can reveal itself, for example, in the meeting of a religious client where the therapist has bad experiences with the church and will have the therapist's own story as a central part of the resonance in work with families who are going through similar processes. The whole interaction in the meeting with the client in question may be coloured by preconceptions or prejudices, and the relational resonance can be understood within this framework. In other instances, the relational resonance can be limited to a certain theme and will not be the headline for the whole collaboration or affect all aspects of the relationship.

Spiritual literacy – creating a sense of safety for the clients

Therapy is a community of the language. We will now introduce another concept, spiritual literacy, which includes both analogical and dialogical perspectives of language. Developing spiritual literacy as therapists may help to create safe therapeutic meetings where clients' spiritual lives can take place (Holmberg, Jensen and Vetere, 2021).

A general definition of *literacy* is the ability to read and write. It is to be literate, having knowledge or skill in a specified field (Oxford English Dictionary, n.d.). The usual meaning is strictly verbal, cognitive or mental; we may think it has to do with words and the verbal skills of reading and writing. In therapy, we need to consider the deeper meaning of the concept. A more inclusive definition can be to recognize the meaning in certain shapes, signs and marks. It is the ability to pick up meaning and intention through tone of voice, facial expression and body language. It is the ability to "read" and sense in human relations, it is about being present and awake bodily, the ability to reach deep levels in humans. However, just as you need letters to learn to read and write, you also need some general knowledge to be a literate therapist. You need knowledge about both research and various interpersonal topics. That does not mean that this general knowledge applies to everyone, but therapists typically need knowledge of the different dimensions of human life.

A Swedish author has written, "Man is like a script, whose content is open only to humans with literacy". There are multiple varieties of humans as a text, varieties of styles and language. To read the human is about exploring meaning and deeper motives. The text becomes a metaphor for a deeper context of meaning. Piltz (1991) says, "There is a tension between the author and the text; the letters can be killed by humans; the text may become a paling (fence) of letters that block communication" (p. 55). In each meeting, we must seek the unique and be awake and open to the individual client. There is a connection between the text, the story, and the reader, and in the dialogue, the text can be framed and rewritten.

Figure 10.1 A map of spiritual literacy in systemic family therapy.

Based on research, we will now present a theory from seven perspectives called a map of spiritual literacy. We will then go back to the client Louise and link this model to her story and her experience of spiritual protection in a life filled with ambivalence and insecurity (Figure 10.1).

Spiritual literacy in practice

Louise has been part of the religious culture for many years. After a break, she now tries to find her way forward. Meeting Louise as a systemic therapist, the first step was to *recognize her spiritual or religious practices and culture*, both the past and present. We do this by listening appreciatively in an accepting, tolerant and respectful way. This is about showing interest, curiosity and acceptance but also acknowledging that this may be important for the therapist as well. Louise can reflect on the therapist. This will hopefully create a sense of security in the therapy room. Through this, power and freedom can be developed, helping her to find her way. The key is knowing there is a room, regardless of whether you talk about it or not.

The next step in the model is *to work systemically in dialogue*. Louise's story is related to body, emotions and relationships, and she mentions her father. Human spiritual life is intertwined with other human perspectives, like that of a couple and family life, religious institutions, their culture and discourses in society. Therapists can explore how spiritual and existential perspectives affect and are influenced by other perspectives in human life. Although Louise does not feel recognized by her parents or their faith, she finds comfort and assistance in her faith and her relationship with God. We believe people live better lives if they live in harmony with their values, and we can explore what gives hope, meaning and perhaps also reconciliation. Systemic questions can help clients develop their perspectives and create change. Louise can reflect on what is experienced as protective and safe for herself. Her experience is that she is not alone in the world.

A good starting point for meeting the spiritual life of clients is *to use the client's resources and language*. Crises, death and suffering can crush all hopes and dreams, and how do we go on in life despite it all? We are all shaped by the stories we tell ourselves or are told by others. Stories made before our birth, by our ancestors, by gender, social class and religious groups. However, there is always more lived experience that has yet to be put in our stories of ourselves. Some are not yet formed. In therapy, we enter stories made and stories in the making and reflect on which stories the client want to be guided by or which histories one desires to resist. Therapists are encouraged to attend to the spiritual dimension of experience to explore issues that constrain adaptation and to draw on spiritual resources that fit clients' preferences within and/or outside organized religion (Walsh, 2009). Having spiritual literacy seems to be open to the different languages of clients and involves being responsive to learning from the client.

Spiritual literacy and personal and professional development

The next steps in the map of spiritual literacy are about the development of the therapist: *Bridging linguistic uncertainty, increasing personal awareness and competence and working with personal hindrances.* As therapists, we are in a position of power. There are often many themes to choose from, and we can easily opt out of clients' spirituality in favour of another theme.

Spirituality seems to be expressed in multiple ways, and different feelings are associated with these words. When a client struggles to find the right phrasing, as therapists, we can look at it as a common concern and go along with the client. Our client Louise had several therapy lessons before she mentioned something about her spiritual life. She wanted to feel safe, to be sure that her therapist could manage her spiritual struggle. Her husband came from a different upbringing and culture, and it was difficult for them to share their disparate spiritual lives. Therefore, the dialogue with the therapist became crucial for her.

Reflecting on their own spiritual life and journey makes therapists more open and sensitive to meeting spiritual clients. Therapists may have many personal hindrances to incorporating spiritual perspectives in therapy, both personal and professional. On a personal level, therapists may feel embarrassed by the topic, thinking it is too personal or they do not have a relationship with spirituality or religiosity. On a professional level, some may feel inexperienced, lacking the knowledge or tools. The therapist can have thoughts about a client that perhaps some clients do not find it important to include spiritual aspects in therapy. If clients do not say anything themselves, it means they do not want to talk about it; it is too private for therapy. For therapists, it will be important to work with these obstacles so that therapists do not themselves become an obstacle to clients' growth and spiritual development.

Conclusions

If there is to be room for spiritual life in therapy for Louise and other clients, the theme needs to be highlighted in our therapeutic environment. The last step in our model is to *break the silence in the public space*, and that means sharing stories, experiences and research so therapists can become more confident in dealing with the topic. Research says that faith, belief in a higher power, prayer and meditative practices, along with congregational support, can be a help in times of crisis (Koenig, 2012). Connection with nature and animals, doing something useful for others and dedication to social justice or climate change activism are all spiritual aspects that may promote meaning and belonging. A relationship with God can be a healing factor, a foundation, a source of vitality and meaning; and for some, it may be crucial when life is at its darkest. This is in many ways a relationship of love, a belief and experience that one is loved just as they are, despite the circumstances. There is someone who wants that person to live and have a good life. There can be a kind of healing power in love, which can make the impossible possible (Aponte, 2009).

In systemic therapy, we try to manage complexity and connect different parameters (Telfener, 2017). The client may frequently sense if therapists are open to the spiritual world. When therapists greet clients with love, wonder and an open heart, and then have a look for greater meaning and connectedness with life, the therapy session can become a healing moment in difficult times.

References

Aponte, H. J. (2009). The stress of poverty and the comfort of spirituality. In F. Walsh (ed.), *Spiritual Resources in Family Therapy* (2nd ed., pp. 125–140). Guilford Press.

Bateson, G. (2000). *Steps to an Ecology of Mind*. University of Chicago Press.

Bourdieu, P. and Nice, R. (1990). *The Logic of Practice*. Polity Press.

Canda, E. R. and Furman, L. D. (2010). *Spiritual Diversity in Social Work Practice: The Heart of Helping* (2nd ed.). Oxford University Press.

Elkaïm, M. (1997). *If You Love Me, Don't Love Me: Undoing Reciprocal Double Binds and Other Methods of Change in Couple and Family Therapy*. Jason Aronson Inc.

Elkins, D. N. (1999). *Beyond Religion: A Personal Program for Building a Spiritual Life Outside the Walls of Traditional Religion*. Quest Books, Theosophical Publ.

Holmberg, Å. (2018). *Making Room for Spirituality? Family Therapists' and Clients' Perceptions and Experiences About Spirituality in Family Therapy* [Doctoral thesis, VID Specialized University].

Holmberg, Å., Jensen, P. and Vetere, A. (2021). Spirituality – A forgotten dimension? Developing spiritual literacy in family therapy practice. *Journal of Family Therapy*, *43*(1), 78–95. https://doi.org/10.1111/1467-6427.12298

Jensen, P. (2008). *The Narratives Which Connect … A Qualitative Research Approach to the Narratives Which Connect Therapists' Personal and Private Lives to Their Family Therapy Practices* [Doctoral thesis, Tavistock and Portman NHS Foundation Trust].

Koenig, King, D. E. and Carson, V. B. (2012). *Handbook of Religion and Health* (2nd ed., pp. XV, 1169). Oxford University Press.

Oxford English Dictionary (n.d.) Literacy. In *Oxford English Dictionary*. Retrieved 16 March 2023 from https://en.oxforddictionaries.com/definition/literacy

Piltz. (1991). *Mellan ängel och best: mænniskans värdighet och gåta i europeisk tradition* (p. 256). Alfabeta.

Rohr, R. (2019). *The Universal Christ: How a forgotten Reality Can Change Everything We See, Hope For, and Believe.* Convergent Books.

Schnell, T. (2011). Individual differences in meaning-making: Considering the variety of sources of meaning, their density and diversity. *Personality and Individual Differences*, *51*(5), 667–673. https://doi.org/10.1016/j.paid.2011.06.006

Swinton, J. (2001). *Spiritual and Mental Health Care: Rediscovering a Forgotten Dimension.* Jessica Kingsley Publisher.

Telfener, U. (2017). Becoming through belonging: the spiritual dimension in psychotherapy. *Australian & New Zealand Journal of Family Therapy*, *38*(1), 156–167. https://doi.org/10.1002/anzf.1199

Walsh, F. (2009). *Spiritual Resources in Family Therapy* (2nd ed., pp. XIX, 412). Guilford Press.

Wampold, B. E. and Imel, Z. E. (2015). *The Great Psychotherapy Debate: The Evidence for What Makes Psychotherapy Work* (2nd ed.). Routledge.

Part III

Safety and security in a couple and family context

Chapter 11

Caregiver roles in children's threat and safety learning

Neuroscientific evidence and real-world implications

Jordan L. Mullins and Kalina J. Michalska

Caregiver-child attachment is foundational to children's fear development (Bowlby, 1969). The attachment bond is thought to serve as a base from which the developing child can begin to learn about the external world, including which aspects of the environment are safe and which pose a threat (Tottenham, 2014). Neuroscientific research draws on threat and safety learning paradigms to chart the development of both normative fear and pathological anxiety. In this chapter we adopt an attachment perspective, leveraging data from neuroscience, evolutionary biology, and experimental psychology to detail how caregivers modulate threat neurocircuitry and associated anxiety trajectories in their children. In doing so, we elucidate the role of caregiving in children's developing understanding of threat, both in the context of laboratory-based experimental paradigms and in the face of real-world threat exposure in the form of ethnic-racial discrimination experiences.

Threat and safety learning

Laboratory threat learning paradigms provide a powerful translational platform for investigating the neural underpinnings of both developmental processes and stress-related disorders, such as anxiety disorders. Fear conditioning, a form of associative learning, is one such widely used experimental paradigm for investigating the psychophysiological processes and neural mechanisms subserving threat learning in a range of mammalian species (Shechner et al., 2014). In classical fear conditioning paradigms, a neutral conditioned stimulus (CS, e.g., light) is repeatedly paired with an aversive unconditioned stimulus (US, e.g., shock). These repeated pairings yield a CS-US association, whereby the previously neutral stimulus is now processed as a threat cue and begins to produce a conditioned response (CR, e.g., freezing behavior). Some paradigms also probe safety learning processes via *two* CSs, one paired with the US (CS+) and another unpaired (CS-; Michalska et al., 2016; Mullins et al., 2021). When the CS+, but not the CS-, elicits a CR, an organism's ability to respond adaptively to future similarly threatening events while maintaining an understanding of situations that remain safe is enhanced. Extinction, on the other hand, is a process during which the CS+ is presented repeatedly in the absence of the US, leading to an attenuated CR. Of

DOI: 10.4324/9781003308096-15

note, extinction does not eradicate the initial learned association between the CS+ and the US. Rather, it creates a new learned association by which the CS+ is now associated with the *absence* of the US (Bouton, 2004). Finally, *extinction recall* occurs when the extinguished CS+ is presented again at a later time, with the general consensus that low levels of fear expression reflect successful extinction recall and high levels of fear expression reflect poor extinction recall (Glenn et al., 2020; 2021; Michalska, et al., 2019).

Associative threat learning processes like conditioning, extinction, and extinction recall are adaptive when executed at a level proportionate to both the likelihood and severity of the potential threat (Fanselow, 2018). However, these forms of learning can also become a source of pathology when they go awry and fear becomes so pervasive that it interferes with normal functioning (Rosen and Schulkin, 1998). A common feature across anxiety disorders is aberrant and excessive anticipatory responding under conditions of threat uncertainty (Grupe and Nitschke, 2013; Michalska et al., 2022) whereby anxious individuals may appraise the unknown probability of a particular outcome (i.e., whether a CS will predict an aversive US) as overly likely (Baker and Galván, 2020). Perturbations in threat learning can occur when, for example, fear conditioned responses are triggered in the absence of any CS-US contingency, or when an individual is impaired in recognizing safety cues, particularly ones resembling previously learned threat cues (Lissek et al., 2005). Understanding the neural mechanisms underlying associative learning of threat and safety can elucidate processes shaping the development of both normative fear and pathological anxiety, the most prevalent form of child psychopathology (Kessler et al., 2012) with diagnostic rates known to increase as children enter adolescence (Canino et al., 2004).

Neural processing of threat

Threat and safety learning involves processing sensory information about the CS and the US. Because these stimuli are frequently presented in distinct sensory modalities (e.g., visual light and tactile shock), they activate different sensory cortices (Shechner, 2014). Neuroimaging research in both animals and humans further implicates a network of regions in threat and safety learning including the amygdala, the medial prefrontal cortex (mPFC), and the hippocampus (Maren, 2011). The amygdala, an almond-shaped structure in the medial temporal lobe, forms the core of the neural network that processes threatening stimuli, including detecting threat and activating fear behaviors in response to dangerous stimuli (Fanselow and LeDoux, 1999). The hippocampus is a highly interconnected region that contributes to the regulation of threat responding by segmenting information about an environmental stimulus and distributing this information to various regions in the brain (Meyer et al., 2019). Given the key role of the hippocampus in disambiguating cues that have different meanings in different contexts (Maren et al., 2013) and that its projections modulate amygdala-prefrontal function by providing information about the extent of threat and safety in the environment (Fanselow, 2000),

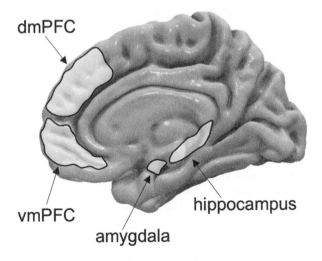

Figure 11.1 Neurocircuitry underpinning threat and safety learning.

the hippocampus is thought to be central for conditioned inhibition. The mPFC receives input from subcortical structures, like the amygdala and hippocampus, which enables the encoding of threat-relevant information to determine behavioral outputs, including the expression and regulation of fear (Alexandra Kredlow et al., 2022) (Figure 11.1).

Animal models of threat and safety learning

A potential fear circuitry in the brain has been elucidated in rodent models, suggesting that information about the CS and the paired US initially converges in the amygdala which is likely involved in both the acquisition and expression of acquired fear (Maren et al., 1996). In other words, sensory information from sensory cortical regions (e.g., visual cortex, auditory cortex) is received by the amygdala which in turn projects to targets in the brainstem that mediate CRs (McDonald et al., 1996). At first, the neutral CS produces weaker amygdala activation relative to the US, but this response is strengthened with repeated CS-US pairings, reflecting a learned association. The *prelimbic region* of the mPFC in rodent brains, homologous to the dorsomedial prefrontal cortex (dmPFC) in human brains, is thought to enhance the expression of fear conditioning via excitatory projections to the amygdala (Sierra-Mercado, Padilla-Coreano, and Quirk, 2011). Importantly, once associations are formed, the CS can elicit a strong amygdala response even in the absence of the US, sending subsequent projections to the brainstem and motor areas that control the expression of behavioral (e.g., freezing), autonomic (e.g., skin conductance response), and endocrinergic (e.g., hormone release) fear responses (LeDoux, 2000). Conversely, during extinction, inhibitory circuits in the amygdala *prevent* neuronal excitation (Royer and Paré, 2002). Simultaneously, the *infralimbic region* of the rodent mPFC, homologous to the ventromedial prefrontal cortex (vmPFC) in humans, attenuates the expression of fear responses through connections with these inhibitory circuits within the amygdala (Quirk and Mueller, 2008). Further contributing to threat and safety learning, the hippocampus facilitates context-specific learning and extinction recall (Corcoran and Maren, 2004). Given the complementary roles the amygdala, mPFC, and hippocampus play in successful conditioning and extinction, disruptions among these networks are consequential for threat and safety learning and anxiety, more broadly.

Models of anxiety emphasize exaggerated associative learning of environmental cues and aversive outcomes (Lissek et al., 2005). As noted above, the amygdala is central to the formation of CS-US associations, particularly in the context of aversive stimuli (LeDoux, 2000). This enhanced learning serves an adaptive function in the case of real threats, but when it persists in neutral or secure contexts, it can result in excessive fear and avoidance, core features of anxiety. In rodents, activity in the amygdala reflects a cue's associability with threat (Holland and Gallagher, 2006) and inhibition of this region is required to prevent freezing responses to a CS+ and allow appropriate avoidance of the US (Moscarello and LeDoux, 2013). This suggests that amygdala hyperactivity can interfere with effective safety learning and exacerbate anxiety and is consistent with work in non-human primates that finds resting amygdala metabolism predicts trait-like anxiety (Fox et al., 2008). Of note, primates with extreme anxious temperament exhibit hyperactivity even in the security of their own homes. Similarly, in mice exposure to neutral tones elicits greater amygdala activity and anxious behavior, particularly when the timing of these tones is unpredictable (Herry et al., 2007). Thus, over-anticipation of even *non-aversive* events implicates amygdala activity and anxiety.

The rodent mPFC-amygdala circuit is involved in learning about and responding to safety in potentially threatening contexts. Electrical stimulation of the rodent vmPFC reduces the expression of amygdala-mediated conditioned fear responses (Milad and Quirk, 2002), while inactivation of this region impairs the acquisition and recall of fear extinction (Sierra-Mercado et al., 2011). Further, animals without a functional hippocampus are unable to contextualize their fear and extinction memories and, instead, respond according to their net experience with the CS (Maren, 2011). This promotes the generalization of fear across multiple contexts, a key symptom of anxiety disorders (Jasnow et al., 2017).

Human studies of threat and safety learning

Complementing animal models of threat and safety learning, human neuroimaging studies likewise show that the amygdala plays a central role in enhancing responsivity to threat and safety (Delgado, Olsson, and Phelps, 2006), while the hippocampus facilitates contextual conditioning and CS-US contingency awareness. Patients with amygdala lesions, for instance, report impairments in fear conditioning (Weike et al., 2005) and amnestic patients with damage to the hippocampus but an intact amygdala show increased autonomic reactivity during threat and safety learning paradigms, despite an inability to explicitly report the CS-US contingency (Fried, MacDonald, and Wilson, 1997). In contrast, patients with damage to the amygdala demonstrate awareness of the CS-US contingencies but fail to show elevated autonomic arousal in response to the CS+ (Phelps, 2006). Similar to patterns of activation observed in rodents during extinction recall, studies in humans also show inhibition of the amygdala coupled with activation of the vmPFC can facilitate regulatory processes crucial to safety learning (Quirk and Beer, 2006). Just as in animals, perturbations in these networks can disrupt threat and safety learning processes and, consequently, maintain or exacerbate anxiety symptoms.

Threat and safety learning in anxious individuals

Theoretical and empirical models posit a central tenet of anxiety in humans is an intolerance of uncertainty (Grupe and Nitschke, 2013; Michalska et al., 2022), defined as the perception of uncertainty as inherently threatening, regardless of the true possibility of threat (Tanovic, Gee, and Joormann, 2018). Individuals who find uncertainty less tolerable exhibit similar amygdala activity in response to both threat and safety during early trials of extinction (i.e., safety learning), whereas individuals who are more tolerant of uncertainty exhibit greater amygdala activity to threat cues compared to safety cues (Morriss, Christakou, and van Reekum, 2015). Anxious individuals thus appear to have select difficulty discriminating between threat and safety and their responses to threat may generalize to stimuli that in fact denote safety (Glenn et al., 2020). This suggests that highly anxious individuals continue to express fear in response to previously learned threat stimuli, despite the absence of threat, possibly as a result of difficulty inhibiting fear expression via elevated amygdala activity and reduced flexibility of amygdala-vmPFC circuitry.

In a study of prefrontal cortex activation during threat appraisal, the point during the recollection of extinguished fears when participants report how afraid they are of a presented CS, anxious adults exhibit reduced activation in the vmPFC relative to non-anxious adults (Britton et al., 2013), suggesting reduced neural engagement during emotional regulatory processes. Interestingly, anxious children exhibit a U-shaped pattern of activation in response to the most extreme CS+ and CS-, suggesting heightened sensitivity to both threat *and* safety conditions and a decreasing ability to regulate in the presence of increasingly similar stimuli (Michalska et al., 2019). Impaired hippocampus-dependent associative learning may be an additional vulnerability factor for anxiety (Lambert and McLaughlin, 2019). Specifically, humans with dysregulated hippocampal function may have difficulty remembering the details of an aversive event, which could contribute to anxiety stemming from the anticipation of a similar event in the future.

Perturbations within and among key neural regions, namely the amygdala, vmPFC, and hippocampus, can disrupt threat and safety learning and subsequently elicit, maintain, or even exacerbate anxiety symptoms. Childhood, in particular, is a period characterized by rapid development of this neurocircuitry (Gogtay et al.,

2004; Wierenga et al., 2014), as well as the emergence of individual differences in threat anticipation and anxiety symptoms (Michalska et al., 2019). Importantly, findings on the neurobiology of fear and anxiety reviewed so far have come from research studying threat or defense responses in isolation from their social context. But as every caregiver knows, children do not acquire knowledge about what is threatening and what is safe in a social vacuum. To more fully characterize such knowledge, it is imperative to consider how caregivers, who play an outsized role in the lives of their children during this time, may regulate children's threat neurobiology and shape their understanding of safety.

Caregiver roles in children's threat and safety learning

Caregiver-child attachment is foundational to children's fear development. Even the earliest psychological theories of attachment posit that a primary driver of attachment formation is a caregiver's ability to modulate fear in their child (Bowlby, 1969). The routine presence of the caregiver, coupled with high levels of warm caregiving, promotes attachment formation (Ainsworth and Bell, 1970; Anisfeld et al., 1990), with sensitive and responsive caregiving fostering secure attachment relationships. The attachment bond is thought to serve as a base from which the developing individual can begin to learn about the external world, including which aspects of the environment are safe and which pose a threat (Tottenham, 2014).

Attachment formation

The attachment bond is a foundation from which future environmental exploration is built, which implies that the formation of this bond is a key precursor to the development of threat and safety learning. In rodents, the threat system is quiescent in early life and neural circuits developing postnatally are biased toward supporting attachment learning and proximity seeking *over* threat learning (Callaghan et al., 2019). For instance, amygdala-dependent learning does not occur in infant rats younger than 10 days of age (Sullivan et al., 2000), despite pups' ability to readily detect aversive stimuli (Collier and Bolles, 1980). It is thought that fear behaviors are not learned or expressed because the amygdala is not actively engaged in contingency learning at this time. Likewise, in human infants, the amygdala is not responsive to threat cues during postnatal development (Graham, Fisher, and Pfeifer, 2013).

In the absence of amygdala-dependent fear learning, competing systems instead produce *preference* behaviors for learned associations, likely supporting pup-mother attachment. These competing systems are the same as those engaged when pups are learning their mother's natural odor (Perry et al., 2016) and begin to orient toward her scent to facilitate attachment formation (Landers and Sullivan, 2012). During this developmental period, threat conditioning thus fails to engage the neural substrates for learning fear responses, and, instead, engages the mechanisms for forming an attachment to a caregiver. This is especially noteworthy because even though attachment has historically been considered innate, such more recent neurobiological evidence indicates a significant amount of learning that activates a biologically predisposed attachment circuit used to initiate and maintain the attachment bond. This work also helps to explain why postnatal infants, both human and nonhuman, readily learn attachments to their caregivers, regardless of the quality of care (Perry, Blair, and Sullivan, 2017). As offspring exit this developmental period, however, variations in caregiving begin to predict differences in threat and safety learning (Callaghan et al., 2019).

Caregiver presence and practices

In childhood, previous goals of attachment formation and proximity seeking are gradually replaced by goals of increasingly independent exploration. In humans, these changes are accompanied by elevated amygdala activity and maturation of the hippocampus and prefrontal cortex, enabling fear learning capacities (Gabard-Durnam et al., 2014; Silvers et al., 2017; Uematsu et al., 2012). Similarly, in young rats, stress hormone (i.e., cortisol) release facilitates amygdala activation allowing fear conditioning to emerge (Moriceau and Sullivan, 2006). At this time, the presence and proximity of a caregiver can predict differential responsivity to threat, in a process known as caregiver or social "buffering", a phenomenon where a caregiver or other significant social figure attenuates stress hormone release by blocking the hypothalamic pituitary adrenal (HPA) axis. One of the most powerful effects of social buffering is maternal social buffering of offspring, whereby the mother acquires the ability to serve as a safe haven or signal safety for the child. In the laboratory, children exhibit lower amygdala reactivity and more mature prefrontal connectivity when viewing pictures of mothers' faces, than when viewing pictures of strangers' faces (Gee et al., 2014). Children with greater attachment security exhibit the most effective amygdala suppression, suggesting secure caregiver attachment supports adaptive threat regulation. Relatedly, children's ability to appropriately inhibit fear-potentiated startle (reflexive eye blinking) is enhanced when mothers are more physically accessible (i.e., just outside the testing room versus down the hall; van Rooij et al., 2017). Animal models arrive at similar conclusions, notably that stress reduction in the parent's presence can block fear conditioning in rat pups through attenuation of amygdala learning-induced plasticity (Moriceau and Sullivan, 2006).

As reviewed above, among rodents, the mere presence of the mother during fear learning causes the infant to approach rather than avoid threat cues. Rodent caregiver deprivation, on the other hand, can result in the early emergence of adult-like fear learning via alterations in fronto-amygdala circuitry (Callaghan and Richardson, 2011) and earlier emergence of amygdala function (Moriceau et al., 2006) and structural maturation (Ono et al., 2008). Neural connectivity is similarly affected in human children experiencing early maternal deprivation (Gee et al., 2013), indicating that maternal deprivation accelerates the development of the threat learning system involving the amygdala. Compared to youth raised by their biological parents, previously institutionalized youth exhibit broader amygdala-hippocampal-PFC network connectivity during threat conditioning, providing further evidence that caregiver absence can alter threat neurocircuitry and threat and safety learning processes (Silvers et al., 2016).

Threat neurocircuitry is not only impacted by caregiver presence, but also by the quality of care received. Children of mothers who exhibit high levels of caregiver warmth display reduced amygdala responsivity to facial emotions relative to children of mothers who endorse low levels of caregiver warmth (Stevens et al., 2021), suggesting maternal warmth helps attenuate threat responsivity in children. Even later in development, adolescents who report receiving more parental support show dampened amygdala reactivity to threat cues (Romund et al., 2016). Conversely, chronic harsh parenting has profound adverse consequences for brain development including reduced amygdala-insula connectivity and less effective deactivation of the medial temporal lobe to threat versus safety stimuli (La Buissonnière-Ariza et al., 2019). Rat pups reared with an abusive mother demonstrate disrupted engagement of the infralimbic cortex, homologous to the human vmPFC, during conditioning and the mother's ability to buffer fear responses is compromised (Robinson-Drummer et al., 2019). Human children suffering physical and sexual abuse exhibit reduced amygdala and hippocampal volume and alterations in physiological responsivity to threat (McLaughlin et al., 2016). Caregiver influences may even extend beyond severe forms of abuse and neglect to more mildly negative caregiving practices. A recent study of fathers and daughters, for instance, suggests that high levels of criticism can subtly impact safety learning in anxious youth (Mullins et al., 2021). Together, these findings illustrate neural mechanisms through which attachment security, caregiver presence and accessibility, and the quality of caregiving practices jointly shape threat and safety learning in children. Of note, the vast majority of this empirical work, is conducted in controlled laboratory settings. How caregiving similarly implicates the neurocircuitry subserving children's understanding of real-world threats is less clear.

Children's understanding of real-world threats

One salient real-world threat that may rewire threat neurocircuitry is ethnic-racial discrimination, the unfair treatment of individuals due to their ethnicity or race (Carter and Forsyth, 2010). The turn of the century has seen compounding, extensive, and harmful effects of ethnic-racial discrimination on mental health during childhood and adolescence (Priest et al., 2013), with higher rates of exposure associated consistently with elevations in anxiety. Far less work explores the neurobiological mechanisms mediating detriments in mental health, and virtually no studies of ethnic-racial discrimination adopt a threat and safety learning perspective that elucidates how caregivers can protect children from the harmful effects of ethnic-racial discrimination. This is especially surprising given experiences of ethnic-racial discrimination are, in fact, instances of learning that condition how future racially charged social interactions are experienced. Indeed, the neural structures supporting the physical component of pain are shared with those supporting the experience of social pain that results from rejection, exclusion, and harassment (Eisenberger, 2012). Repeated encounters with and anticipation of ethnic-racial discrimination shape how children understand their experiences, form expectancies about future encounters, and monitor and prepare themselves for social interactions in the social environments they inhabit (Blair and Raver, 2012). Thus, neural circuits involved in threat and safety detection are critical for monitoring the environment for potential social threats and coordinating neurophysiological responses. When these systems are perturbed by chronic stressors like ethnic-racial discrimination, this can engender anxious hypervigilance, or excessive anticipatory threat responding, a core feature of pathological anxiety. Thus, embedding the study of ethnic-racial discrimination into a theoretical framework centered on laboratory-based threat and safety learning can help clarify neurobiological mechanisms by which real-world experiences of ethnic-racial discrimination contribute to anxiety.

Neurobiological consequences of discrimination

Emerging functional and structural neuroimaging evidence documents detrimental and compounding effects of ethnic-racial discrimination on the neural architecture subserving threat and safety learning (Hobson et al., 2022). Individuals who report higher levels of intersectional discrimination exposure (racism, sexism, heterosexism) exhibit heightened spontaneous amygdala activity and greater functional connectivity with neighboring regions during resting state fMRI (Clark, Miller, and Hegde, 2018). Additionally, participants subjected to racially motivated social exclusion demonstrate higher levels of dmPFC and vmPFC activation than during experimental conditions of social inclusion (Masten, Telzer, and Eisenberger, 2011), demonstrating effects of racial bias on neural regions linked to social distress and emotion regulation. Structural investigations posit similarly consequential effects of ethnic-racial discrimination, with one study showing smaller hippocampal volumes in children residing in regions with more prejudicial social policies and attitudes relative to youth living in lower stigma contexts (Hatzenbuehler et al., 2021) and another study documenting larger amygdala volumes in adults exposed to higher levels of sexism, racism, and ageism (Rosario et al., 2020). Further, people at risk of ethnic-racial discrimination are particularly attuned to cues that signal certain social situations as threatening or safe, suggesting that ethnic-racial discrimination exposure also implicates threat-relevant attentional processes (Purdie-Vaughns et al., 2008). This work, while modest in scale, suggests the neural substrates underlying laboratory-based threat learning are a reliable proxy for real-world threats like exclusion, harassment, and discrimination. Examining whether caregivers have the capacity to play an equally influential role in real-world threat learning as they do in the laboratory could inform preventive efforts targeting how the toll discrimination takes on anxiety may be offset.

Caregiving in the context of discrimination

A nascent literature articulates the shortcomings of an attachment framework that does not adequately attend to the social context of attachment formation between caregivers and children of color (Stern, Barbarin, and Cassidy, 2022). Families of color both face unique sociocultural stressors that may tax the caregiver-child relationship and also possess rich cultural resources to buffer and counter such stressors. Caregivers of color face the undue burden of providing their children with protection and safety in the face of powerful threats like intergenerational trauma of discrimination, ongoing racist policies that disproportionately harm people of color, and daily experiences of mistreatment based on race and ethnicity. Importantly, for youth of color, caregiver attachment security may be an especially robust predictor of well-being due to greater activation of the attachment system triggered by discrimination-related stress (Parade, Leerkes, and Blankson, 2010). Therefore, if threat and safety learning research is to make meaningful progress in characterizing caregiver roles in children's understanding of real-world threats, like ethnic-racial discrimination, and their potential influence on threat neurocircuitry and anxiety, we must as a field increase our attention on attachment relationships in caregiver-child dyads of color and other historically marginalized groups.

Caregiver socialization efforts are the primary mechanism through which children understand and practice responding to experiences of ethnic-racial discrimination (Smalls-Glover et al., 2013). Importantly, the efficacy of caregiver socialization messages about external threats hinges on the quality of the attachment relationship (Darling and Steinberg, 1993), such that children may respond more positively to caregiver ethnic-racial socialization if they themselves are in a responsive caregiving environment (Smalls, 2009). It is, thus, unsurprising that caregiver efforts to protect children from the deleterious effects of ethnic-racial discrimination are best practiced in the context of positive caregiving practices. Specifically, caregivers who are engaged in warm, supportive relationships with their children tend to provide them with cultural socialization and ethnic-racial pride messages that exhibit the most consistently protective effects (Smalls, 2009). While effects of discrimination on mental health are more severe at higher levels of exposure, nurturant and involved caregiving and caregiver closeness have been shown to attenuate these costs (Brody et al., 2006). For example, high ethnic pride is associated with high parental acceptance, which is, in turn, linked to reduced anxiety in children (Gray, Carter, and Silverman, 2011). Further, children of parents who endorse high levels of cultural pride reinforcement messages have significantly lower anxiety scores relative to children of parents who endorse low levels of these messages (Bannon et al., 2009). Caregivers who practice appropriate monitoring of and involvement with their children also transmit more frequent cultural socialization messages (Murry et al., 2014). Importantly, these ethnic-racial socialization efforts executed in a positive caregiving environment predict better child psychological well-being in the context of ethnic-racial discrimination (Varner et al., 2018). Together, these findings suggest that secure attachment relationships and high-quality caregiving practices serve to protect children from the costs of ethnic-racial discrimination on mental health. We contend that caregivers who facilitate their children's understanding of and responding to these unique and potent threats place them on a trajectory for adaptive threat and safety learning that may protect against the development of anxiety. Given the speculative nature of our argument, empirical testing represents immediate next steps for future work.

In conclusion, the current chapter draws on data from neuroscience, evolutionary biology, and experimental psychology to make a case for the study of discrimination from a threat and safety learning perspective. Clarifying whether exposure to ethnic-racial discrimination alters the neurocircuitry involved in learning about and responding to threat and identifying aspects of caregiving that play into these processes will provide new insights into the neural mechanisms of ethnic and racial health disparities and ways in which they can be offset. Future work should empirically test altered threat neurocircuitry as a neurobiological pathway by which ethnic-racial discrimination disrupts threat and safety learning and elevates anxiety, and how caregivers can buffer these effects. Shifting political climate and positive momentum notwithstanding, structural inequality and ethnic-racial discrimination are significant, historic barriers with limited short-term solutions. As we work towards systemic structural change, it is imperative we simultaneously identify and leverage proximal means to protect children from the harmful effects of ethnic-racial discrimination.

References

Ainsworth, M. D. and Bell, S. M. (1970). Attachment, exploration, and separation: illustrated by the behavior of one-year-olds in a strange situation. *Child Development, 41*(1), 49–67.

Alexandra Kredlow, M., Fenster, R. J., Laurent, E. S., Ressler, K. J., and Phelps, E. A. (2022). Prefrontal cortex, amygdala, and threat processing: Implications for PTSD. *Neuropsychopharmacology, 47*(1), 247–259. https://doi.org/10.1038/s41386-021-01155-7

Anisfeld, E., Casper, V., Nozyce, M., and Cunningham, N. (1990). Does infant carrying promote attachment? An experimental study of the effects of increased physical contact on the development of attachment. *Child Development, 61*(5), 1617–1627. https://doi.org/10.1111/j.1467-8624.1990.tb02888.x

Baker, A. E. and Galván, A. (2020). Threat or thrill? The neural mechanisms underlying the development of anxiety and risk taking in adolescence. *Developmental Cognitive Neuroscience, 45*, 100841. https://doi.org/10.1016/j.dcn.2020.100841

Bannon, W. M., McKay, M. M., Chacko, A., Rodriguez, J. A., and Cavaleri, M. (2009). Cultural pride reinforcement as a dimension of racial socialization protective of urban African American child anxiety. *Families in Society, 90*(1), 79–86. https://doi.org/10.1606/1044-3894.3848

Blair, C. and Raver, C. C. (2012). Child development in the context of adversity: Experiential canalization of brain and behavior. *The American Psychologist, 67*(4), 309–318. https://doi.org/10.1037/a0027493

Bouton, M. E. (2004). Context and behavioral processes in extinction. *Learning & Memory, 11*(5), 485–494. https://doi.org/10.1101/lm.78804

Bowlby, J. (1969). *Attachment*. New York: Basic Books.

Britton, J. C., Grillon, C., Lissek, S., Norcross, M. A., Szuhany, K. L., Chen, G., Ernst, M., Nelson, E. E., Leibenluft, E., Shechner, T., & Pine, D. S. (2013). Response to learned threat: An FMRI study in adolescent and adult anxiety. *The American Journal of Psychiatry, 170*(10), 1195–1204. https://doi.org/10.1176/appi.ajp.2013.12050651

Brody, G. H., Chen, Y. F., Murry, V. M., Ge, X., Simons, R. L., Gibbons, F. X., Gerrard, M., & Cutrona, C. E. (2006). Perceived discrimination and the adjustment of African American youths: A five-year longitudinal analysis with contextual moderation effects. *Child Development, 77*(5), 1170–1189. https://doi.org/10.1111/j.1467-8624.2006.00927.x

Callaghan, B., Meyer, H., Opendak, M., Van Tieghem, M., Harmon, C., Li, A., Lee, F. S., Sullivan, R. M., and Tottenham, N. (2019). Using a developmental ecology framework to align fear neurobiology across species. *Annual Review of Clinical Psychology, 15*, 345–369. https://doi.org/10.1146/annurev-clinpsy-050718-095727

Callaghan, B. L. and Richardson, R. (2011). Maternal separation results in early emergence of adult-like fear and extinction learning in infant rats. *Behavioral Neuroscience, 125*(1), 20–28. https://doi.org/10.1037/a0022008

Canino, G., Shrout, P. E., Rubio-Stipec, M., Bird, H. R., Bravo, M., Ramirez, R., … and Martinez-Taboas, A. (2004). The DSM-IV rates of child and adolescent disorders in Puerto Rico: Prevalence, correlates, service use, and the effects of impairment. *Archives of General Psychiatry, 61*(1), 85–93. https://doi.org/10.1001/archpsyc.61.1.85

Carter, R. T. and Forsyth, J. (2010). Reactions to racial discrimination: Emotional stress and help-seeking behaviors. *Psychological Trauma: Theory, Research, Practice, and Policy, 2*(3), 183–191. https://doi.org/10.1037/a0020102

Clark, U. S., Miller, E. R., and Hegde, R. R. (2018). Experiences of discrimination are associated with greater resting amygdala activity and functional connectivity. *Biological Psychiatry, 3*(4), 367–378. https://doi.org/10.1016/j.bpsc.2017.11.011

Collier, A. C. and Bolles, R. C. (1980). The ontogenesis of defensive reactions to shock in preweanling rats. *Developmental Psychobiology, 13*(2), 141–150. https://doi.org/10.1002/dev.420130206

Corcoran, K. A. and Maren, S. (2004). Factors regulating the effects of hippocampal inactivation on renewal of conditional fear after extinction. *Learning & Memory, 11*(5), 598–603. https://doi.org/10.1101/lm.78704

Darling, N., & Steinberg, L. (1993). Parenting style as context: An integrative model. *Psychological Bulletin, 113*(3), 487–496. https://doi.org/10.1037/0033-2909.113.3.487

Delgado, M. R., Olsson, A., and Phelps, E. A. (2006). Extending animal models of fear conditioning to humans. *Biological Psychology, 73*(1), 39–48. https://doi.org/10.1016/j.biopsycho.2006.01.006

Eisenberger N. I. (2012). The pain of social disconnection: examining the shared neural underpinnings of physical and social pain. *Nature Reviews Neuroscience, 13*(6), 421–434. https://doi.org/10.1038/nrn3231

Fanselow, M. S. (2000). Contextual fear, gestalt memories, and the hippocampus. *Behavioural Brain Research, 110*(1–2), 73–81. https://doi.org/10.1016/s0166-4328(99)00186-2

Fanselow M. S. (2018). The role of learning in threat imminence and defensive behaviors. *Current Opinion in Behavioral Sciences, 24*, 44–49. https://doi.org/10.1016/j.cobeha.2018.03.003

Fanselow, M. S. and LeDoux, J. E. (1999). Why we think plasticity underlying Pavlovian fear conditioning occurs in the basolateral amygdala. *Neuron, 23*(2), 229–232. https://doi.org/10.1016/s0896-6273(00)80775-8

Fox, A. S., Shelton, S. E., Oakes, T. R., Davidson, R. J., and Kalin, N. H. (2008). Trait-like brain activity during adolescence predicts anxious temperament in primates. *PloS One*, *3*(7), e2570. https://doi.org/10.1371/journal.pone.0002570

Fried, I., MacDonald, K. A., and Wilson, C. L. (1997). Single neuron activity in human hippocampus and amygdala during recognition of faces and objects. *Neuron*, *18*(5), 753–765. https://doi.org/10.1016/s0896-6273(00)80315-3

Gabard-Durnam, L. J., Flannery, J., Goff, B., Gee, D. G., Humphreys, K. L., Telzer, E., Hare, T., and Tottenham, N. (2014). The development of human amygdala functional connectivity at rest from 4 to 23 years: A cross-sectional study. *NeuroImage*, *95*, 193–207. https://doi.org/10.1016/j.neuroimage.2014.03.038

Gee, D. G., Gabard-Durnam, L. J., Flannery, J., Goff, B., Humphreys, K. L., Telzer, E. H., Hare, T. A., Bookheimer, S. Y., and Tottenham, N. (2013). Early developmental emergence of human amygdala-prefrontal connectivity after maternal deprivation. *Proceedings of the National Academy of Sciences of the United States of America*, *110*(39), 15638–15643. https://doi.org/10.1073/pnas.1307893110

Gee, D. G., Gabard-Durnam, L., Telzer, E. H., Humphreys, K. L., Goff, B., Shapiro, M., Flannery, J., Lumian, D. S., Fareri, D. S., Caldera, C., and Tottenham, N. (2014). Maternal buffering of human amygdala-prefrontal circuitry during childhood but not during adolescence. *Psychological Science*, *25*(11), 2067–2078. https://doi.org/10.1177/0956797614550878

Glenn, D. E., Feldman, J. S., Ivie, E. J., Shechner, T., Leibenluft, E., Pine, D. S., Peters, M. A. K., and Michalska, K. J. (2021). Social relevance modulates multivariate neural representations of threat generalization in children and adults. *Developmental Psychobiology*, *63*(7), e22185. https://doi.org/10.1002/dev.22185

Glenn, D. E., Fox, N. A., Pine, D. S., Peters, M. A. K., and Michalska, K. J. (2020). Divergence in cortical representations of threat generalization in affective versus perceptual circuitry in childhood: Relations with anxiety. *Neuropsychologia*, *142*, 107416. https://doi.org/10.1016/j.neuropsychologia.2020.107416

Gogtay, N., Giedd, J. N., Lusk, L., Hayashi, K. M., Greenstein, D., Vaituzis, A. C., Nugent, T. F., 3rd, Herman, D. H., Clasen, L. S., Toga, A. W., Rapoport, J. L., and Thompson, P. M. (2004). Dynamic mapping of human cortical development during childhood through early adulthood. *Proceedings of the National Academy of Sciences of the United States of America*, *101*(21), 8174–8179. https://doi.org/10.1073/pnas.0402680101

Graham, A. M., Fisher, P. A., and Pfeifer, J. H. (2013). What sleeping babies hear: A functional MRI study of interparental conflict and infants' emotion processing. *Psychological Science*, *24*(5), 782–789. https://doi.org/10.1177/0956797612458803

Gray, C. M. K., Carter, R., and Silverman, W. K. (2011). Anxiety symptoms in African American children: Relations with ethnic pride, anxiety sensitivity, and parenting. *Journal of Child and Family Studies*, *20*(2), 205–213. https://doi.org/10.1007/s10826-010-9422-3

Grupe, D. W. and Nitschke, J. B. (2013). Uncertainty and anticipation in anxiety: An integrated neurobiological and psychological perspective. *Nature Reviews Neuroscience*, *14*(7), 488–501. https://doi.org/10.1038/nrn3524

Hatzenbuehler, M. L., Weissman, D. G., McKetta, S., Lattanner, M. R., Ford, J. V., Barch, D. M., and McLaughlin, K. A. (2022). Smaller hippocampal volume among Black and Latinx youth living in high-stigma contexts. *Journal of the American Academy of Child and Adolescent Psychiatry*, *61*(6), 809–819. https://doi.org/10.1016/j.jaac.2021.08.017

Herry, C., Bach, D. R., Esposito, F., Di Salle, F., Perrig, W. J., Scheffler, K., Lüthi, A., and Seifritz, E. (2007). Processing of temporal unpredictability in human and animal amygdala. *The Journal of Neuroscience, 27*(22), 5958–5966. https://doi.org/10.1523/JNEUROSCI.5218-06.2007

Hobson, J. M., Moody, M. D., Sorge, R. E., and Goodin, B. R. (2022). The neurobiology of social stress resulting from Racism: Implications for pain disparities among racialized minorities. *Neurobiology of Pain, 12,* 100101. https://doi.org/10.1016/j.ynpai.2022.100101

Holland, P. C. and Gallagher, M. (2006). Different roles for amygdala central nucleus and substantia innominata in the surprise-induced enhancement of learning. *The Journal of Neuroscience, 26*(14), 3791–3797. https://doi.org/10.1523/JNEUROSCI.0390-06.2006

Jasnow, A. M., Lynch, J. F., 3rd, Gilman, T. L., and Riccio, D. C. (2017). Perspectives on fear generalization and its implications for emotional disorders. *Journal of Neuroscience Research, 95*(3), 821–835. https://doi.org/10.1002/jnr.23837

Kessler, R. C., Petukhova, M., Sampson, N. A., Zaslavsky, A. M., and Wittchen, H.-U. (2012). Twelve-month and lifetime prevalence and lifetime morbid risk of anxiety and mood disorders in the United States. *International Journal of Methods in Psychiatric Research, 21*(3), 169–184. https://doi.org/10.1002/mpr.1359

La Buissonnière-Ariza, V., Séguin, J. R., Nassim, M., Boivin, M., Pine, D. S., Lepore, F., Tremblay, R. E., and Maheu, F. S. (2019). Chronic harsh parenting and anxiety associations with fear circuitry function in healthy adolescents: A preliminary study. *Biological Psychology, 145,* 198–210. https://doi.org/10.1016/j.biopsycho.2019.03.019

Lambert, H. K. and McLaughlin, K. A. (2019). Impaired hippocampus-dependent associative learning as a mechanism underlying PTSD: A meta-analysis. *Neuroscience and Biobehavioral Reviews, 107,* 729–749. https://doi.org/10.1016/j.neubiorev.2019.09.024

Landers, M. S. and Sullivan, R. M. (2012). The development and neurobiology of infant attachment and fear. *Developmental Neuroscience, 34*(2-3), 101–114. https://doi.org/10.1159/000336732

LeDoux J. E. (2000). Emotion circuits in the brain. *Annual Review of Neuroscience, 23,* 155–184. https://doi.org/10.1146/annurev.neuro.23.1.155

Lissek, S., Powers, A. S., McClure, E. B., Phelps, E. A., Woldehawariat, G., Grillon, C., and Pine, D. S. (2005). Classical fear conditioning in the anxiety disorders: A meta-analysis. *Behaviour Research and Therapy, 43*(11), 1391–1424. https://doi.org/10.1016/j.brat.2004.10.007

Maren, S., Aharonov, G., Stote, D. L., and Fanselow, M. S. (1996). N-methyl-D-aspartate receptors in the basolateral amygdala are required for both acquisition and expression of conditional fear in rats. *Behavioral Neuroscience, 110*(6), 1365–1374. https://doi.org/10.1037//0735-7044.110.6.1365

Maren, S. (2011). Seeking a spotless mind: Extinction, deconsolidation, and erasure of fear memory. *Neuron, 70*(5), 830–845. https://doi.org/10.1016/j.neuron.2011.04.023

Maren, S., Phan, K. L., & Liberzon, I. (2013). The contextual brain: Implications for fear conditioning, extinction and psychopathology. *Nature Reviews Neuroscience, 14,* 417–428. https://doi.org/10.1038/nrn3492

Masten, C. L., Telzer, E. H., and Eisenberger, N. I. (2011). An FMRI investigation of attributing negative social treatment to racial discrimination. *Journal of Cognitive Neuroscience, 23*(5), 1042–1051. https://doi.org/10.1162/jocn.2010.21520

McDonald, A. J., Mascagni, F., and Guo, L. (1996). Projections of the medial and lateral prefrontal cortices to the amygdala: A Phaseolus vulgaris leucoagglutinin study in the rat. *Neuroscience, 71*(1), 55–75. https://doi.org/10.1016/0306-4522(95)00417-3

McLaughlin, K. A., Sheridan, M. A., Gold, A. L., Duys, A., Lambert, H. K., Peverill, M., Heleniak, C., Shechner, T., Wojcieszak, Z., and Pine, D. S. (2016). Maltreatment exposure, brain structure, and fear conditioning in children and adolescents. *Neuropsychopharmacology*, *41*(8), 1956–1964. https://doi.org/10.1038/npp.2015.365

Meyer, H. C., Odriozola, P., Cohodes, E. M., Mandell, J. D., Li, A., Yang, R., ... and Gee, D. G. (2019). Ventral hippocampus interacts with prelimbic cortex during inhibition of threat response via learned safety in both mice and humans. *Proceedings of the National Academy of Sciences*, 116(52), 26970-26979. https://doi.org/10.1073/pnas.1910481116

Michalska, K. J., Benson, B., Ivie, E. J., Sachs, J. F., Haller, S. P, Abend, R., McFarlin, D. R., Urbano Blackford, J., and Pine, D. S. (2022). Neural responding during uncertain threat anticipation in pediatric anxiety. *International Journal of Psychophysiology*, In Press. https://doi.org/10.1016/j.ijpsycho.2022.07.006

Michalska, K. J., Feldman, J. S., Ivie, E. J., Shechner, T., Sequeira, S., Averbeck, B., Degnan, K. A., Chronis-Tuscano, A., Leibenluft, E., Fox, N. A., and Pine, D. S. (2019). Early-childhood social reticence predicts SCR-BOLD coupling during fear extinction recall in preadolescent youth. *Developmental Cognitive Neuroscience*, *36*, 100605. https://doi.org/10.1016/j.dcn.2018.12.003

Michalska, K. J., Shechner, T., Hong, M., Britton, J. C., Leibenluft, E., Pine, D. S., and Fox, N. A. (2016). A developmental analysis of threat/safety learning and extinction recall during middle childhood. *Journal of Experimental Child Psychology*, *146*, 95–105. https://doi.org/10.1016/j.jecp.2016.01.008

Milad, M. and Quirk, G. (2002). Neurons in medial prefrontal cortex signal memory for fear extinction. *Nature*, *420*, 70–74. https://doi.org/10.1038/nature01138

Moriceau, S. and Sullivan, R. M. (2006). Maternal presence serves as a switch between learning fear and attraction in infancy. *Nature Neuroscience*, *9*(8), 1004–1006. https://doi.org/10.1038/nn1733

Moriceau, S., Wilson, D. A., Levine, S., and Sullivan, R. M. (2006). Dual circuitry for odor-shock conditioning during infancy: Corticosterone switches between fear and attraction via amygdala. *The Journal of Neuroscience*, *26*(25), 6737–6748. https://doi.org/10.1523/JNEUROSCI.0499-06.2006

Morriss, J., Christakou, A., and van Reekum, C. M. (2015). Intolerance of uncertainty predicts fear extinction in amygdala-ventromedial prefrontal cortical circuitry. *Biology of Mood & Anxiety Disorders*, *5*, 4. https://doi.org/10.1186/s13587-015-0019-8

Moscarello, J. M. and LeDoux, J. E. (2013). Active avoidance learning requires prefrontal suppression of amygdala-mediated defensive reactions. *The Journal of Neuroscience*, *33*(9), 3815–3823. https://doi.org/10.1523/JNEUROSCI.2596-12.2013

Mullins, J. L., Zhou, E., Glenn, D. E., Moroney, E., Lee, S. S., and Michalska, K. J. (2021). Paternal expressed emotion influences psychobiological indicators of threat and safety learning in daughters: A preliminary study. *Developmental Psychobiology*, *63*(7), e22205. https://doi.org/10.1002/dev.22205

Murry, V. M., Berkel, C., Simons, R. L., Simons, L. G., and Gibbons, F. X. (2014). A twelve-year longitudinal analysis of positive youth development among rural African American males. *Journal of Research on Adolescence*, *24*(3), 512–525. https://doi.org/10.1111/jora.12129

Ono, M., Kikusui, T., Sasaki, N., Ichikawa, M., Mori, Y., and Murakami-Murofushi, K. (2008). Early weaning induces anxiety and precocious myelination in the anterior part of the basolateral amygdala of male Balb/c mice. *Neuroscience*, *156*(4), 1103–1110. https://doi.org/10.1016/j.neuroscience.2008.07.078

Parade, S. H., Leerkes, E. M., and Blankson, A. N. (2010). Attachment to parents, social anxiety, and close relationships of female students over the transition to college. *Journal of Youth and Adolescence, 39*, 127–137. https://doi.org/10.1007/s10964-009-9396-x

Perry, R. E., Al Aïn, S., Raineki, C., Sullivan, R. M., and Wilson, D. A. (2016). Development of odor hedonics: Experience-dependent ontogeny of circuits supporting maternal and predator odor responses in rats. *The Journal of Neuroscience, 36*(25), 6634–6650. https://doi.org/10.1523/JNEUROSCI.0632-16.2016

Perry, R. E., Blair, C., and Sullivan, R. M. (2017). Neurobiology of infant attachment: Attachment despite adversity and parental programming of emotionality. *Current Opinion in Psychology, 17*, 1–6. https://doi.org/10.1016/j.copsyc.2017.04.022

Phelps E. A. (2006). Emotion and cognition: Insights from studies of the human amygdala. *Annual Review of Psychology, 57*, 27–53. https://doi.org/10.1146/annurev.psych.56.091103.070234

Priest, N., Paradies, Y., Trenerry, B., Truong, M., Karlsen, S., and Kelly, Y. (2013). A systematic review of studies examining the relationship between reported racism and health and wellbeing for children and young people. *Social Science & Medicine (1982), 95*, 115–127. https://doi.org/10.1016/j.socscimed.2012.11.031

Purdie-Vaughns, V., Steele, C. M., Davies, P. G., Ditlmann, R., and Crosby, J. R. (2008). Social identity contingencies: How diversity cues signal threat or safety for African Americans in mainstream institutions. *Journal of Personality and Social Psychology, 94*(4), 615–630. https://doi.org/10.1037/0022-3514.94.4.615

Quirk, G. and Mueller, D. (2008). Neural mechanisms of extinction learning and retrieval. *Neuropsychopharmacology, 33*, 56–72. https://doi.org/10.1038/sj.npp.1301555

Quirk, G. J. and Beer, J. S. (2006). Prefrontal involvement in the regulation of emotion: Convergence of rat and human studies. *Current Opinion in Neurobiology, 16*(6), 723–727. https://doi.org/10.1016/j.conb.2006.07.004

Robinson-Drummer, P. A., Opendak, M., Blomkvist, A., Chan, S., Tan, S., Delmer, C., Wood, K., Sloan, A., Jacobs, L., Fine, E., Chopra, D., Sandler, C., Kamenetzky, G., and Sullivan, R. M. (2019). Infant trauma alters social buffering of threat learning: Emerging role of prefrontal cortex in preadolescence. *Frontiers in Behavioral Neuroscience, 13*, 132. https://doi.org/10.3389/fnbeh.2019.00132

Romund, L., Raufelder, D., Flemming, E., Lorenz, R. C., Pelz, P., Gleich, T., Heinz, A., and Beck, A. (2016). Maternal parenting behavior and emotion processing in adolescents-An fMRI study. *Biological Psychology, 120*, 120–125. https://doi.org/10.1016/j.biopsycho.2016.09.003

Rosario, M. A., Ayoub, A., Alotaibi, R., Clark, U. S., and Schon, K. (2020). Perceived control attenuates the relationship between experiences of discrimination and left amygdala volume in older adults. *Alzheimer's & Dementia, 16*(5), e045394. https://doi.org/10.1002/alz.045394

Rosen, J. B. and Schulkin, J. (1998). From normal fear to pathological anxiety. *Psychological Review, 105*(2), 325–350. https://doi.org/10.1037/0033-295x.105.2.325

Royer, S. and Paré, D. (2002). Bidirectional synaptic plasticity in intercalated amygdala neurons and the extinction of conditioned fear responses. *Neuroscience, 115*(2), 455–462. https://doi.org/10.1016/s0306-4522(02)00455-4

Shechner, T., Hong, M., Britton, J. C., Pine, D. S., and Fox, N. A. (2014). Fear conditioning and extinction across development: Evidence from human studies and animal models. *Biological Psychology, 100*, 1–12. https://doi.org/10.1016/j.biopsycho.2014.04.001

Sierra-Mercado, D., Padilla-Coreano, N., and Quirk, G. J. (2011). Dissociable roles of pre-limbic and infralimbic cortices, ventral hippocampus, and basolateral amygdala in the expression and extinction of conditioned fear. *Neuropsychopharmacology*, *36*(2), 529–538. https://doi.org/10.1038/npp.2010.184

Silvers, J. A., Insel, C., Powers, A., Franz, P., Helion, C., Martin, R. E., Weber, J., Mischel, W., Casey, B. J., and Ochsner, K. N. (2017). vlPFC-vmPFC-amygdala interactions underlie age-related differences in cognitive regulation of emotion. *Cerebral cortex (New York, N.Y.: 1991)*, *27*(7), 3502–3514. https://doi.org/10.1093/cercor/bhw073

Silvers, J. A., Lumian, D. S., Gabard-Durnam, L., Gee, D. G., Goff, B., Fareri, D. S., Caldera, C., Flannery, J., Telzer, E. H., Humphreys, K. L., and Tottenham, N. (2016). Previous institutionalization is followed by broader amygdala-hippocampal-PFC network connectivity during aversive learning in human development. *Journal of Neuroscience*, *36*(24), 6420–6430. https://doi.org/10.1523/JNEUROSCI.0038-16.2016

Smalls, C. (2009). African American adolescent engagement in the classroom and beyond: the roles of mother's racial socialization and democratic-involved parenting. *Journal of Youth and Adolescence*, *38*(2), 204–213. https://doi.org/10.1007/s10964-008-9316-5

Smalls-Glover, C., Williams, J. L., Zuckerman, A., and Thomas, D. (2013). Parental social-ization in response to racism. In M. S. Harris (ed.), *African American Perspectives: Family Dynamics, Health Care Issues and the Role of Ethnic Identity* (pp. 47–70). Hauppauge, NY: Nova Science Publishers Inc.

Stern, J. A., Barbarin, O., and Cassidy, J. (2022) Working toward anti-racist perspectives in attachment theory, research, and practice. *Attachment & Human Development*, *24*(3), 392–422. https://doi.org/10.1080/14616734.2021.1976933

Stevens, J. S., van Rooij, S., Stenson, A. F., Ely, T. D., Powers, A., Clifford, A., Kim, Y. J., Hinrichs, R., Tottenham, N., and Jovanovic, T. (2021). Amygdala responses to threat in violence-exposed children depend on trauma context and maternal caregiving. *Development and Psychopathology*, 1–12. Advance online publication. https://doi.org/10.1017/S0954579421001085

Sullivan, R. M., Landers, M., Yeaman, B., and Wilson, D. A. (2000). Good memories of bad events in infancy. *Nature*, *407*(6800), 38–39. https://doi.org/10.1038/35024156

Tanovic, E., Gee, D. G., and Joormann, J. (2018). Intolerance of uncertainty: Neural and psychophysiological correlates of the perception of uncertainty as threatening. *Clinical Psychology Review*, *60*, 87–99. https://doi.org/10.1016/j.cpr.2018.01.001

Tottenham N. (2014). The importance of early experiences for neuro-affective development. *Current Topics in Behavioral Neurosciences*, *16*, 109–129. https://doi.org/10.1007/7854_2013_254

Uematsu, A., Matsui, M., Tanaka, C., Takahashi, T., Noguchi, K., Suzuki, M., and Nishijo, H. (2012). Developmental trajectories of amygdala and hippocampus from infancy to early adulthood in healthy individuals. *PloS One*, *7*(10), e46970. https://doi.org/10.1371/journal.pone.0046970

van Rooij, S. J., Cross, D., Stevens, J. S., Vance, L. A., Kim, Y. J., Bradley, B., Tottenham, N., and Jovanovic, T. (2017). Maternal buffering of fear-potentiated startle in children and adolescents with trauma exposure. *Social Neuroscience*, *12*(1), 22–31. https://doi.org/10.1080/17470919.2016.1164244

Varner, F. A., Hou, Y., Hodzic, T., Hurd, N. M., Butler-Barnes, S. T., and Rowley, S. J. (2018). Racial discrimination experiences and African American youth adjustment: The role of parenting profiles based on racial socialization and involved-vigilant parenting.

Cultural Diversity and Ethnic Minority Psychology, *24*(2), 173–186. https://doi.org/10.1037/cdp0000180

Weike, A. I., Hamm, A. O., Schupp, H. T., Runge, U., Schroeder, H. W., and Kessler, C. (2005). Fear conditioning following unilateral temporal lobectomy: dissociation of conditioned startle potentiation and autonomic learning. *The Journal of Neuroscience*, *25*(48), 11117–11124. https://doi.org/10.1523/JNEUROSCI.2032-05.2005

Wierenga, L., Langen, M., Ambrosino, S., van Dijk, S., Oranje, B., and Durston, S. (2014). Typical development of basal ganglia, hippocampus, amygdala and cerebellum from age 7 to 24. *NeuroImage*, *96*, 67–72. https://doi.org/10.1016/j.neuroimage.2014.03.072

Chapter 12

"Beyond sensitivity"

Understanding caregiving compromises in adverse contexts using the Meaning of the Child Interview

Ben Grey

Introduction

Mary Ainsworth's role in highlighting and evidencing the role of parental sensitivity as the bedrock of child attachment (Ainsworth et al., 1978/2015) was revolutionary in the context of an academic environment and wider culture saturated in behaviourism, which virtually equated sensitive responding with spoiling children (Grossmann et al., 2013). However, its subsequent influence in child welfare settings has created the risk that attachment theory can be used in a one-dimensional way to blame parents and obscure the contribution of social context to relational "insecurity" and developmental difficulties in children (White et al., 2020). Such misuse, however, ignores the contribution of attachment theory in understanding how human relationships adapt and survive dangerous environments (Crittenden 2016), which, as Bowlby recognised includes the social and material conditions in which parents seek to care for their children (Duschinsky 2020).

This chapter develops these insights in relation to the Meaning of the Child Interview (MotC: Grey and Farnfield, 2017), a procedure for analysing parenting interviews, and a case example of a family struggling with the behaviour of their 6-year-old child who has a diagnosis of autism, to show the potential of attachment theory to link internal meaning making with both past and present context. The MotC was developed within clinical practice, seeking to use the potential of attachment theory not just to label risk in vulnerable families, but to understand better the relationships of those who are struggling.

Parental sensitivity

Bowlby's systemic insights notwithstanding, conceptualisations of parental sensitivity have largely focussed on whether the parent is providing the foundations of secure attachment, despite the recognition that "security" is not always optimal in all situations. For example, Forslund et al.'s (2021, p. 18) influential consensus of prominent attachment researchers, notes that diverse, *even insecure*, patterns contribute to a child's "survival and adaptation to varying caregiving and contextual conditions" given that resources and adversity are not distributed equally.

DOI: 10.4324/9781003308096-16

However, these writers (p. 30) define the assessment of caregiving in terms of "safe-haven provision":

> The parent's ability to understand and respond effectively to the child's needs, to know and value the child, and to be consistently in charge in the relationship.

This definition returns attention very squarely to an *ability* that resides in the parent rather than to the "varying ... contextual conditions" in which secure attachment may not be adaptive. For example, trusting that others will respond empathically to an open communication of your frustrations may be dangerous in some relationships in so-called safe societies, let alone more obviously dangerous ones. If "insecure" attachment strategies may be adaptive to difficult contexts, then the same must be true for parenting. Different and "non-sensitive" patterns of caregiving, which may not offer a "safe-haven", may be adaptive in adverse circumstances; they may prepare the child to manage dangerous environments where there is no true "safe-haven" for anyone, adult or child. Such caregiving might also enable the parent to continue to parent as best they can with minimal resources.

This chapter suggests that *compromised caregiving* may better capture the active way in which parents interact with their particular context to offer the best chances to their offspring, whilst enabling parents' continuing functioning and management of their wider relationships. Acting upon limited information, parents prioritise and respond to aspects of reality that have informed their survival and ability to manage the particular dangers that have loomed large in their experience. That is, their actions are based on an interpretation of their current context through the lens of their past (Crittenden, 2016). In addition, parents need to continue to survive and function in order to continue to care for their child, or in extremis, raise other children. Whether explicitly acknowledged or not, all parents to a greater or lesser extent face a trade-off between their own survival needs and the caregiving impulse to ensure the survival of their offspring. Given the importance of adequate parental functioning to the survival chances of the child, this dilemma can become acute in dangerous situations and environments.

The caregiving motivational system

Bowlby envisaged the parental *caregiving* system as the mirror image of the child *attachment* system (Duschinsky, 2020). Child attachment was conceived as staying safe by regulating *proximity* with the attachment figure. The caregiving system was based on the *retrieval* instinct of the caregiver: how far can the parent "let the child go" and explore the world, whilst still being able to remove the child from trouble when needed. Especially as the child gets older and the immediate physical presence of the caregiver becomes less important, retrieval and proximity are better seen as metaphors for the regulation of parental *availability*. Specifically, what level of psychological availability and attentiveness is needed to reassure the child that the parent can offer protection and support when needed, and the parent that the child will fall in quick enough with this to ensure his or her safety? The parent balances their instinct to protect the children with the child's need for independence and a concern for their wider development, and the parents' need to negotiate the world around the child.

Adaptive caregiving strategies

However, weighing up these goals in particular contexts, with shifting danger and our necessarily limited perspective on reality, is a more complex business. In the real-world, human beings need to make compromises in order to react quick enough to protect themselves and their young. From the child's point of view, Ainsworth's work began to formally outline the two basic defences or compromises for the child, namely Type A (commonly called avoidant) attachment, where the child keeps a level of distance, particularly emotionally, in order to remain close enough to the attachment figure for protection whilst minimising the chances of rejection, and Type C (commonly called ambivalent), where the child seeks to ensure continuing closeness to a parent whose availability is uncertain, often by engaging in a continuous struggle with the attachment figure (Ainsworth et al., 1978). George and Solomon (2008) extended this approach to caregiving, identifying the mirror patterns in parents of "distanced protection", where the caregiving system is deactivated, and the umbilical cord stretched (called here *Unresponsive*, or *child-led* parenting), and "close protection" (*Controlling*, or *parent-led* parenting), where the child is kept on a metaphorical short leash. There is a third option of "flexible" caregiving (here *Sensitive*, or *collaborative* parenting): trying to stay open to the situation and select the best option in the moment, attending when the child needs help, and facilitating independence when the child can manage. The Meaning of the Child Interview (MotC) terms of *Sensitivity*, *Unresponsiveness*, and *Control* are drawn from Crittenden's CARE-index (Crittenden, 2007). The CARE-Index operationalises Ainsworth's thinking on parental sensitivity in a short, videoed episode of parent-infant play. Critically, it examines parent-child interaction dyadically, in terms of how child and parent behaviour are connected (or not) to each other, rather than conceptualising sensitivity as an individualised trait or capacity.

Compromised caregiving in the MotC

Without losing the focus this work gave to the representational world of the parent, we wish to link it further with the parents' participation in the outside world, making explicit the external context in which these relationship patterns are situated. We will focus on Unresponsive and Controlling patterns, as the child-protective intentions and positive aspects of the compromises these parents are making are less intuitively obvious, and less frequently stressed.

Controlling, parent-led caregiving

Parents using a *controlling* strategy of caregiving devote resources to keeping the child in line and attentive to them and are hyper-aware of the dangers the world presents to the child, seeking to *make sure* that they are able to protect the child. For this reason, it is a *parent-led* strategy of caregiving. The child's separateness is experienced as threatening of the parents' ability to protect the child. Parent-led caregiving tends to implicitly assume or explicitly state that the world is a hostile place that their child cannot manage alone. There is an assumption that the parent alone can offer the child what they need. If the parent does not (micro)manage the child and their environment, they (and the family) may get hurt. If the child is overly differentiated or separated from the parent, s/he may get "picked off" by outside threats.

The *key parental role* is to monitor and maintain the child's close alignment to the parent, so that the parent can always be on hand to ensure their safety. This can be done either by selectively focussing on countering the child's attempts to individuate, seen in frustration or even hostility towards the child, or selectively emphasising their closeness and connection (how they are the same) blurring the gap between parent and child in ways that may seem enmeshed.

The *advantage* of this strategy is that the parent can be always "on hand" to deal with any threat posed to the child and can tackle problems that the child cannot manage alone. The parent is more equipped than the child to manage the world and better able to *make sure* of their safety. This is a (nearly) "always on" strategy – activated quickly and terminated slowly. The fear of the child struggling, failing, missing out, or getting themselves in trouble is highly motivating, such that parents remain actively monitoring the child and situation, even when the child is safe. That way they can be ready for problems and dangers as they arise. For the child, it can be reassuring to have so much parental availability, attention, and ultimately protection.

The difficulty or risk is, first, that this is potentially overwhelming for the parent, leaving them depleted in their ability to attend outside of the relationship. This can cause resentment in the parent (which the child may also pick up on). Such resentment can fuel the negative side of the strategy, where alignment with the parent is enforced more punitively or emotively (either through harsh parenting, or emotional plays for increased closeness). This pressurises the child not to differentiate in any way that might put them at risk from the parent as well as the outside world. Second, the pattern necessarily involves rejection of the child's separate self, potentially negatively impacting the child's sense of their own competence and value.

Unresponsive, child-led caregiving

Parents using an *unresponsive* strategy intuitively recognise that they cannot always be around to protect their children who will need to learn to manage without them.

They may devote more resources to managing the world outside the family, telling themselves not to "interfere" with the child's development and independence. It is a *child-led* strategy; children are seen as possessing what they need to develop, so long as the parent manages the outside world and doesn't inflict their own needs on their offspring. The parent-child umbilical cord is stretched as far as it will go to facilitate maximum independence and free up the parent to attend to dangers outside the parent-child relationship. Parents tend to implicitly assume that their child knows best and can handle situations themselves better using their own resources, which it is essential that they develop and utilise. There is a corresponding distrust in what the parent has to offer the child.

The *key parental role* is to hasten the child's ability to manage by themselves. This may lead to a prioritisation of encouraging competence (e.g., educational achievement or learning practical skills) over nurture (attending to the child's feelings or experience). Nurture may lead to dependence upon the parent, whilst competence helps the child manage the world successfully.

The *advantage* is that the strategy allows the parent to attend to other threats and their own functioning – facilitating the child's developing her/his own independent resources, and rationing their availability to the child for *when it is really needed*. The caregiving system is activated late and terminated early, conserving resources. For the child, the strategy offers increased opportunities for self-mastery and independence.

The *difficulty or risk* is that the child will also experience a lack of nurture, support, connection, and potentially a felt or real lack of protection. The more the parent attends away from the child, the less quickly they are able to respond to sudden and unexpected threats to the child or serious distress. This can leave the child dealing with threats and problems they cannot manage despite the parents' better intentions. Even where the child is safe, because the parent is elsewhere a lot of the time (psychologically if not physically), much of the child's world remains invisible to the parent, and so by extension to the child also. Lacking an effect upon others, such children can at worst become invisible to themselves – and struggle to develop a coherent or complete sense of self. They can gain a superficial competence, but one that is externally defined and motivated by social rules or powerful others.

Self-protection vs. child-protection

The evolutionary function of attachment is to stay alive long enough to reproduce and pass on your genes (Crittenden 2016). However, these two goals can and often do conflict – that is, the impulse to nurture and protect the child, can conflict with or threaten the parent's impulse to survive. Whilst in extremis, parents may sacrifice themselves to save their children, all or most parents experience a competing impulse to protect themselves (and go on to raise other children), rather than risk no-one surviving and no future offspring. In practice it is difficult to disentangle these two instinctive responses. We are likely to dress up self-protection in terms of child-protection to avoid being shamed, and because sometimes we do need to prioritise ourselves as parents to keep our children safe.

The social context of caregiving

It is here that critical differences between the attachment and caregiving systems become clear. For the child (especially the infant) the parent is (for the most part) their whole world. Whilst age introduces a wider and more complex set of relationships, until adolescence these are largely mediated through the parent. However, the management of the outside social world and other relationships for the child is integral to parental caregiving in a way that it is not for child attachment, for whom "management" only of the parent and other key relationships are key.

This means that to truly understand caregiving we need to understand the historical and social context in which the parent is situated, along with the cultural discourses parents use to give meaning to their experience and the power relationships that inform them. It can be useful to think about these as a series of embedded circles containing and shaping the basic parent-child relationship, informing every aspect of it (Figure 12.1).

In one parent-child relationship, managing the tensions in the spousal relationship may be so critical to the safety of mother and child, that this is what primarily informs the caregiving pattern, but this is also mediated by the wider social situation, which informs those tensions. For example, a mother's attention is so devoted to managing her frequently violent partner (who in turn protects her and her child perhaps from a very dangerous external gangland, violence-dominated, social context), that she has little parental resources remaining for the comfort and wider

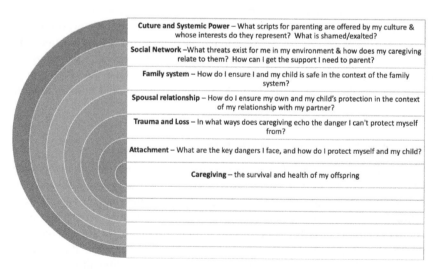

Figure 12.1 The embedded Meaning of the Child.

protection of her child. This, at least from her perspective, may be the best compromise she can make in the current circumstances (even if her pattern is classified as *unresponsive*). Her partner may be hypervigilant to challenges to his authority, and feel he must assert power and dominance, and to "make sure" his child and partner toe the line (so he can protect them), as this may be his best chance of fighting off an ever-present danger of physical attack and potential exploitation (even though this compromise would be classified as *controlling*). Cultural narratives encouraging women to organise their identity around pleasing their spouse, and men to see their value in terms of their strength and status outside the home, socially sanction the mother sacrificing her own and her child's safety, and the father's aggressive "protection" of the family status. They also make the process less visible by normalising it. Context is key to understanding the meaning of caregiving for each parent.

Case example

The following example is drawn from the interviews of two parents of a child with a diagnosis of autism. The family was part of a wider study of families who have a child with this diagnosis, and a multi-family intervention aimed at supporting them (Dallos, Grey, and Stancer, 2022; Grey, Dallos, and Stancer, 2021). In these studies, we looked at how parental trauma can transform how problems are maintained and intensified in the lives of the families where a child had an autism diagnosis. We also drew attention to how the social discourse around autism, by locating relational problems entirely as an individual irreversible disorder, helped ease the sense of blame felt by the parents we studied, but also robbed them of much of their interpersonal influence as a parent. Parent-child interaction was stripped of any relational and personal meaning, being seen only as a "symptom" of autism. Parents were left managing dysfunctional behaviour rather than relating to their children. In this chapter, our focus is on the contextual nature of parental caregiving, however, rather than the difficulties presenting around autism.

Family context

Dave and Denise, live with their two sons, Jim (aged 6) and Ollie (aged 4). Denise's side of the family live nearby and see them regularly.

Parental attachment and caregiving

Dave: Feeling "on a prison ship"

Dave describes a family history as "quite a happy childhood" but a father prone to anger, and a mother whose attention was devoted to Church activities. Dave noted that "in my childhood we did have a lot of running around after other people and us feeling slightly neglected" but commented: "I like the way she's like really caring for other people".

Dave's mother's strict and socially isolating kind of religion placed him in situations where he felt humiliated and trapped:

> [My] mother was a constant embarrassment, to be honest … one day I'm going to be free of this woman, I can start living.

Unfortunately, Dave's experience of being a parent is exchanging one kind of imprisonment for another:

> You just feel hemmed in like you're … on a ship, a prison ship or something, trapped with them and you can't get away and it's all a bit much and you're trying to drive a car and they're like (makes wailing noise), and you're like can't take any more of this, my head's gonna pop.

The over-riding theme of Dave's MotC is a sense of feeling trapped in the relationship with Jim. He tries to avoid getting angry with Jim and this is at some cost to him. He describes that he feels shaky and upset after Jim's "meltdowns" and that he has to use anti-depressants to cope. In MotC terms, this is unresponsive, "child-led'" parenting, seeing himself as a threat to the child and aiming not to impose his feelings on his child like his father did. He hankers after an outdoor, "free", activity-based and without the kind of claustrophobic intensity of his own childhood, but his desire to be a good parent places him right back in the same situations of being socially shamed that his mother placed him in:

> I was in Homebase today, and a lady had a young lad … and he was … playing up around the shop and stuff, … whizzing around say, on the wheelie thing … and I just thought, he's just got autism.

Therefore, although Dave is working hard to be more in control of his temper than his father, his desperation to break-free results in lapses that intensify his feelings of shame:

> I couldn't control it, … just feeling like, you know, I should be controlling this, I should be a parent, that sort of stuff, putting myself under pressure, but it is what it is really.

Thinking in terms of the social context, the discourse of autism is employed by Dave's unresponsive pattern to strip away the personal rupture inherent in his conflict with his son ("*it* is what *it* is really"), by removing his and his child's behaviour from any relational or interpersonal context ("he's just got autism"). His child is a "locked inside his own head" and unreachable – so separate, Dave feels unable to act as a parent to Jim:

there's lots of people with mental illness and autism and they're all sort of locked inside their own head and stuff … you feel you're just not getting through to him.

This has the effect of making the whole problem feel inevitable and irresolvable – for Dave, there is no escape.

Denise: "Fighting a fire"

A significant part of Denise's childhood had been that her brother suffered from mental health problems, which continue to impact on Denise's life and that of her parents. Denise's interview tended to minimise difficulties and portray her childhood as happy, although showing an undercurrent of fear not fully acknowledged. Denise was the "good" child, with a twin brother who had constant problems:

Once my brother just kinda flipped out a bit about something around his anxiety, and I think he, he did break my mum's glasses once, um I think I was there, and I remember sort of thinking, it was a bit upsetting to see your parent, you know, being sort of attacked because you know you want to see that they're all together and they're fine … but on the whole he would actually be sort of violent, that would make us feel unsafe, though um it was more just sort of this anxiety, and … he was more sort of shy with it on the whole rather than kind of very angry with it.

Denise's language is minimising ("bit upsetting", "flipped out a bit", "more sort of shy") but there is an undercurrent of fear and danger ("flipped", "attacked", "violent"), which she is reluctant to stay with, perhaps because to focus on her vulnerability and fear might overwhelm her, and undermine her role of being the supportive, helpful one who holds everything together.

Significantly, Denise appears to be repeating the same role in her parenting, in that she is trying to hold things together by focussing on her task rather than her feelings, and is not able to draw any hope of things getting better from her own family:

it can feel a bit like fighting fire sometimes because it's kind of desperation because … literally things are starting to fly around and get broken, and you think um someone is really going to get hurt or something is really going to get broken in a minute, and you have to sort of drop everything and whatever you're doing and sort of calm things down um so um it can just make you feel a bit frazzled (laugh).

There are a range of adversarial images of it being a "battle", "struggle", "fighting a fire", "like a roller coaster" in ways that echo the unresolved sense of danger from her own childhood. At the same time Jim is not personally present in this picture (notice that "someone" and "something" will get hurt or broken, without anyone particular doing these things). Denise is only present in the more distant "you", and with the emotional impact minimised ("sort of calm things down", "a bit frazzled"). Like Dave, she appears to have developed a way of distancing from Jim. The socially provided autism discourse helps to ameliorate her anger, by externalising the problem as "autism" rather than Jim personally, and recruiting her childhood role as the family fire-fighter, the one who "calms things down". However, at the same time it renders Denise external to the situation, trying desperately to predict what he will do next and running after him, as if he were an out-of-control missile, rather than seeing herself as participating in a relationship with her son. She is "desperate", because in re-enforcing her child-led, unresponsive strategy, Denise is not present as a parent with a power to influence and resolve the conflict and ruptures in her family, until she comes in from the outside, "fire-fighting" to "calm things down". The metaphor is telling, as fire fighters have no part in fire itself, or the circumstances that led to it, but are external and can only arrive once things are already out of control.

Family relationships: "A battle ... you just can't control"

Whilst both parents frequently mention the stress and strains of parenting, there is very little reference to either of them seeking support from the other. It seems the core of their shared experiences is that Jim is frustrating, like a battle, promoting a sense of helplessness and exhaustion. However, both parents described problems situated within family processes which actively involved Ollie, Jim's sibling, who does not have an autism (or any other) diagnosis:

> They'll feed off each other like Jim'll react to Ollie, Ollie will get in a state, Jim won't like the noise, Jim'll kick off and then Ollie will just um react to that and you just can't control the situation (laughs), you just got to ride it out and stuff.

The children are seen as feeding off each other, a typical family process. However, for Dave and Denise, instead it is Jim's autism that is the problem, and that there is nothing you can do about it but try and "ride it out".

For Jim and Ollie their central experience of such a child-led pattern must be their parents' constant fear of them; a sense of being too powerful, of being uncontained, unprotected, and uncomforted. This could lead to them exacerbating their difficult behaviour to draw their parents in to "drop everything" and "try and calm things down". By becoming angry, the children would feel more powerful and in control of a fearful world. This partially succeeds in drawing in the parents to manage them physically but exacerbates the fear of their parents (Dave that he will lose control of himself, and Denise that she will lose control of the family situation), adding fuel to the fire. The children are only partially reassured by their parents containing behaviour, as their high arousal is not addressed or seen, perpetuating the cycle.

Looking at all of this, the embedded MotC (Figure 12.2) for Denise and Dave can be more specifically written as Figure 12.2.

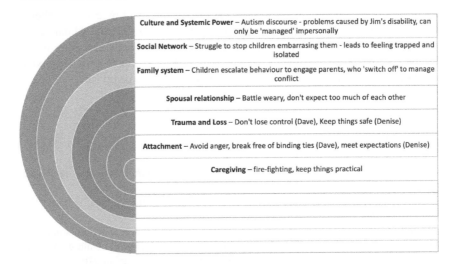

Figure 12.2 Dave and Denise's embedded MotC.

Conclusion

Our analysis of Dave and Denise's situation shows an overly *child-led* family system, as the parents must try and switch off emotionally to manage the family conflict, and the children escalate behavioural attempts to be seen and engage their parents. However, this unresponsiveness is motivated "from below" by Dave's fear of losing it like his father and being trapped by closeness to his mother, and Denise's role of avoiding her feelings to manage the conflict in her family origin. It is also entrenched "from above" by the culturally available discourses about autism, which by locating the problem as an impersonal and individualised brain impairment not as "naughtiness" (an internal motivation). This robs the children's behaviour of any interpersonal significance, likely intensifying Jim and Ollie's sense of not being seen. For Dave and Denise, these discourses help them manage the social embarrassment and potential blame in caring for Jim, as well as avoid angry feelings that might (and for Dave sometimes do) overwhelm them. However, these compromises leave them trapped and desperate, as there is no room in this for parental influence, the ability to make things different by helping manage and contain their child(ren)'s feelings.

The example helps illustrate how attachment and caregiving analysis of discourse, whilst illuminating internal representations, do not make parental sensitivity and internal capacity of the parent, but a feature of a wider social network, incorporating a present context as well as past history. Unresponsiveness and Control are compromises that parents instinctively as well as consciously make to find what passes for safety in dangerous contexts, whilst holding themselves together in the meantime. Without losing awareness of the impact upon children, this kind of analysis can make these compromises explicit, highlighting both the "payoff" that keeps the system going, as well as the price being paid by each member of the family, which might be too high. It draws attention to the external dangers in the past and present social environment that may be sustaining such compromised caregiving. This potentially opens the way for collaborative intervention in finding alternatives or possibilities for change that might otherwise be invisible.

References

Ainsworth, M., Blehar, M., Waters, E., and Wall, S. (1978/2015). *Patterns of Attachment: A Psychological Study of the Strange Situation*. Erlbaum.

Crittenden, P. M. (2007). *CARE-Index: Infant and Toddlers Coding Manual*. Unpublished manuscript, Family Relations Institute.

Crittenden, P. M. (2016). *Raising parents: Attachment, Representation, and Treatment* (2nd ed.). Routledge.

Dallos, R., Grey, B., and Stancer, R. (2022). Anger without a voice, anger without a solution: Parent–child triadic processes and the experience of caring for a child with a diagnosis of autism. *Human Systems*, 26344041221115256. https://doi.org/10.1177/263440 41221115255

Duschinsky, R. (2020). *Cornerstones of Attachment Research*. Oxford University Press. https://doi.org/10.1093/med-psych/9780198842064.001.0001

Forslund, T., Granqvist, P., van IJzendoorn, M. H., Sagi-Schwartz, A., Glaser, D., Steele, M., Hammarlund, M., Schuengel, C., Bakermans-Kranenburg, M. J., Steele, H., Shaver, P. R., Lux, U., Simmonds, J., Jacobvitz, D., Groh, A. M., Bernard, K., Cyr, C., Hazen, N. L., Foster, S., … Duschinsky, R. (2021). Attachment goes to court: Child protection and custody issues. *Attachment & Human Development*, 1–52. https://doi.org/10.1080/14616 734.2020.1840762

George, C. and Solomon, J. (2008). The caregiving system: A behavioral systems approach to parenting. In J. Cassidy and P. Shaver (eds), *Handbook of Attachment: Theory, Research, and Clinical Applications* (Vol. 2nd, pp. 833–856). Guilford Press.

Grey, B., Dallos, R., and Stancer, R. (2021). Feeling "like you're on … a prison ship" – Understanding the caregiving and attachment narratives of parents of autistic children. *Human Systems*, 26344041211000200. https://doi.org/10.1177/26344041211000202

Grey, B. and Farnfield, S. (2017). The Meaning of the Child Interview: A new procedure for assessing and understanding parent–child relationships of "at-risk" families. *Clinical Child Psychology and Psychiatry*, 22(2), 204–218. https://doi.org/10.1177/135910451 6633495

Grossmann, K. E., Bretherton, I., Waters, E., and Grossmann, K. (2013). Maternal sensitivity: Observational studies honoring Mary Ainsworth's 100th year. *Attachment & Human Development*, 15(5–6), 443–447. https://doi.org/10.1080/14616734.2013.841058

White, S., Wastall, D., Matthew, G., and Walsh, P. (2020). *Reassessing Attachment Theory in Child Welfare*. Policy Press; 1st edition.

Chapter 13

Safety in the home-school system with relation to autism

The SwiS* approach

Tara Vassallo, Rudi Dallos, and Rebecca Stancer

Autism and attachment in the school context

Reflecting the theme of this book, this chapter explores how an attachment perspective helps us think about 'safety', 'danger', and 'risk', not just in terms of the physical, but also emotional and relational dangers. The loss of affection, loneliness, and isolation are amongst the greatest dangers that we can experience. We will use the example of autism to discuss children's challenges and dilemmas in the context of feelings of safety, particularly in terms of managing transitions between home and school. We will illustrate these issues with reference to an approach we have developed: SAFE with Schools (SwiS), an attachment-narrative-based systemic family therapy programme for parents and teachers of autistic children.

All children want and need to feel safe and secure. Feeling secure is the foundation for exploration, to go out into the world and gain the necessary experience that shapes our development (Ainsworth, 1973). Leaving the security of home, for example, to access school, occurs frequently for most young children, and can represent a significant attachment situation for them (Barrett, Dadds, and Rapee, 1996). Most children navigate this well and can confidently make the transition smoothly. However, for autistic children, such transitions are often challenging, and difficulties associated with these, enduring (Vassallo, Dallos, and Mckenzie, 2020).

Autistic children can find school 'anxiety provoking' for a variety of reasons. The unpredictability of the school day, a lack of understanding of the autistic perspective, social demands, and sensorial overload, can combine to make navigating the school environment extremely challenging. Therefore, having an attachment figure available in school offering a continued attachment response, is necessary for children to feel reassured. However, contrasting attachment responses from parents and caregivers at school, who each have their own attachment needs (*and do not simply provide a secure context for the child to develop*), can be confusing and contribute to children feeling unsafe and becoming anxious (Dallos, 2014). This can escalate aspects of autistic experience to become challenging, in turn leading to

---

* SwiS (SAFE with Schools) is an attachment-narrative based systemic family therapy programme of support for parents and teachers of autistic children.

DOI: 10.4324/9781003308096-17

a 'totalising' discourse from caregivers, that frames the child's difficulties as being predominantly 'caused' by their autism and therefore 'their problem'. By siting the difficulty 'within the child' it places the responsibility for problems too much on their shoulders and can lead to increased risks for such children. Even to the extent that when they experience dangerous events such as 'bullying', this can often be 'dismissed' or 'diluted' by others as not 'really' bullying. Rather, that because they are autistic, any social relationship difficulties must be 'their misunderstanding' of social interaction since 'they' do not understand teasing, joking, or 'banter' from other children (Buglass et al., 2021; Canavan, 2015).

Attachment figures: home and school

Apart from time with parents, school is the second largest amount of time children spend with influential, significant adults. In some cases, with the demands of work on parents, who may be overwhelmed, stressed, and tired, the actual contact and attention given to children may on occasion be greater from caregivers in school, than they are able to receive from their parents. Given 'time spent caregiving' is influential in the development of a child's attachment hierarchy (Cassidy, 2016, p. 15), should we therefore consider teachers and other school staff as temporary or 'ad-hoc' attachment figures? How are the bonds they form with children similar or different to those children form with their parents, and importantly how do teachers and parents work together to meet the child's needs?

As Verschueren and Koomen (2012) identify, despite the school context being unconducive to maintaining an 'enduring tie' between child and teacher (*as teachers change relatively frequently*), the 'different' emotional investment in children between teachers and parents, and the lack of exclusivity of the child-teacher relationship (*sharing the teacher with many other students*), there are certain factors that might precipitate 'ad-hoc' attachment relations, specifically the vulnerability of the child. The levels of anxiety experienced by autistic children, makes for a more frequently activated attachment system, in terms of seeking comfort and support with emotional regulation (McKenzie and Dallos, 2017). Similarly to parents, emotionally responsive teachers create a 'safe-haven' in the classroom, and an ongoing 'secure-base' from which children can explore the social world of school, together with the provision of emotional comfort, particularly in new or difficult situations. This suggests the potential for an attachment component to the child-teacher relationship (Morris-Rothschild and Brassard, 2006).

School and home of course present some similar but also different priorities in the lives of children, beyond children's educational needs. Schools also serve to socialise children into the moral values, norms, and expectations of a given culture (Puspitasari et al., 2021). Some rules are taught 'explicitly', such as conduct in the classroom or playground. However, some important rules are 'implicit', for example how we show our emotions, express our need for comfort, and seek safety. These are imparted not just by teachers, but by other children, that is, whether some forms of comfort-seeking are seen as overly needy, selfish, attention seeking, hurtful of others and so on (Puspitasari et al., 2021). Differences between autistic and non-autistic communication, including emotional responding, can create misunderstanding and conflict, making it difficult for schools to offer a 'place of safety' for autistic children, free from bullying and discrimination. For many schools in the UK, national policies for inclusion, pose considerable challenges in terms of meeting that agenda, as policies are not matched with funding and resource, particularly specialist staff training, as well as educational and environmental adaptions (Glazzard, 2011). Therefore, the experience for some autistic children and their families may be that they do not receive adequate protection and care at school and therefore do not experience school as a 'safe place' (McKinlay et al., 2022).

How teachers respond to children is influenced by their own preferred self-protective attachment strategies. Interestingly, as discussed later in the chapter, studies have found high incidence of avoidant patterns of attachment in teachers (Acer and Akgun, 2010; Kepalaitė, 2012; Morris-Rothschild and Brassard, 2006). This could mean, that a teacher with a more avoidant attachment style may feel more emotionally compatible with a child who is quiet, withdrawn, or shows less emotion. Unfortunately, the emotional needs of these children can also be overlooked, as those who do not make a fuss, are at risk of becoming 'invisible'. In contrast, children who are more activated, exuberant, or emotionally volatile, are more likely to be noticed, but also become seen as 'problematic' by teachers who do not share their anxious-ambivalent orientation. However, both sorts of children can be seen as 'seeking safety and protection', but in different ways.

First days at school

What are your memories of your first day at school or nursery? Can you remember what happened? How did you feel?

I remember my first day at nursery school aged about four. A female approached us, and I think could see that I was frightened and tried to reassure me. I remember a mixture of concern from my mother but also a sense of foreboding about the situation, as if she may have had anxieties about taking me, wondering how I would cope, since it was not long since she had separated from my father and perhaps realised that I may still have been anxious about separations. However, she did not really have an alternative since she needed to work to support us. This dilemma is of course common for parents, and young children who are not yet at a developmental stage to be able to understand this, may feel upset and abandoned. As she left, I started to cry, and I think I was fairly inconsolable. The memory is vague, but the embodied feeling of that experience is still available to me. I am pretty sure that she had to return sometime later and take me home, and going forward, I think my attendance at nursery was patchy as my grandmother stepped in to look after me.

Attachment relations – parent-teacher-child

This little scenario highlights a triadic process between parent, teacher, and child. How did they communicate and co-ordinate how my feelings were managed? Was there a shared perception of the best way to manage my feelings? How was this communicated? In some cases, where a child may protest at being left and become distressed, teachers may feel parents are being too indulgent with the child, or alternatively parents may feel that teachers are too unsympathetic or critical of them. A dynamic can rapidly start to be constructed in this period, which for many children can appear frightening and highly distressing, particularly if attitudes from each caregiver toward the other, are negative.

Attachment can be understood as consisting of two inter-dependent processes: exploration and comfort-seeking. The top part of the diagram (Figure 13.1) represents the attachment figures providing a 'secure-base' from where a child can feel confident enough to be able to explore the world, learn and take risks. It includes a sense of knowing that the caregiver is there, available, keeping an eye on them, and recognising their efforts and achievements.

Parents need to prepare children for separation in terms of anticipating how they will feel, challenges they might encounter, such as navigating school, coping strategies they will use, including who they will turn to for support if needed. The bottom part of the diagram represents the return to the 'safe-haven', coming back for care and comfort after adventures and perhaps experiences of anxieties and mishaps. An important aspect of the 'safe-haven' is that attachment figures help the child organise and make sense of their experiences by assisting the child to identify and name their own feelings, think about the intentions and feelings of others, and what they have learnt from the event. They also need help to develop plans and strategies for dealing with similar events in the future.

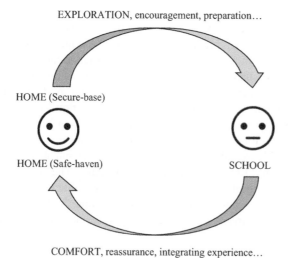

Figure 13.1 Exploration, comfort, and separation for school.
Source: Personal collection.

Moving between home and school is challenging for all children, since there are differences in rules about what is acceptable and not acceptable at school, compared to what they are familiar with at home. There are also different expectations of what they are required to do. In addition, they now must learn to relate to a wider group of children, as opposed to just siblings or even perhaps no others at home. The stresses of these demands can become particularly apparent at 'points of transition' between the home and school systems, such as going to school in the morning and returning home in the afternoon.

Families frequently describe their children as reluctant to get ready for school in the mornings, finding ways to delay getting out of bed or getting dressed, resist eating their breakfast and avoid getting their school materials ready. These can be indicators of the anxiety and apprehension children feel about going to school and likewise, returning home, what they are bringing back from school to home, in terms of stress from the day or explanations of difficulties experienced at school (Figure 13.2). The home and school systems not only have different rules regarding behaviours but also about how attachment needs are expressed and met. A teacher may oversee 30 or more children, hence there is much more competition for their attention and care. A child must learn that they cannot rely on the teacher in the same way as they can their parents if they feel upset, anxious, hurt, or are feeling ill. This will impact children according to their dominant attachment styles. For example, children with secure experiences may be more able to tolerate unavailability, confident that their needs will eventually be met at home. Whereas children

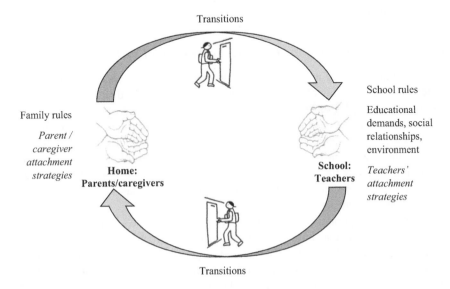

Figure 13.2 Home–school systems.

Source: Personal collection.

who have learnt avoidant 'de-activating' attachment strategies may 'appear' to be able to cope with teachers being less available, but are possibly at risk of becoming withdrawn (Kennedy and Kennedy, 2004). However, children with anxious-ambivalent 'hyper-activating' strategies may find the delay in responding to their needs difficult to manage. A danger for them can be they may come to be regarded as demanding and disruptive, becoming emotionally dysregulated as they oscillate between comfort-seeking and withdrawing. Consequently, ambivalent responses from the teacher may escalate their responses, potentially leading to meltdown (Kulig and Saj, 2021).

Teaching staff also have their own preferred attachment orientations. It is naïve to assume that all or most teachers employ secure strategies. Several studies indicate that teachers vary considerably in their attachment styles and in some cases the levels of insecurity displayed can be surprisingly high. A study of trainee teachers found that only 11 of 91 showed clearly secure strategies (Acer and Akgun, 2010). In a subsequent study, Kepalaitė (2012) likewise indicated that in a sample of 145 teachers, only 13 indicated secure attachment styles. In both studies teachers demonstrated a greater likelihood of employing dismissing attachment strategies. Furthermore, research studies indicate that teachers' strategies influence how they interact with their pupils, particularly in relation to how they manage conflicts. Morris-Rothschild and Brassard (2006) found that teachers who used anxious or avoidant attachment styles were less able to develop mutually satisfactory forms of compromises with children and more likely to attempt to withdraw from the situation or attempt to overly exert control. These studies point to the importance of considering teachers' own attachment strategies in shaping how they respond to children in their classroom.

Attachment dilemmas in the child-home-school system

Children must manage an enormously complex set of variables both in terms of differentiating the rules of home and school, but also likely differences between the attachment styles of their parents and teachers. This may become even more confusing for children as they may be influenced by an 'implicit' assumption that teachers are secure stable attachment figures, therefore internalise difficulties that arise in the classroom as predominantly caused by themselves, rather than also being influenced by their teacher and their reciprocal relationship. A further layer of complexity is that their teacher and the child's parent may also differ in their preferred attachment styles (Figure 13.3).

A child may experience a dilemma in trying to resolve the competing messages regarding attachment seeking that their teacher and parent provide. For example, a young mother (Val) was anxious that her 5-year-old son (Jake) was shy, anxious and would not be able to cope well with school. Her own attachment history had featured a difficult relationship with her son's father and Val also felt anxious about her competence as a mother. Jake at home was still occasionally wetting

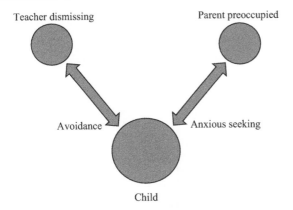

Figure 13.3 An approach-avoidance attachment dilemma for child, between parent and teacher.

Source: Personal collection.

himself and Val let him continue to wear pull-ups. She asked the school if they could accommodate this, but felt their reaction was to treat her as an over-anxious mother, and instead, in her view, took a 'tougher' stance with Jake that she did not, so he had 'no choice' but to control himself. He did initially manage to do this, but the trade-off was increased anxiety and 'withdrawal' for Jake. Val described her son as very anxious when he came home, worried whether he could manage to stay dry in school and avoid the humiliation of a toilet accident. Though understandable, the teacher's apparently more 'dismissing' orientation to Val's preoccupied style was not only posing difficulties emotionally for Jake, that is, he became very quiet and withdrawn at school, but also increasingly made Val feel that she was being viewed by the school as neurotic and difficult. A conflict between school and home appeared to be developing and Jake was becoming increasingly more aware of this, which in turn was contributing to an increased sense of unsafeness for him, leading to a resistance to leave his mother and refusing to go to school.

Development of SwiS – building parent-teacher relationships

We have developed the SwiS approach which aims to help construct a sense of safety not only for the children, but also for parents and teachers. We initially found that for families and school staff there could be difficulties in understanding each other's needs and situations, which frequently led to criticism of each other's responses (Vassallo, Dallos, and Mckenzie, 2020). For example, teachers expressed concern and even disapproval around the quality of parenting, if children were not as they saw it 'school ready'. Likewise, parents felt teachers' lack of understanding

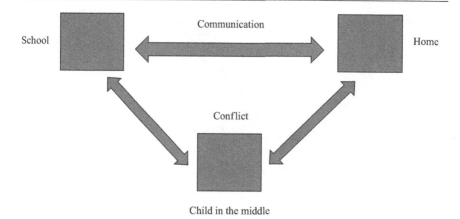

Figure 13.4 Triadic process – Facilitating communication in the school-home-child triangle.

Source: Personal collection.

of their child's autistic perspective and how they should be supported, exacerbated the challenges around autism, which had a cascading impact on not only the child, but the whole family, adding to difficulties at home. Interaction between parents and teachers was often 'crisis-activated', that is, requiring 'urgent' after-school or extra-ordinary 'meetings' only when something had gone wrong (Figure 13.4), making them inherently negative and reactive, rather than proactive, preventative, and rooted in a shared understanding of the child.

Summary of SwiS

Teaching staff (teachers and/or teaching-assistants) and parents as caregivers to the autistic child, meet in a group (up to six parent-teacher units) and work together across two all-day sessions. These two days are deliberately structured to support relationships, promote effective communication, share knowledge and experience of autism, develop understanding of systemic practice and attachment theory, and enable both types of caregivers to unpack difficulties they face, by engaging in specific, shared, problem-solving activities.

Attachment theory

Attachment theory is used to explore negative feelings of failure and blame that have typically become a part of the parental experience raising an autistic child. For example, parents often report 'feelings of blame', where 'insecure attachments' are frequently cited during interactions with professionals, as contributing to difficulties or even 'causing' autism. These unhelpful assumptions have led many parents to avoid discussions of attachment altogether. SwiS offers a safer representation of attachment theory using the Circle of Security's (CoS) visual depiction of attachment (Marvin et al., 2002). Autistic children often experience high levels of anxiety, therefore the return/reunion aspect of CoS, where the caregiver offers comfort and support to help organise the child's feelings, is particularly important (Adams, Young, and Keen, 2019). The CoS is discussed in terms of the challenges of home-school separations, extended to include the demands and supports from the school context and the caregiving teacher (Figure 13.5). As the child leaves the safety and security of their home 'secure-base', the teacher then receives them into their care and acts as a form of attachment figure, offering a temporary 'safe-haven' throughout the day until the child returns home again, back to their secure-base.

Parents and teachers are encouraged to be 'aware' of what happens to the child within the circle, that is, if the child experiences something challenging in school, it is important that information is shared with parents, similarly with teachers, if something happens at home, as the effects of distress in one context are likely to transfer across contexts, impacting the other. Therefore, to properly support the child, transparent parent-teacher communication and understanding about the child is paramount. Personal reflections are encouraged to be reflexive regarding parents' and teachers' own attachment needs, including their needs for love and approval from the children they share care of.

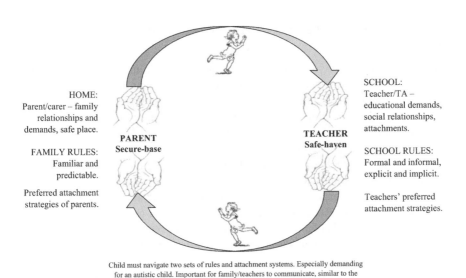

Child must navigate two sets of rules and attachment systems. Especially demanding for an autistic child. Important for family/teachers to communicate, similar to the need for parents and grandparents to be consistent and in agreement with one another.

Figure 13.5 The extended secure circle includes both the parent and the teacher/ home and school.

Source: Personal collection.

SwiS Day-1

This starts with sharing some personal details and experiences of their children, including their child's interests, and what a typical day might look like in school and at home. Parents and teachers often only have scant knowledge of each other's contexts and experiences. What they do know of each other might be gleaned from meeting one another during drop-off or pick-up, from brief parent-teacher meetings, or from disclosures from children about school at home, or vice versa.

SHARING UNDERSTANDINGS OF AUTISM

Teachers and parents frequently differ in their understanding of theories and approaches to assist autistic children. Often parents have developed sophisticated and extensive knowledge through their own efforts to support their child. Parents and teachers have the opportunity to empathise with their child's perspective, for example exploring patterns and cycles of difficulty, how particular stressors, such as mismatched communication, might ignite conflict with other children and staff, or how the busy class environment might exacerbate struggles with sensorial overload, interrupting schoolwork, and increasing anxiety, which might then be released at home without warning, disrupting the peace and safety of their usual secure-base.

TRACKING: A SYSTEMIC–RELATIONAL PERSPECTIVE: POSITIVE AND PROBLEMATIC CYCLES

Parents and teachers are encouraged to reflect on difficult interactions they sometimes find themselves unhelpfully drawn into. A non-blaming stance is encouraged, by building on their existing expertise. Parents and teachers are invited to start by analysing a video depicting a common problematic home-school cycle for an autistic child; a father struggling to persuade his son to attend class. They are encouraged to engage in a collaborative problem-solving activity together, supported by use of a systemic/attachment mapping diagram, exploring the relational processes and attachment dynamics at play in the situation. They are asked to focus on specific instances of interactions with the child at school and at home and map these in terms of sequences of actions between the child and caregiver. By outlining the idea of 'attempted solutions', parents and teachers can consider how positive intentions driving our attempts to resolve difficulties, may unintentionally inflame situations (Figure 13.6).

Often 'time out' is used for autistic children, not as punishment, but a de-escalation strategy, that time away from the situation will give the child a low arousal 'space' where they can regulate their emotions. This technique is often used so that children who are highly anxious and either 'melting-down', or at risk of doing so, can go somewhere and be free from extraneous sensorial input,

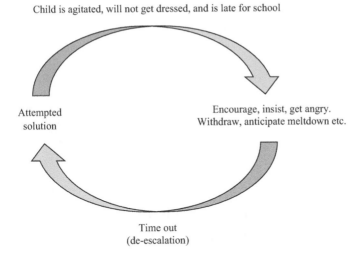

Child is agitated, will not get dressed, and is late for school

Attempted
solution

Encourage, insist, get angry.
Withdraw, anticipate meltdown etc.

Time out
(de-escalation)

Figure 13.6 Attempted solutions and escalation of problems.

Source: Personal collection.

that might otherwise add to or maintain their distress, preventing them from calming down. However, this potentially misses a connection opportunity, and consequentially may leave a child feeling rejected and isolated, with no-one available to help them organise their feelings, negating their attachment needs 'in the moment'.

Teachers and parents also share examples of 'exceptions' when they have resolved such situations, having recognised signs of escalation and used positive strategies to support their child. They also explore how a lack of shared detailed information between them might inadvertently contribute to any escalation, reinforcing cycles of difficulty.

Tracking initially focuses parents and teachers on *positive* interactions which are mapped as a circular pattern. This enables caregivers to 'slow down' so they might reflect in detail on what 'exactly' happened, and what both they and the child might be feeling at each point. Within everyday interactions, we rarely have the opportunity for such reflection, and can find ourselves 'repeating' and getting 'stuck' in familiar, but negative patterns. By starting with a positive episode, parents and teachers are not only encouraged to acknowledge their ability to alter interactions with their child and change the outcome, but also review what they are already doing well and be confident in that. This can help them contemplate ways to manage more challenging interactions, rather than attributing problems to 'autism' and therefore beyond their influence. Figure 13.7 is an example of a familiar situation for parents, teachers, and children, that of being late for school due to ongoing child anxiety and eventual school refusal.

Child gets up asks mum "*is it school today?*" Mum says "*yes*" – child runs and hides in room

Child distressed all day – vows not to go to school tomorrow

Mum gently helps child dress. Now late, mum rushes to make breakfast - child gets undressed

Teacher is annoyed punishes child for being late and having wrong shoes - loses their playtime

Dad reassures child. Helps them dress, brush teeth, & get down for breakfast

Receptionist takes child to class but leaves without explaining shoes or lateness to the teacher

Tracking a circularity

…Late for school

Child in distress, protesting they want to stay home, but complies & eats breakfast

Get to school late. Teacher is busy. Mum quickly explains lateness & shoes to receptionist

Mum clears breakfast & asks child to put on shoes – child complies but can't find them

Parents still cross but reassure child it will be okay – they will speak to the teacher

Child gets upset, says no as they will be in trouble with teacher & lose play time

Now late for school, dad is cross, shouts child must wear their trainers

Child crying, parents get frustrated & also look for shoes but can't find them either

Figure 13.7 Tracking – Slowing things down; exploring positive and negative cycles.

Source: Personal collection.

The child, who was feeling unsafe about school, retreated to the safety of their bedroom. Parents were experiencing the challenge of seeing their child distressed and the impact on their day from school refusal, and the teacher, frustration at having their class disrupted by lateness and uniform transgressions. Without the benefit of shared information between parent and teacher, the earlier positioning of 'poor parenting' and 'lack of teacher understanding' might persist between caregivers. However, by breaking down what happened, both caregivers could 'slow down' and share all the information, identifying critical moments where the trajectory of the situation could be changed along with the outcome. From this, they worked on a solution of communication together to avoid similar difficulties in the future. Parent-teacher units were able to do this for situations at home, at school, and for those that crossed the two contexts.

SwiS Day-2

Day-2 builds on the activities of Day-1, especially sharing the use of tracking. The focus of the second day is to soften some of the 'problem-saturated' and rigidly medical discourses that surround experiences of autism. As a result of frustration, sense of blame and failure, parents and teachers can retreat into negative views of autism, especially in terms of their abilities to communicate and connect with children.

THE CHILDREN'S WORLDS: NARRATIVES OF AUTISM, SAM-SELF AUTISM MAPPING

Many difficulties, including autism, can become 'totalising' (Anderson, 2016; McKenzie and Dallos, 2016; White and Epston, 1990) in that a narrow understanding of the label can serve to limit the child's identity and potential growth. More broadly, diagnostic labels can hold multiple and sometimes conflicting meanings between parents and teachers. SAM supports parents and teachers to talk openly about what autism means to them in the context of the child they care for, using a visual and playful activity (Figure 13.8). They are also invited to produce visual representations (externalisation) of the autistic perspective, that is, using playdough/ drawing, and use this to open conversations with the child at home or school, to enhance understanding of the child's perspective (Vassallo, 2023). For example, a common view of a child's diagnosis of autism, is that their 'brain is wired differently'. This may lead to a fixation on established difficulties, overlooking talent, ability, and feelings, becoming focused on negative characteristics or stereotypes, or at risk of making sweeping assumptions.

Parents and teachers are invited to discuss how they see autism using the visual depiction of SAM, but also to think about how their child would see themselves. Parents and teachers can reflect on the similarities and differences between their perceptions but are also encouraged to reflect about the child's perceptions. This is especially important, since there can be a drift towards regarding the children as 'hard to understand because of autism', abandoning attempts to mentalise about them (Slade, 2009).

SAM can help ease into conversations, allowing parents and teachers the space to consider aspects of autism that are less problematic or even helpful, enabling them to explore the uniqueness of their child and the positives that often accompany autism. SAM allows some 'loosening of thinking' particularly about negative aspects of autism, for example, when given the space to reflect on individual characteristics, some children have observed that autism enables their talents, such has having great 'attention to detail', noticing what others miss. It might also account for their 'excellent memory', being able to recall important and interesting facts, making them experts in areas of 'particular interest' and so on. These conversations reframe ideas of autism slightly, opening everyone up to the advantages of autism, rather than remaining 'stuck' with negative thinking. It also enables identification

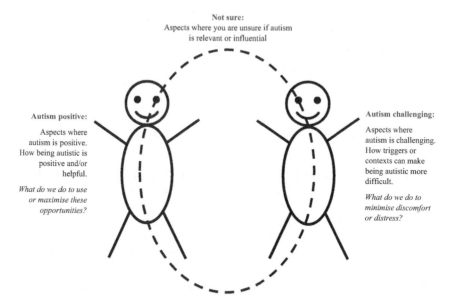

Figure 13.8 Self autism mapping – SAM.

Source: Personal collection.

of external influences, where challenges are more often socially constructed, rather than because the child is autistic. A common outcome from SAM undertaken with children is the identification of specific difficulties such as social anxiety and struggles developing friendships. These can be discussed as both general fears that children experience, as well as aspects that are more specific to autism.

Discussion

We have suggested that one approach to helping children with a diagnosis of autism, their families, and their teachers, is to facilitate communication between all of them. For Bowlby (1982), open communication was synonymous with secure attachment. However, as we suggest in this chapter, 'increased communication' is not necessarily enough for parents and teachers to produce the relationship and connection needed, to facilitate effective joint problem-solving around the child they care for. What may be necessary is that parents and teachers have available a continuing format, utilising concepts and techniques from systemic and narrative therapies and attachment theory. We have found that offering such a format can alter dynamics between parents and teachers, from a sense of helplessness, failure, and mutual blame, to one of mutual co-operation and constructive problem-solving. In our experience, some of the negative cycles of mutual-blaming, mistrust, and miscommunication between teachers and parents, may be exacerbated by a sense of hopelessness and helplessness on both their parts about what they can do to resolve problems involving their children. Having a format to assist their mutual problem-solving can help change cycles between them, from negative to positive ones.

It must be acknowledged there are operational considerations to implementing programmes such as SwiS. When approaching schools, we have found teachers interested in the programme, often cite lack of resources, time to engage in training, and a general sense of being overwhelmed and exhausted by the demands of their job, as barriers. It is important to recognise these organisational pressures and be aware that suggesting an approach such as SwiS, without commitment from the school management to support it, can feel like yet another pressure on teachers. Additionally, teachers raised concerns that despite SwiS techniques being helpful with certain children, they felt anxious about embracing them, concerned that resolving 'some' problems, might, during this time of economic pressure, be over-generalised by school management, that they were 'coping well enough' and result in the rejection of much needed extra resource, applied for to support other children in their class. Such Catch-22 dilemmas were frequently apparent in our contact with teachers. They are significant barriers to positive change in schools and are centrally connected to issues of safety for all concerned: children, teachers, and parents.

The danger, as widely documented, is that the home-school system can become increasingly risk-averse and crisis-activated. By waiting until problems such as school anxieties, relationship breakdowns at school, and related problems at home escalate, means problems can become fixed and solutions harder to find. Co-operation, communication and early problem-solving through systemic action, is pragmatically better for all, but also morally necessary, especially to offer vulnerable children a better experience of the home-school context.

We are in the process of generating research on the effectiveness and applicability of SwiS, with our intention to make it widely available to parents and teachers. Please contact us for further information.

References

Acer, D. and Akgun, E. (2010). Determining attachment styles of the pre-school teacher candidates. *Procedia-social and Behavioral Sciences*, 2(2), 1426–1431.

Adams, D., Young, K., and Keen, D. (2019). Anxiety in children with autism at school: A systematic review. *Review Journal of Autism and Developmental Disorders*, 6(3), 274–288.

Ainsworth, M. (1973). The development of infant-mother attachment. In B. Caldwell and H. Ricciuti (Eds.), *Review of Child Development Research* (Vol. 3, pp. 1–94). University of Chicago Press.

Anderson, H. (2016). Postmodern/poststructural/social construction therapies: Collaborative, narrative, and solution-focused. In T. Sexton and J. Lebow (Eds.), *Handbook of Family Therapy* (First ed., pp. 182–204). Routledge.

Barrett, P. M., Dadds, M. R., and Rapee, R. M. (1996). Family treatment of childhood anxiety: A controlled trial. *Journal of Consulting and Clinical Psychology*, *64*(2), 333–342.

Bowlby, J. (1982). *Attachment and Loss: Vol. 1. Attachment*. London: Hogarth Press.

Buglass, S. L., Abell, L., Betts, L. R., Hill, R., and Saunders, J. (2021). Banter versus bullying: A university student perspective. *International Journal of Bullying Prevention*, *3*(4), 287–299.

Canavan, C. (2015). *Supporting Pupils on the Autism Spectrum in Primary Schools*. Routledge.

Cassidy, J. (2016). The Nature of the Child's Ties. In J. Cassidy and P. R. Shaver (Eds.), *Handbook of Attachment: Theory, Research, and Clinical Applications* (Third ed.). Guildford Press.

Dallos, R. (2014). Assessing attachment in families: Beyond the dyads. In S. Farnfield and P. Holmes (Eds.), *The Routledge Handbook of Attachment: Assessment* (pp. 192–209). Routledge.

Glazzard, J. (2011). Perceptions of the barriers to effective inclusion in one primary school: Voices of teachers and teaching assistants. *Support for Learning*, *26*(2), 56–63.

Kennedy, J. H. and Kennedy, C. E. (2004). Attachment theory: Implications for school psychology. *Psychology in the Schools*, *41*(2), 247–259.

Kepalaitė, A. (2012). Links between teachers' attachment style and social interest. *Social Welfare: Interdisciplinary Approach*, *2*, 38–47.

Kulig, B. and Saj, T. (2021). Trauma-informed alternative care: How to care for a child affected by trauma. *Trauma-informed Caregivers – Investment to Better Child Development* (pp. 1–34). Nordic Council of Ministers, Poland, https://wioskisos.org/wp-content/uploads/2021/12/trauma-informed-alternative-care-final-eng.pdf

Marvin, R., Cooper, G., Hoffman, K., and Powell, B. (2002). The Circle of Security project: Attachment-based intervention with caregiver-pre-school child dyads. *Attachment & Human Development*, *4*(1), 107–124.

McKenzie, R. and Dallos, R. (2016). 'I just like Lego!' Self-Autism Mapping as a non-totalizing approach. *Context*, *144*, 21–23.

McKenzie, R. and Dallos, R. (2017). Autism and attachment difficulties: Overlap of symptoms, implications and innovative solutions. *Clinical Child Psychology and Psychiatry*, *22*(4), 632–648.

McKinlay, J., Wilson, C., Hendry, G., and Ballantyne, C. (2022). 'It feels like sending your children into the lions' den' – A qualitative investigation into parental attitudes towards ASD inclusion, and the impact of mainstream education on their child. *Research in Developmental Disabilities*, *120*, 104128. https://doi.org/https://doi.org/10.1016/j.ridd.2021.104128

Morris-Rothschild, B. K. and Brassard, M. R. (2006). Teachers' conflict management styles: The role of attachment styles and classroom management efficacy. *Journal of School Psychology*, *44*(2), 105–121.

Puspitasari, D., Widodo, H. P., Widyaningrum, L., Allamnakhrah, A., and Lestariyana, R. P. D. (2021). How do primary school English textbooks teach moral values? A critical discourse analysis. *Studies in Educational Evaluation*, *70*, 101044.

Slade, A. (2009). Mentalizing the Unmentalizable: Parenting Children on the Spectrum. *Journal of Infant, Child, and Adolescent Psychotherapy*, *8*(1), 7–21. https://doi.org/10.1080/15289160802683054

Vassallo, T. (2023). Fostering home–school relationships: SAFE with Schools (SwiS). In R. Dallos (Ed.), *Attachment Narrative Therapy: Applications and Developments* (First ed., pp. 195–228). Palgrave/Macmillan. https://doi.org/https://doi.org/10.1007/978-3-031-12745-8

Vassallo, T., Dallos, R., and Mckenzie, R. (2020). Parent and teacher understandings of the needs of autistic children and the processes of communication between the home and school contexts. *Autism – Open Access*, *10*(4). https://doi.org/doi.org/10.35248/2165-7890.20.10.262

Verschueren, K. and Koomen, H. M. (2012). Teacher–child relationships from an attachment perspective. *Attachment & Human Development*, *14*(3), 205–211.

White, M. and Epston, D. (1990). *Narrative Means to Therapeutic Ends*. WW Norton & Company.

Chapter 14

"and nothing but the Truth"

Chip Chimera

Introduction

This chapter is written from the perspective of 25 years of experience in working with the Courts in England as an expert witness in family proceedings. As a systemic psychotherapist my expertise is in understanding family dynamics, deconstructing the meanings of those dynamics and belief systems in the family, assessing the potential outcome of intervention, and the impact on the child of either intervening or not intervening.

Increasingly the nature of the work in the UK family courts has been with families where there has been prolonged conflict between the parents in relation to contact with the children. This pattern of increased litigation has also occurred in much of Europe and the rest of the world. Either an allegation of parental alienation has been made or the court has determined that parental alienation is present. Systemic therapists are often asked to provide therapy for such families in the hope of changing family dynamics. This chapter is written from the perspective of working with the children caught up in such allegations. It is my intention to also write in due course from the perspectives of each of the parents and the practitioners trying to help. However, in this chapter the focus is on how safety and protection, comfort, and reassurance, or rather the lack of it, can be understood from the position of the child, and the impact of the wider context on them. Of course, in focussing on the child, inevitably other perspectives will need to be considered, or at least named. In this chapter, reference to the "child" includes all the children in the family, recognising that there is often more than one and they will have different attachment experiences in the same family.

The motivation for this chapter in this book emanates from the practice experience of trying to help highly disturbed, unhappy, and struggling children who have rejected a parent for reasons which do not stand up to scrutiny and do not make sense. The context of rejection is the insecure attachment to the other parent and the threat of loss or damage to the safety, protection comfort, and reassurance on which they believe they must rely. They believe this requires the exclusion of a once-loved parent, no matter how strong the previous relationship, or how much they felt love from and to that other parent.

DOI: 10.4324/9781003308096-18

Parental alienation

For clarity, this concept does not include any situation in which a parent has behaved in ways which warrant the child's avoidance and rejection: this is "justified estrangement". Where children have been hurt and parents have been emotionally, physically or sexually abusive, children need a very different kind of therapeutic input. Such parents need to be appropriately dealt with by the law and offered individual therapeutic help before they can safely be with their children.

Definitions of parental alienation have proven difficult. In the context of this chapter, alienation is defined as the active turning of a child or children by one parent against the other parent. This involves the conscious or unconscious disregard for the needs of the child in relation to the rejected parent: the failure to see the child as a separate person in their own right with needs different to those of the parent influencing them.

Alienation does not, contrary to some reports, have a gender bias: men and women are equally capable of using the children against the other parent. However, in our culture and in the context of divorce and separation, it is more usual for the children to be resident with their mother. Often the resident parent, for reasons I will explore below, has the most influence on the children. However this is not always the case and there have been many instances of the non-resident parent turning the children against the parent they live with on a day-to-day basis.

There has been much debate about the concept since it was first defined by Richard Gardner in the 1980s (Gardner, 1998). He put the name "parental alienation syndrome" to this pattern of interaction in high conflict post separation disputes between parents over contact with the children. The pattern has been seen over generations and is not a new phenomenon. Literature has many stories of children being used as weapons by their parents, from Philip Pullman's Lyra to Euripedes' story of Medea who murders her two sons in an act of revenge against Jason, their father. Other images of children being influenced against a parent abound in fiction and popular cultural stories: the films *Hook*, and *Mrs Doubtfire* being some relatively recent examples. These and other mass media examples often make useful resources for interventions with families. They show how unscrupulous adults, Captain Hook in the case of "Hook", attempt to turn children against otherwise loving parents. Mrs Doubtfire shows the somewhat fanciful lengths to which a father might go to be near his children.

In relation to court proceedings, Cafcass (Children and Family Court Advisory and Support Service) have defined parental alienation as "the unjustified resistance or hostility from a child towards one parent as a result of psychological manipulation by the other parent" (Cafcass, 2021). Cafcass is the agency which represents children in family court cases in England. They independently advise the family courts about what is safe for children and in their best interests.

Other descriptions have been tried. "Resist/refuse dynamics" has been used to describe the behaviour of the children. This places responsibility with the child, not the parent whose actions maintain the dynamic. "Implacable hostility to contact" has also been used, especially during a time when there was considerable opposition to the term "alienation". It begs the question of whose implacable hostility and again the boundaries between adult responsibility and child behaviour can become blurred.

There is now a plentiful and growing body of research into the many aspects of alienation (see Sillars, 2022, for a comprehensive list of literature including many peer-reviewed journal articles), yet there is a vocal minority of people who insist that it does not exist or that it is a false concept with no scientific base made up by men (fathers) to control women (mothers) (Birchall, 2021; Barnett, Riley, and Katherine, 2021). That faction continues to deny the scientific findings.

The Diagnostic and Statistical Manual of Mental Disorders, Fifth Edition (DSM-5), whilst not having a specific category of alienation, has three categories which may appropriately be used:

1 Child affected by parental relationship distress (DSM-V CAPRD). (CAPRD is Child Affected by Parental Relationship Distress. V61 is the internal reference in the DSM.) "This category should be used when the focus of clinical attention is the negative effects of parental relationship discord (e.g., high levels of conflict, distress, or disparagement) on a child in the family, including effects on the child's mental or other medical disorders."

    • This is identified as a relationship problem. William Bernet and his colleagues have elaborated on the importance of this category in understanding alienation and highlighted four specific presentations (Bernet, Wamboldt, and Narrow,2016).

2 Parent-child relational problem (V61.20). Heyman et al. (2009) describe these as "clinically significant behavioural or psychological syndromes or patterns that occur between or among individuals and that are associated with present distress or disability or with a significant increased risk of suffering death, pain, disability, or an important loss of freedom" (p. 7).

3 Child psychological abuse (V995.51). Slep and her colleagues have written in Family Process about the complexities in this criterion (Slep, Heyman, and Foran, 2015).

To help these children good assessment is essential, using all the tools at the disposal of professionals, including formal attachment assessments, such as the Adult Attachment Interview (AAI) (Crittenden and Landini, 2011), or the Meaning of the Child Interview (MotC) (Grey and Farnfield, 2017).

Systemic, attachment, and trauma theory

Children caught up in the intense post separation conflicts between their parents are subjected to a myriad of confusing and disturbing communications from one parent, sometimes both parents, about the other. A multi-modal approach is necessary to understand the processes and forces that are at work, with no one modality holding all the answers. Systems theory, attachment, and the neurobiology of trauma all help to piece together the puzzle that is alienation. All families are unique and all have a different story to tell. However, there are distinct patterns, separate to the content embedded within them, which help practitioners.

Systems theory has several related constructs which help navigate the child's experience. In the systemic literature patterns where a child becomes aligned with one parent against another were identified early. Murray Bowen first described the concept of *triangulation* in relation to family functioning as a normative and stabilising pattern. He proposed that a two-person system was unstable and that a third person was required to achieve and maintain balance (Bowen 1978, 1983, 1985).

> It [the triangle] is considered the building block or "molecule" of larger emotional systems because a triangle is the smallest stable relationship system. A two-person system is unstable because it tolerates little tension before involving a third person. A triangle can contain much more tension without involving another person because the tension can shift around three relationships. If the tension is too high for one triangle to contain, it spreads to a series of "interlocking" triangles. Spreading the tension can stabilize a system, but nothing is resolved.
>
> (www.thebowencenter.org/)

Jay Haley, another early pioneer, and family therapy theorist, named the "perverse triangle" which would generate a "pathological" system, "one resulting in continual conflict" (Haley, 1981, p. 100). He further defined the characteristics of such a triangle as:

- One member of the triangle being from a different generation,
- This generating a power imbalance,
- Two members of the triangle forming a coalition against the other,
- The coalition is denied,
- The coalition persists over time and becomes rigid. (ibid.)

Minuchin described "rigid triangles" where

> each parent demands that the child side with them against the other parent. Whenever the child sides with one, he is automatically defined as attacking the other. ... the child is paralysed. Every movement he makes is defined by one parent as an attack. ... The rigid triad can also take the form of a stable coalition. One of the parents joins the child in a rigidly bounded cross-generational coalition against the other parent.
>
> (Minuchin, 1974, p. 102)

Byng-Hall brought attachment thinking into systems theory. His identification of intergenerational scripts adds a further systemic dimension to our understanding of these processes by showing how patterns and meanings are transmitted across generations. Additionally, his concept of the child as "distance regulator" elaborated the ideas of triangulation as a way of maintaining stability in the parental relationship, whether positive or negative, through the engagement of the child in conflict between the parents (Byng-Hall, 1995).

Dallos and Vetere have taken the notion of triangulation further in linking attachment theory and systemic thinking and connect it specifically to the dilemmas faced by children in divorce and separation of their parents (Dallos and Vetere, 2012).

As modern attachment theory has been integrated more fully into systemic thinking and practice, issues of safety, comfort, and protection have become of increasing interest to family therapists:

- How do families "do" safety?
- What happens when someone in the family needs comfort?
- How is protection addressed and who protects whom from what?

Theories which focus on the individual are not sufficient to understand what happens when children are used as weapons. John Bowlby identified the absolute importance of thinking relationally when trying to understand children's behaviour from the very beginnings of the exploration of attachment (Bowlby, 1979).

The double bind theory of Bateson and his colleagues (Bateson et al., 1972) provides a helpful bridge to shed light on communication which seems counter-intuitive and at times incomprehensible. The pattern, described below, incorporates the constructs previously described. Although there has been much criticism of double bind theory as a cause of mental disorder, it is immensely helpful in unravelling the patterns of communication (Gibney 2006). Whilst it was originally understood as communication between a dyad, here it is expanded to include the other parent (Figure 14.1).

First a word on terminology. The person who is starting the alienation process may be male or female. The couple may be married or in a civil partnership or unmarried. "AP" (alienating parent) is used here to distinguish between the person who is maintaining the hostility through the children and "TP" (targeted parent) the person who wants to maintain the relationship with their children. Some people use perpetrator and victim. Whatever terminology is used is problematic. This terminology is used with the intention of remaining gender neutral.

This diagram illustrates the communication which both triangulates the child into the conflict whilst purporting to focus on the child's needs, and installs the double bind process. It identifies stages in the process which are expanded below:

1   Alienating parent (AP) feels threatened. There may be many reasons for this. Assessment as to underlying causes is crucial in understanding this phenomenon. There may be many contributing factors, often going back to childhood.

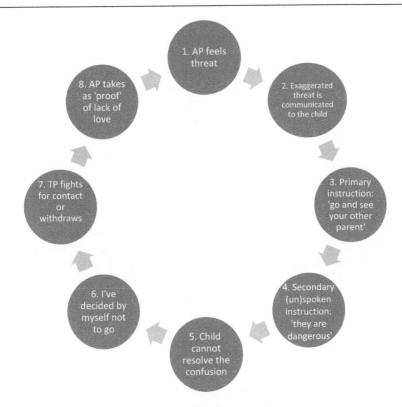

Figure 14.1 A triangular understanding of the double bind process.

Very often the feeling of threat has been evident during the relationship between the parents predating separation, sometimes for many years.

2 The threat is exaggerated and communicated to the child. The threat may be communicated in overt or covert ways. Sometimes the AP will say frightening things directly to the child, for example the other parent "may run away with you and I will never see you again." It is also possible that children will be aware of what has been said to other adults. For instance, schools may be told that the other parent is violent, when this has not been previously alleged and was not a reason for the separation. Children may also overhear conversations between other family members criticising the TP. These first two stages are contextual factors which need in depth assessment. Extended family, social networks, GP's and schools are all essential in a thorough assessment.

3 The primary instruction. This is the first layer of the double bind. "Go and see your other parent". It is almost always qualified in some way. The AP may say that the court is instructing it. They may say it is their own wish. One family where the AP had grown up in care said overtly to the children how much they

wished the children to have a relationship with both parents as that had been denied to them when they were little. This is an example of how transgenerational scripts (Byng-Hall, ibid.) may have a strong role in assessment and understanding the alienation process. Here the AP seemed to have a corrective script, i.e. they wanted their children to have a different experience than they had and could see that their experience had not been helpful. However as assessment progressed it became clear that other processes were preventing the corrective experience and a replicative script was in process.

4 Secondary instruction: "they are dangerous". The next layer of the double bind is the secondary instruction. It carries the information that the other parent is dangerous, either to the AP, or to the child themselves. Here is where attachment theory meets systems theory. The implied danger can come in many forms. It is striking how often the child has some form of vulnerability either physical or psychological. There are often co-morbid psychiatric diagnoses such as ASD or ADHD, or the child is developing symptoms. Sometimes there is a vulnerability in the AP, either through illness or disability. At this level coalitions become a focus of attention. The child may also have a parental role in caring for the parent in an inverted hierarchy, where the child has taken on a protective role for that parent or is in some ways responsible for their wellbeing. Family roles may have changed when the relationship between the parents failed. AP and child demonstrate enmeshment (Minuchin, 1974) where it is not possible to separate out distinct needs.

5 The child's inability to resolve the confusion or ask for clarification. At this stage the developmentally immature child cannot resolve the confusion and cannot ask for clarification. They are left to figure things out for themselves. However the context for their decision making is that it happens within an important relationship in which the child is dependent on the adult. The power dynamic is immanent in the system with the adult AP in the powerful position in the relationship.

Attachment theory helps us assess the child's main attachment figure as the AP. It is the AP they turn to for protection from harm and to keep them safe. When the AP highlights danger, the attachment system turns on. Safety becomes the primary concern. Anxiety heightens and fear of losing the AP may become prominent. If the child's attachment strategies are focused on the protection of the AP they will be highly conflicted and not know which of the instructions to follow. The contradictions are:

a My parent on whom I depend for everything and who loves me is sending me into a situation they have connoted as unsafe and I may be harmed,

b My other parent may be dangerous and I also have good memories of them, don't I? Sometimes they have been angry, and I have had nice times with them. They also say they love me.

Research on memory has shown just how easily it can be manipulated. Children can have very clear memories of things which never happened. The work of Elizabeth

Loftus and John Palmer on eyewitness testimony in criminal trials (Loftus and Palmer, 1974; Loftus, 2013) has shown how unreliable memory can be and how open to the power of suggestion. More recently Julia Shaw (2016) has shown how easy it is to implant a memory of something which has never happened. Distortions are also prevalent in the memory systems and help us understand the development of attachment strategies (Crittenden and Landini, 2011; Crittenden, 2016).

 c The AP may deliberately withdraw at this point in order not to appear to be influencing the child.

 d Without help to find a way through the morass, the child is alone to decide. Dichotomous thinking, i.e. splitting the world into right and wrong, may be a helpful, sometimes the only, way out. "My other parent cannot be good if my main attachment figure says they are not. They must be bad." Habitual dichotomous thinking has been associated with many mental health difficulties in adulthood (Bonfá-Araujo, Oshio, and Hauck-Filho, 2022).

6 I have decided by myself. Having absorbed the information that the other parent is bad or dangerous, the child decides "all by myself that I don't want to go. And I will never see that other parent again. I cannot trust them." This is the "independent thinker" phenomenon identified by Gardner and seen so often in the severe cases of alienation. Often there may be something that happened: the other parent got a birthday wrong, or let them down on some occasions, or bought them the wrong thing, or didn't spend enough time with them. This then becomes the reason for never wanting to see them again.

Paradoxically, at this stage the AP and the child can appear to be in a battle, with the AP insisting that they go to see the other parent and the child becoming angry with the AP for insisting. "If they (the other parent) are so great, you go and see them then!" Parents, who may truly be unaware of the conundrum the child is facing, will point to this stage and suggest to the professional that they "just ask the child". The child will explain why they do not want to see the other parent.

Professionals witnessing this process can become confused as the reasons given and behaviour shown are contradictory and do not make rational sense. The child's presentation and insistence that they will not go can be convincing. Surely that other parent must have done something terrible. The "truth" seems elusive, obscure, and unclear.

Encouraging the AP to exercise parental authority and ensure the child gets to the other parent often makes things worse. Using rational arguments such as comparing it with other situations in which the child might be reluctant, for example going to school or going to the doctor, do not work. At this stage direct work with the child or work with the AP will often result in escalation of hostility of the child toward the TP.

7 Targeted parent fights or withdraws. The TP is now faced with a dilemma, the child is in distress at the thought of coming to see them. They are often mystified

and cannot understand why, when they previously had a good relationship, they do not want to see them, or their grandparents or aunts, uncles or cousins. They do not want to cause the child more distress, they simply want a relationship with their child.

8 Alienating Parent connotes the decision of the targeted parent as "proof" of lack of love by the targeted parent. At this level the triangulation is complete. The risk here is that the AP will make it clear to the children that the TP is even more dangerous by taking the AP to court. If the TP withdraws and allows the no contact to continue it will be "proof" that the TP doesn't love the child enough to keep trying, that they have given up and do not really love them. No matter what the TP does it will be construed as wrong.

And the process continues. Many non-professional people, and professionals new to this work believe that if left alone, given time, not pressurised, the child will "come round" and want to see their other parent. However, research in this area has shown this does not happen without considerable help (Baker, 2007). Baker's research has shown that once alienated, children do not in general "come round". The alienation continues well into adulthood and may never be resolved. Research demonstrates that many children who are alienated realise as adults that they did not want their parent to give up trying to see them (Baker, 2007; Clawar and Rivlin, 2013).

The importance of an understanding of neurobiology

When assessing or trying to help repair the relationships practitioners will notice an increase in symptoms in the child which can become alarming and dangerous. Children may become emotionally dysregulated, start to restrict food intake, self-harm, withdraw and become distressed or develop dysregulated behaviour difficulties which need to be assessed by a relevant mental health professional. Where a diagnosis is given, such as ADHD, these are based on behavioural criteria and do not usually address the underlying causes. It is of crucial importance that the child or children be helped off the psychiatric trajectory.

An ability to notice when the child is becoming physically overwhelmed is essential for practitioners. A good knowledge of limbic system responses such as amygdala hijack (Goleman, 1996), the window of tolerance (Siegal, 1999) and the workings of the vagal system (Porges, 2017) can help practitioners to help children recover their equilibrium. Amygdala hijack refers to the danger reaction which is activated in the brain when the person perceives themselves to be at immediate risk. The subcortical brain functions take over: fight, flight, or freeze responses are activated. At those moments higher brain functions, that is, the ability to think rationally, go offline. The remedy is to make the person safe. The experience of road rage is an example of amygdala hijack that most of us will have experienced.

Space prevents a full discussion; however, many exercises and techniques can be introduced to help children and adults when arousal levels are too high. There is no specific list. Exercises need to be devised and adapted for each specific family's needs. Examples can be found and can be found in the literature for neurological understandings, trauma, critical thinking and relationship building as well as the traditional systemic sources.

These exercises help calm the amygdala and the vagal system and bring the body and brain back to normal functioning. Such resources emphasise the importance of healthy relationships for healthy development. Bringing relationships back to health is the challenge.

Intervention

As yet there are no hard and fast rules for intervention in situations of severe alienation. There is considerable knowledge of what does not work. Traditional family therapy, that is, get them into a room to discuss their beliefs and feelings and generate good mutual understandings and child focused parental behaviours, is not only ineffective, it usually makes things worse. Children tend to become more entrenched in their positions.

There are several intensive tailor-made programmes for severe alienation which have been evaluated: Turning Points for Families (Harman, Saunders, and Afifi, 2021) and Family Bridges (Warshak, 2018). These involve the temporary transfer of the child's residence to the TP for a minimum of 90 days and the reintroduction of the child to the TP via an initial intensive programme, usually over four days. There has been much controversy about these programmes. Harman, Saunders, and Afifi found that the Turning Points for Families programme caused no traumatic harm to children, addressing a concern which had been raised. Family Bridges was assessed as highly successful in reunifying the children with the rejected parent so long as there was no contact with the AP during the programme. Work with the AP needs to take place during the 90 days, if they are willing, to ensure that alienation processes do not start again. The Anna Freud Centre has also developed a model of intervention (Asen and Morris, 2020) applying principles of mentalisation. This has yet to be independently evaluated.

Some of the intervention programmes have been taught internationally. However, most practice in these programmes occurs in the USA and Canada. Although knowledge of the dynamics of alienation is growing, there are few recognised training courses. As elaborated below, most intervention for sever alienation consists of psychoeducation, developing critical thinking skills and therapy for individuals as well as subgroups of the family.

It is essential that people intervening in these families have the required knowledge and expertise to help. Having undertaken an assessment for court, the expert witness needs to state how they see the situation, reporting the "truth" as they see it in all its complexity. This often means stating uncomfortable findings and justifying the reasons for those. They must take a position. For that reason, the expert cannot be the main therapist for the family. They have lost sufficient neutrality, no matter how accurate or otherwise their report. The ability to form a therapeutic alliance with all members of the family is severely compromised.

To be effective for children caught up in the conflict, therapy needs to be muti-modal and involve a team of practitioners. This should include as a minimum:

- A systemic family therapist with specialist training in alienation, to work with the TP and the child(ren) both separately and together. This person would also work with the wider network: extended family and school.
- A separate therapist for the AP with specialist training in alienation and expertise in dealing with complex personalities.
- Depending on severity, the children may need separate specialist input from a therapist who works with children and has knowledge and experience of the impact of alienation.

There should be a care coordinator which could be the original assessor. The team would need to meet regularly. Good supervision is essential. These interventions are very expensive as they require highly skilled individuals. At time of writing there is no specific National Health Service (NHS) provision for these families in the UK. The Child and Adolescent Mental Health Service (CAMHS) within the NHS may get involved when children develop severe symptoms, however there is no specific training for CAMHS practitioners to deal with this complex presentation.

The intervention itself needs to address all the elements of the double bind process identified above and every other relevant issue. Intervention is multi-factorial and consists of:

- Psychoeducation on the process and impact of alienating behaviours. This should be provided for the whole family as well as separate input aimed at the child's developmental age and for the TP. The AP, if they are willing to under-take therapy, would need separate sessions.
- Critical thinking skills for the child to help them unravel the confusion of mixed messages. The aim would be to understand that the adults have positions based on their experience which may be different from the child's, and to resolve the dichotomous thinking. It needs to be age appropriate.
- Therapeutic input for the child to help with self-regulation.
- A protected space to think, reflect, and develop reflective processing. This needs to be a safe space and one in which safety can be experienced. Often the children do not understand what psychological safety truly means and may not have experienced it for a long time if ever.
- Specific trauma-oriented therapy, such as EMDR, may be needed.

Conclusion

Systems in which alienation is present are fear organised systems. Everyone is afraid of something and this fear organises behaviour. The AP's fears are often driving the system and need to be assessed and understood in each case separately. The TP's fears are of losing the loving relationship with the child forever.

Professionals are often attacked using the same strategies as are used against the TP, generating fear of complaints being made and of attacks on professional integrity. Often the child at the centre of it all bears the fear for all to see. Like the canary in the mineshaft, they are the first to show distress, and the mental health sequelae of being caught in the crossfire can be profound (Baker, 2007).

This chapter has focused understanding on the position of the child caught up in intense processes of parental hatred. The children are tortured and suffer in immeasurable ways. Their safety, protection, and comfort are severely compromised in the face of extreme relational danger. They are often seeking the truth. Many children have said explicitly that they don't know which parent to believe. The aim of intervention is for the children to find their truth, their whole truth in the light of their love for both parents and the ability to have a meaningful relationship with both parents and all of their family.

References

American Psychiatric Association. (2013). *Diagnostic and Statistical Manual of Mental Disorders* (5th ed.). https://doi.org/10.1176/appi.books.9780890425596

Asen, E. and Morris, E. (2020). *High-Conflict Parenting Post-Separation: the making and Breaking of Family Ties.* London: Routledge.

Baker, A.J.L. (2007). *Adult Children of Parental Alienation Syndrome: Breaking the Ties that Bind.* New York: W.W. Norton.

Barnett, A., Riley, A., and Katherine. (2021). Experiences of Parental Alienation Interventions, in Mercer, J. and Drew, M. (eds) *Challenging Parental Alienation New Directions for Professionals and Parents.* New York: Routledge.

Bateson, G., Jackson, D.D., Haley. J., and Weakland, J.H. (1972). Toward a Theory of Schizophrenia, in Bateson, G. (ed.) *Steps to an Ecology of Mind.* New York: Ballantine Books.

Bernet, W., Wamboldt, M. Z., and Narrow, W. (2016). Child Affected by Parental Relationship Distress. *Journal of the American Academy of Child and Adolescent Psychiatry*, 55(7), 571–579.

Bonfá-Araujo, B., Oshio, A., and Hauck-Filho, N. (2022). Seeing Things in Black-and-White: A Scoping Review on Dichotomous Thinking Style. *Jpn Psychol Res.* www.onlinelibrary.wiley.com/doi/epdf/10.1111/jpr.12328 accessed 16.12.22.

Birchall, J. (2021). *"Parental Alienation": A Dangerous and Harmful Concept.* www.womensaid.org.uk/parental-alienation-a-dangerous-and-harmful-concept/ accessed 12/11/22.

Bowen, M (1978, 1983, 1985). *Family Therapy in Clinical Practice.* Maryland: Rowman and Littlefield Pub, Inc.

Bowen Centre website: www.thebowencenter.org/triangles, accessed 13/11/22.

Bowlby, J. (1979). *The Making and Breaking of Affectional Bonds.* London: Routledge.

Byng-Hall, J. (1995). *Re-Writing Family Scripts.* New York: Guilford.

Cafcass, (2021). www.cafcass.gov.uk/2021/01/14/cafcass-reissues-position-on-parental-alienation/ accessed on 13/11/22.

Clawar, S. S. and Rivlin, B. V. (2013). *Children Held Hostage* 2nd edn. American Bar Association.

Crittenden, P. M. (2016). *Raising Parents: Attachment, Representation, and Treatment* 2nd edn. London: Routledge.

Crittenden, P. M. and Landini, A. (2011). *Assessing Adult Attachment: A Dynamic Maturational Approach to Discourse Analysis.* New York: W.W. Norton.

Dallos, R. and Vetere, A (2012). Systems Theory, Family Attachments and Processes of Triangulation: Does the Concept of Triangulation Offer a Useful Bridge? *Journal of Family Therapy, 34*, 117–137.

Euripides (2020). *Medea: Translation by Gilbert Murray.* Ottawa, ON: East India Publishing Company.

Gardner, R.A. (1998). *The Parental Alienation Syndrome: A Guide for Mental Health and Legal Professionals.* Cresskill, NJ: Creative Therapeutics.

Gibney, P. (2006). The Double Bind Theory: Still Crazy-Making After All These Years, *Psychotherapy In Australia, 12*, 3 https://search.informit.org/doi/10.3316/informit.5458 22294870607 accessed 5.12.22.

Goleman, D. (1996). *Emotional Intelligence: Why It Can Matter More than IQ.* London: Bloomsbury.

Grey, B and Farnfield S (2017). The Meaning of The Child Interview (MotC) – The initial validation of a new procedure for assessing and understanding the parent-child relationships of 'at risk' families, *Journal of Children's Services, 12*, 1, 16–31.

Haley, J (1981). *Reflections on Therapy and Other Essays.* Chevy Chase, MD: The Family therapy Institute of Washington DC.

Harman, J.J., Saunders, L., and Afifi, T. (2021). Evaluation of the Turning Points for Families (TPFF) program for severely alienated children. *Journal of Family Therapy, 44*, 2, 279–298.

Heyman R. E., Smith Slep A. M., Beach S. R., Wamboldt M. Z., Kaslow N. J., and Reiss D. (2009). Relationship Problems and the DSM: Needed Improvements and Suggested Solutions. *World Psychiatry, 8*(1):7–14. Accessed 13/11/22.

Loftus, E (2013). How Reliable Is Your Memory? Ted Talk www.ted.com/talks/elizabeth_loftus_how_reliable_is_your_memory?language=en accessed 29.12.22.

Loftus, E and Palmer, J. (1974). Reconstruction of Automobile Destruction: An Example of the Interaction Between Language and Memory. *Journal of Verbal Learning and Verbal Behavior, 13*, 585–589 www.demenzemedicinagenerale.net/images/mens-sana/AutomobileDestruction.pdf accessed 29.12.22

Minuchin, S. (1974). *Families and Family Therapy.* London: Tavistock Publications.

Porges, S. W. (2017). *The Pocket Guide to Polyvagal Theory: The Transformative Power of Feeling Safe.* New York: W.W. Norton.

Pullman, P. (1995). *Northern Lights.* 1st ed. London: Scholastic.

Shaw, J (2016). *The Memory Illusion*, London: Penguin Books.

Siegel, D. (1999). *The Developing Mind: How Relationships and the Brain Interact to Shape Who We Are.* New York: Guilford.

Sillars, A (2022). *Parental Alienation Literature List ... 2016 And Beyond.* www.amandasillars.com/blog/f/parental-alienation-literature-2016-and-beyond accessed 13.11.22.

Slep, A. M. S., Heyman, R. E., and Foran, H. M. (2015). Child Maltreatment in DSM-5 and ICD-11. *Family Process, 54*(1), 17–32.

Warshak, R. A. (2018). Reclaiming Parent–Child Relationships: Outcomes of Family Bridges with Alienated Children. *Journal of Divorce & Remarriage, 60*(8), 645–667, DOI: 10.1080/10502556.2018.1529505

Chapter 15

Second Phase Parenting

Attachment and parenting adult children

Myrna Gower

Introduction

The stories about the relationships between parents and adult children often pose questions about safety and security. At first glance, these stories may sound predictable and quite in line with expectations associated with lifecycle events, for example the anguish surrounding children leaving home; the partnering and marrying of adult children; birth of the next generation; illness; aging; death and so on. However, adult families as a place of safety and security seems to defy simplicity in real life. We don't seem to get it right. Instead, unexpected complexity becomes des rigueur inviting conflicts, misunderstandings, intense disappointments, unresolved differences and even estrangement. Parenting adult children or this second phase of parenting is most often experienced as a roller coaster ride.

Independence (from whom and from what one may ask) still seems to hold up as the highest success marker for parents and adult children no matter that lived experience evidences ongoing contact; proximity and interdependence between parents and adult children (Gower, 2011). This research has progressed to reconsider these limiting beliefs and has instead highlighted several opposing constructs such as 'closeness and distance' or 'obligation and entitlement' to be integral to parents' relationship with adult children. These constructs confirm the ongoing relationship and offer further evidence to support the integration of 'being connected' into wider narratives of parenting adult children.

From time immemorial people have gathered together, especially in times of increasing uncertainty. Our use of the term 'family' is in constant flux and expanding all the time. It is commonplace that who is considered to be included in a family remains those related to each other and usually inhabiting the same household. Without a closer re-examination of the meanings attributed to 'family', these leading dogmas could help to explain why adult children are in the main, understood to be 'outside of the family' and in that sense seemingly of lesser relevance and of such limited research interest. The Church of England Children's Society recently redefined what it means by the word family as: 'An emotionally supportive network of adults and children, some of whom live together or have lived together'

DOI: 10.4324/9781003308096-19

(Worldwide Words, accessed 2022). Whilst arguably spartan in what it includes, the wider context of families is acknowledged in this brief description. It is heart warming that this volume includes the widest contexts within which we are protected and has invited deliberations of this relationship between parents and their adult children into the very core of considerations on safety, danger and protection in the family, community and the world.

In search of a family relationship framework pertinent to second phase parenting

In searching for a family relationship framework pertinent to parenting adult children, an exploration of existing theories and models of parenting was the first port of call. McDermott (2002) offers a most helpful overview of traditional models of parenting. On reviewing the theories he outlines, the substantial differences in the ways in which infants, children, teenagers and adults relate shows to be the challenge if we are to consider transposing any of the ideas into an adult child context. Exchanging the word 'child' for 'adult child' does not suffice and nor do any of these theories apply in their entirety to the task of parenting adult children.

Of the theoretical models reviewed, attachment studies have been heavily influential in systemic practices. This was initiated by early conversations between John Bowlby himself and child psychiatrist and family therapist John Byng-Hall at the Tavistock Clinic in London as they debated attachment and the wider context of family. Attachment studies have taken a firm place in systemic literature and practice (Dallos and Vetere, 2022; Byng Hall, 1995, 2002) and offer a natural fertile ground for further development into this domain of adult relationships.

With this in mind we will:

A first look at what it is like to review theory and to identify differences between early childhood development and how that could apply in adult relating
B look at four attachment styles transposing these into the adult parenting situation
C define the position of parenting adults in the lifecycle of the family and
D identify several typical behavioural elements of the relationship between parents and adult children reflecting implications for their attachment.

In developing such a framework, the first scaffold to go up will need to be a description of 'family' that will allow parenting adult children to have a place 'at the table'.

In an extensive study of what families look like today, The Children's Commissioner for London (UK) found that it was more about the quality of family relationships rather than about the composition of the family that defined what 'family' meant to respondents in their study (The Independent Family Review, 2022).

These four themes below were present in all forms of the families studied and extends appropriately to the relationship between parents and adult children:

- the emotional importance of connection within families
- shared experience of family life
- unconditional support within families
- strong, positive and enduring relationships found in families.

Reviewing theory and identifying differences between early childhood development models and how that could apply in adult relating

It is when describing specific parent-adult child behaviours that the differences become more explicit although underlying principles from models of parenting young children continue to inform the adult interaction. For example, how often parents see their adult children has been of considerable interest to early studies on adult children (Umberson, 1992; Ermisch, 2004; Strauss, 2009).

One of the properties of attachment theory is 'proximity maintenance' where the child strives to stay near the caregiver in order to keep safe (Bowlby, 1988). Aviezer's (2002) study of children on Kibbutzim reported on the price paid for the 'collective's interference in natural formation processes' (p. 448). In these studies she was talking about emotional availability and proximity of the infant child to the parent as the fundamental variable.

The emotional availability and proximity of parents to their adult children is claimed here to be equally fundamental to the evolution of this relationship. Transferring the idea of 'proximity maintenance' to the adult parenting context up to midlife and beyond conjures up numerous examples of how parents and their adult children stay in touch. This is typified by factors such as multigenerational living, daily contact, weekly visiting, infrequent contact, telephone and media contact, family and religious rituals, geographic distances that do not easily permit gathering, erratic or restricted contact and so on. These examples (and of course there will be more) will each be populated by complexity and ambivalences but will also reflect some well-negotiated and pleasing connectedness within the context of mutually independent and separate lifestyles. To illustrate: A young teacher aged 32 talked to me about having to often visit his mother after work as his mother lived alone. He felt angry and resentful that she did not build a friendship circle and depended instead on his companionship. She was a capable woman and he became impatient with her demands on him. He did enjoy her cooking and was glad to know that she was alright. As she was a retired teacher, he valued talking about his pupils and often did marking with her when visiting. His mother told me it felt unfair that she had to tolerate her son's impatience. She believed that she asked little of him; protected him from her worries and was always there for him when he called for her support.

Differences in the theories and models of parenting young children and those that might pertain to parenting adult children on early examination can be indistinct. It is on deeper examination that significant differences are revealed. As in the example, proximity to a young child is defined very differently from suitable proximity with an adult child but both could equally reflect a securely attached relationship. With young children there is an expectation that suitable proximity can be built. With parents and adult children, we seem to have no such expectation. This leaves us much work to do in defining theoretical ideas to this end and then in attempting their application.

Looking at four attachment styles transposing these into the adult parenting situation

Bowlby (1969) defined attachment as a special type of affectional bond between the parent and child. This requires a specific person who is consistent (not inter-changeable); who is emotionally significant and who produces a desire to maintain proximity (Bowlby, 1969; Edwards, 2002). Involuntary separation from this person would almost always result in distress. Bowlby saw the seeking of security and comfort as ever present. He considered the development of basic trust to be central to (a child's) development.

This definition of attachment applies well to the relationship between parents and adult children. However, parents and their adult children seem unclear as to how to maintain such affectional bonds. All are aware that these are emotionally significant relationships but how to manage these seems to be based on 'try as you go'. One mother of middle-aged children explained that she and the father loved visiting their children but enjoyed being able to leave when they wished. The children often complained that the parents did not visit enough and wanted them to stay longer. To keep contact inevitably builds or at the least helps to sustain the attachment. The question becomes how often to see or be with the children and on what terms. Staying away and having too little contact can result in distress for both yet frequency of contact can generate conflict.

The seeking of comfort and security remains the ever-present challenge. John Byng-Hall (1995) in his work on the family as a secure base described attachment styles (Bowlby, 1969; Ainsworth, 1978) as a guide for clinicians to recognise them as part of family patterns of interaction. These styles of attachment are well known. The novelty of their representation here lies in considering these styles of relating with adult children with the word 'adult' put into the text as a way to experiment with re assigning meanings as you read.

Securely attached (adult) children: Byng-Hall exemplifies these (adult) children as often appearing to have fun together with their parents at home. Attachment studies have proposed that relationships provide not only a secure base for the (adult) child but also a source of great pleasure. The (adult) child begins to feel worthy of attention, building feelings of self-worth and self-esteem. Communications are warm and sensitive. Parents are free to move apart and then come together again but most important of all is the parents' physical and emotional availability at times of the (adult) child's distress. This conveys the message that they can depend on their parents and find comfort from them.

Illustration: John and Anne live an hour's commute from their middle-aged son Brian and his family. Brian and his wife June both work and their children, now entering their teens, are usually taken up with their school and social interests. Although still both employed, John and Anne enjoy flexible hours. They usually do the travelling if they wish to see the children albeit tiring and oftentimes inconvenient and are called on to assist when needed. Brian is especially appreciative of his father's counsel on financial worries. They all particularly enjoy eating together and take turns preparing food (ala bake-off) when visiting John and Anne.

Insecure/Avoidant attached (adult) children: Byng-Hall explains the use of a similar pattern of transactional style to those of disengaged relationships. This shared parent-(adult) child attachment strategy 'is to maintain distance both physically and emotionally in order to reduce the likelihood of emotional outbursts that might lead to rejections or painful reminders. The price is a loss of sensitive care for the (adult) child when it is needed' (Byng- Hall, 1995, p. 111). Although apparently independent, the (adult) child is not adaptable.

Illustration: Sisters Jemi and Ramina left home soon after leaving school. Their mother was a heavy drinker and their parents had always fought in their presence. The girls would get caught up in these running battles escaping to friends' houses for solace. Now in their early 30s both girls are partnered but have no wish for children. They have moved to another city and rarely visit their parents. Ramina has recently had to have emergency surgery for a burst appendix. Neither parent came to visit or offered assistance.

Insecure/ ambivalent attached (adult) children with an insecure attachment display a similar pattern or transactional style to those of enmeshed relationships. These (adult) children often look over-close but parents may well be observed to be unavailable and this invites clinging. Although the mother is committed to parenting, she may be emotionally unavailable.

Illustration: Now in her 50s, Sadie is the younger of two siblings. From the earliest she could recall, she ensured that she was at her mother's side. She remembers her inability to separate from her mother and the desperate home-sickness she would experience if ever she was away from her mother. No matter how unreliable her mother seemed to be, no matter that she rarely was able to soothe Sadie's angst, Sadie desperately tried to please her mother in spite of her mother's regular admonishment of her. She remained living at home until her early 30s when she attempted to marry. Sadie's efforts to separate were constantly thwarted by her mother who disapproved of any of Sadie's choices and most of all then said that Sadie was not the daughter she thought she would be. Sadie herself has not successfully partnered and has no children. She looks after her now aging mother who makes considerable demands of Sadie. Sadie gets little acknowledgement. She feels like a bad daughter. Both of her siblings now live abroad and have families of their own.

If Sadie had been securely attached to her mother feeling lovable and loved, she would have been able to understand the criticism and demands of her mother in a different way. The narrative of Sadie not being good enough would have been replaced by understandings of her mother's complaints without having to blame herself. Describing therapeutic intervening is beyond the scope of this chapter but suffice it to say that the role of the systemic therapist in developing the new narrative breaks the patterns of secure anxious attachment through the therapy. Developing the relationship with her father helped to build Sadie's resilience in re-storying the attachment with her mother. The role of the therapist was crucial in promoting safety and security allowing Sadie to be able to begin enjoying being with her mother.

Sadie has now been able to move to a home of her own and has a renewed sense of self. Through the therapy, Sadie has been able to set new boundaries such that she now no longer, feels that she constantly lets her mother down.

Disorganised/unresolved attached (adult) children. Byng-Hall (1995) suggests that at home there are moments when the parent may dissociate and this could be frightening for the (adult) child. As this is triggered by an internal event in the mother (or caregiver), which the (adult) child cannot anticipate, any reunion with the parent becomes unpredictable.

Illustration: The father of three sons died suddenly aged 62. Two of the sons were married but the youngest (and his mother's favourite), Rajan, was a single man of 34 who remained with his mother during this grieving time. Rajan began to date and it became known to his mother that he and his new girlfriend (who he subsequently married) had spent three nights away together with his then girlfriend prior to marriage. His mother's rage was incandescent. She alleged that he had broken her trust and belief in him and that he had disrespected all her and the community's moral codes and had shamed her. Rajan continued to care for his mother till her death in her 90s. The relationship became deeply conflictual over the ensuing decades. His mother constantly criticised him and his family and she maintained that if only he had been a daughter it would never have been like this.

Space allows for only some brief recounting of Bowlby and John Byng-Hall's work, however these exemplars highlight attachments styles between parents and adult children and offers, where necessary, some direction for the potential building and reparation of these attachments.

The family lifecycle and parenting adult children

In lifecycle descriptions parenting in relation to adult children seems to have been subsumed by the popularly assumed need for adult children to individuate, to leave home and then for parents to make suitable adjustments to 'the empty nest' and following on from this, for old age (Hayley, 1973; Erikson, 1985; Carter and McGoldrick, 2005; McGoldrick, Giordano and Garcia-Preto, 2005). No matter that this relationship can be one of the longest lasting of which we are part, the processes involved in ongoing parenting as children become adults are not recognised in the family lifecycle.

Stages of parenting adult children

In order to consider the integration of second phase parenting into the family life-cycle, qualitative research revealed very different parenting requirements over time. This led to parenting adult children being acknowledged as a life phase and for meaningful inclusion, it required that it be differentiated into the following stages (Gower, 2011).

Parenting emerging adults

Children are living at home longer and are often financially dependent on their parents. This is an extended time period (Arnot, 2000) and can last for 10 years and more.

Parenting in the middle years

Aspects relating to middle parenting years concentrate on the midlife support of adult children, parenting strategies and a review of social structure as a way of understanding intergenerational quality.

Parenting older children

When parents become elderly or ill, the balance of the relationship with adult children alters; intergenerational ambivalence increases (Pillemer and Suitor, 2002) and the power and emotional dynamics between elderly or ill parents and adult children have to be negotiated in the face of expectations and/or necessity of care.

Of particular note is that each stage is determined by the age of the children. Parenting a 25-year-old is quite different from the task of parenting a 40-year-old or a 65-year-old. The identification of a lifecycle position will be an essential component in a reparative dialogue within both clinical or non-clinical conversations.

Where attachment narratives are explored, the identification of the stage of parenting is necessary if key transitions in the relationship are to be supported. The leaving home of a young emerging adult will require very different attention compared to the demands of the relationship between parents and their middle-aged children with children of their own.

Vulnerable parents of adults will need to adjust to increasing levels of ambivalence in their relationship with their adult children but all the time appreciating the connectedness between them.

Some typical behavioural elements of the relationship between parents and adult children reflecting implications for their attachment

Punishment in second phase parenting

How do parents of adults show their disapproval?

The threat of abandonment in attachment narratives has an undeniable emotional force giving rise to intense anxiety.

- Carol (aged 61) regularly calls her 93-year-old mother to confide in her about her failing marriage. Her mother offers little consolation, criticising her daughter, and the calls regularly end abruptly. Each time, Carol cries bitterly that she is unloved. Such disapproval immediately triggers anxious behaviours for which she is medicated.
- Renata's parents were very upset that they had not been included on her family holiday and for two months they have refused to speak to Renata.
- Each time that Josh calls his mother she says that she will not answer if he does not visit.
- Jemi and Ramina's parents say if their daughters will not make an effort to see them then why should they be bothered.
- After an argumentative visit Sadie's mother told her not to come to her house as she maintains that Sadie keeps on interfering.

Each of these examples (and there are multitudes) raised intense discomfort, distress, fear and sadness. The significant enhancement of anxiety has an immediate impact on the quality of the ongoing attachment.

Money as a force

As parents of adults, it seems that we continue to experience ourselves as central in the relationship with our adult children (Gower and Dowling, 2017). As children mature, the levels of parental influence alters but financials being the biggest reported worry for all, continue to exert sway.

- Sadie's mother keeps threatening to write her out of her will, generating feelings of rejection and failure.
- There is a constant question so many parents seem to ask and that is, 'When do we stop paying?'. Who pays and what it means will likely be reflective of the occurring attachment style, e.g. generosity, agreed sharing, pleasurable giving, withholding and disapproving, disengagement with no contribution considered and expectations of payback be it financial or in kind.
- Parental legacies are promised but parents who do not approve of the ways in which children run their finances or disapprove of their choices will often not provide financial benefits until their demise. This can be a powerful withholding.

Normative intergenerational ambivalence

From the time where parents and adult children are able to use adult frames of reference, it would seem reasonable to assume that differences should be more easily negotiated; but how often one says to children that when they grow up they will understand, only to ultimately discover this does not happen.

Luescher and Pillemer (1998) highlight that major family transitions have an ambivalent quality as they typically involve losses and gains. As a general concept Luescher and Pillemer (1998) used the term 'intergenerational ambivalence to designate contradictions in relationships between parents and adult offspring that cannot be reconciled' (p. 416).

Illustration: Rajan has found no way to convince his mother that she need not feel shame on account of his early courting of his wife and especially now that he has three children to whom she is very attached. She remains adamant in her view and should the subject arise, she reminds him in no uncertain terms of her disapproval and her shame. Rajan himself cannot accept his mother's disapproval and constant remonstrating over this historical circumstance and it frequently leaves each exasperated and unhappy.

Ambivalence can increase around times of lifecycle transitions and parents tend to hold on to influential roles. How to identify the different positions and to respect their presence without trying to eliminate one or the other becomes key to the evolution of the relationship.

The tensions between two conflicting elements or forces that emerge are not viewed as polarised positions. In the face of powerful social discourses, however, it is difficult as a clinician, let alone as a parent or as an adult child, to avoid looking for preferred positions where one idea takes precedence over another.

The desire to please

When adult children were asked to name their top joys of being adult children the most highly reported category was their wish to please their parents (Gower and Dowling, 2008). Whilst this may seem a perfunctory outcome, it has an important element of surprise when introduced in the midst of intergenerational argument and it often proves to be new information into a conversation that can make a difference.

Do attachments patterns remain inflexible

It is not always clear if attachment patterns remain inflexible once adulthood is attained.

Much more research is now needed so that we can study the attachment between parent and adult child as a changing process. It is in the sharing of attachment narratives (Byng-Hall, 2002, 2008; Dallos and Vetere 2022) that family members follow their understandings of the relating between them and how each reacts with the other. When new narratives are explored, family members can share preferences and in so doing provide an enhanced sense of security. Byng-Hall considers that the reliable network of attachment relationships is important *at whatever age* and encourages their exploration again in the belief that change in attachment behaviours is possible.

Discussion and conclusion

This chapter incorporates research evidenced descriptions of second phase parenting: affirming this life-time relationship; that independence is an insufficient description to define its success and that connectedness is at the heart of this primary attachment.

Attachment styles and how some of these ideas fit well in the context of parenting adult children is a new initiative and paves the way for much more expansive study.

Whilst attachment styles are viewed as having been established during childhood generally, remaining typical and fixed through adult years, this discussion underscores the potential or even the inevitable that this relationship continues to build during adulthood. There are strong indications that if damaged the attachment could repair. Clinical interventions now recognise the theoretical premise that significant intergenerational ambivalence in this relationship (and particularly in middle and older stages of parenting) is inevitable and cannot necessarily be resolved. This will usher in a different way of acknowledging intergenerational differences where we no longer have to argue our positions as to whose is right in order to be able to have a relationship with one other.

The evolution of the attachment at each stage of the parent-adult child relationship is central in creating the safety of the family base. This will defend against using estrangement as a solution in the face of disagreements which then perpetuates insecurity. Schism and separation are supported by old narratives of independence as the highest organising principles of success for adults and still remain familiar principles to which many adult families seem to use as their default button, particularly in times of conflict

The COVID pandemic put families together in ways that countered narratives of separation and individuation and enforced unimaginable intensity of togetherness. The pandemic mandates meant no choice but for us to negotiate togetherness. This turmoil required generational gathering as people merged into 'legal bubbles' to survive the lockdown against contact with others. The horror of the elder generation being isolated, unprotected, vulnerable and without care and connection brought public outrage. Loved ones having to die alone has left unbearable grieving. Never before had there been mandatory generational separation from family members. Never before had the importance of relating with older parents been given such public prominence.

Now that the restrictions that obliged and insulated togetherness as well as imposed separation from parents and adult children have lifted, we are left reflecting on these disrupted attachment experiences in ways we could never have anticipated. So many relational strategies usually employed to be able to manage our relationships were crashed and may never be retrieved. The use of avoidance, secrecy and estrangement were sorely challenged in the face of 24/7 sharing of personal lived hours. We found ourselves reviewing the meanings of our relationships with the outside world unwittingly being confronted by feelings of anxiety and a desperate need for safety, comfort and protection. This all occurred at the same time as having to live without people for whom we yearned. This has led to many moments of sadness as we had to cope with the loss of contact from those to whom we felt closest. The bewilderment and confusion, the uncertainty and fears lived over endless months, has left significant psychological damage in its wake. It has left us evaluating our connectedness to others; to multigenerational responsibilities and questioning how to find safety and protection within our communities.

The Ukrainian war has seen thousands of migrants seek safety. Three generations of families, principally of women as men of fighting age have had to remain behind, have travelled together. Anecdotal reporting reveals this to be a vital modus operandi to their being able to cope and survive. Multigenerational attachment has been absorbed into the UK as commonplace, admired and supported by those willing to temporarily house multigenerational families. We know the tragedy of migrant families being separated. We know the drastic difficulties of single young migrant men being able to manage and banding into groups in order to cope.

People worldwide have witnessed the mourning of the death of Queen Elizabeth II. This public family has been incorporated into personal psychological experience of so many in the UK and beyond. As leaders of the world arrived at Westminster Abbey for the Queen's funeral, the BBC broadcaster Huw Edwards said, referring to the Royal family members, 'everybody is here'! This was the first time that there had been such a family procession behind the gun carriage as the world said 'goodbye' to the Queen. The Royal family were reported to have made monumental efforts to come together.

The most poignant moments of vigil were the king and his siblings guarding their mother. Then came the vigil from the next generation: grandchildren of the Queen: all adult children of the Queen's children. This multigenerational family has been subjected to scrutiny with tens of hundreds of citizens queueing for hours to pay their respects. What is undeniable was the impact of the generational togetherness we witnessed. The relationships were made visible and there were few who did not opine on the relationships between the royal parents and their adult children. Hours of documentaries and reams of written words on this family filled ten intensive days of public mourning in which many citizens and beyond were participant.

When reflecting on the pandemic, the war in Ukraine and public and private grief, multigenerational family structure has been respected. A secure base beyond the nuclear family, where adult attachments have prevailed, has proven a relief and has been acknowledged as such. Students isolated in halls at universities around the country continue to struggle with the implications of having been cut off and isolated during COVID. Reports of having enjoyed the togetherness of COVID are multiple and the lasting impact of new connections between all generations is commonplace.

Definitions of 'what is family' that are fixed and that depend on specific structures will inevitably exclude so many people. That family is about strong and long-lasting relationships, being able to rely on one another and being able to spend time together makes possible the inclusion of an ongoing attachment between parents and adult children. We know that descriptions of the relationship between parents and adult children is deeply culturally bound. The above characterisation of 'family' is culturally inclusive. It is action driven and is in continual movement.

So many of the ideas evidenced about parenting adult children can sound so ordinary and obvious yet they continue to remain silenced and outside of the current zeitgeist. Existing dominant ideas and beliefs, often counter to different cultural practices and values, continue to hold pathologising narratives about adult children and how parenting children stops when children grow up.

References

Ainsworth, M., Blehar, M., Waters, E. and Wall, S. (1978) *Patterns of Attachment: A Psychological Study of the Strange Situation*. Hillsdale, NJ: Lawrence Erlbaum Associates.

Arnett, J. (2000) Emerging adulthood: A theory of development from the late teens through the twenties. *American Psychologist*, 55: 469–480.

Aviezer, O., Sagi, A. and van IJzendoorn, M. (2002) Balancing the family and the collective in raising children: Why communal sleeping in kibbutzim was destined to end. *Family Process*, 41: 435–454.

Bowlby, J. (1969) *Attachment and Loss: Volume 1. Attachment*. New York: Basic Books.

Bowlby, J. (1988) *A Secure Base: Clinical Applications of Attachment Theory*. London: Routledge.

Byng-Hall, J. (1995) Creating a secure family base: Some implications of attachment theory for family therapy. *Family Process*, 34: 45–58.

Byng-Hall, J. (2002) Relieving parentified children's burdens in families with insecure attachment patterns. *Family Process*, 41: 375–388.

Byng-Hall, J. (2008) The crucial roles of attachment in family therapy. *Journal of Family Therapy*, 30: 129–146.

Carter, B. and McGoldrick, M. (2005) *The Expanded Family Life Cycle: Individual, Family and Social Perspectives* (3rd edn). USA: Addison Wesley.

Dallos, R. and Vetere, A. (2022) *Systemic Therapy and Attachment Narratives: Applications in a Range of Clinical Settings*. Abingdon, UK: Routledge.

Edwards, M. (2002) Attachment, mastery and interdependence: A model of parenting processes. *Family Process*, 41: 389–404.

Erikson, E. (1985) *The Life Cycle Completed: A Review*. New York: Norton.

Ermisch, J. (2004) Parent and Adult-child Interactions: Empirical Evidence from Britain. Institute of Economic and Social Research Working Papers Number 2004-02, University of Essex.

Gower, M. (2011): Parenting Adult Children. A qualitative study of narratives of intergenerational attachment. Department of Psychosocial Studies School of Social Science, History and Philosophy, Birkbeck University of London. (A dissertation submitted for the degree of Doctor of Philosophy).

Gower, M. and Dowling, E. (2008) Parenting adult children – invisible ties that bind? *Journal of Family Therapy*, 30: 425–437.

Gower, M. and Dowling, E. (2017) Second phase parenting: Narratives of parenting when children become adults. In A. Vetere and E. Dowling (eds) *Narrative Therapies with Children and Their Families*. UK: Routledge.

Haley, J. (1973) *Uncommon Therapy*. New York: Norton.

Luescher, K. and Pillemer, K. (1998) Intergenerational ambivalence: A new approach to the study of parent-child relations in later life. *Journal of Marriage and the Family*, 60: 413–425.

McDermott, D. (2002) *Theoretical Background: Perspectives Informing Parent Education*. [Online]. www.parentingproject.org/background.htm (accessed 6 February 2005).

McGoldrick, M., Giordano, J. and Garcia-Preto, N. (2005) (eds) *Ethnicity and Family Therapy*. New York: Guilford Press.

Pillemer, K. and Suitor, J. (2002) Explaining mothers' ambivalence toward their adult children. *Journal of Marriage and Family*, 64: 602–613.

Strauss, M. (2009) Bungee families. *Psychotherapy Networker*, 33: 18–20.

The Children's Commissioner. (2022) The Family Review. www.childrens commissioner. gov.uk/family/family-review/ (accessed 03/10/2022).

Umberson, D. (1992) Relationships between adult children and their parents: Psychological consequences for both generations. *Journal of Marriage and Family*, 54: 664–674.

Worldwide Words. *Family.* (2022) www.worldwidewords.org/topicalwords/tw-fam1.htm (accessed 09/01/2022).

Chapter 16

Polyamorous relationships

Inspirations in the search for new ways of understanding safety and security

Szymon Chrząstowski

During my childhood Poland was one of many countries under the thumb of the Soviet Union. The Berlin Wall is a well-known symbol of this period. History is filled with many examples of walls that were meant to ensure security (Eveleigh, 2016). For many readers brought up in Western Europe, the Berlin Wall might seem a symbol of oppression and harm, but in me it aroused at the time curiosity about what lay beyond the wall. My curiosity was also stimulated by one of the first and most important books I read during my childhood *My Family and Other Animals* by Gerald Durrell. The main character, a 10-year-old boy, spends his days exploring Corfu and is fascinated by its natural history. Corfu is portrayed in Durrell's story as a safe haven and secret garden, waiting to be discovered.

I think that the urge to peep over a fence or wall in order to see what lies on the other side is present in many people, and it is this curiosity that invites me to reflect on polyamorous relationships. They have become a permanent part of what we understand as different forms of adults being together in the contemporary world. On the other hand, we are also faced with different kinds of walls in our heads, which are fixed ways of thinking or even prejudices that shape our thoughts. However, walls are not just there for us to try to topple them, but, most importantly, to reflect upon them. Polyamorous relationships challenge current ways of thinking about security in relationships. Reflections on security in polyamorous relationships topple walls (especially cultural ones) but also prompt thoughts on the limitations of different concepts, including those that are vital to psychotherapy, such as a couple, a relationship, and a family.

As a psychotherapist and researcher, I deal with the psychological aspects of safety and security. I am interested in polyamorous relationships from this perspective. Polyamorous relationships challenge the limitations of current thinking about safety and security. The creators of attachment theory focussed on relationships in dyads (Bowlby, 1988/2005), leading to the conviction that this theory did not have the capacity to explain the functioning of polyamorous relationships (cf. Fern, 2020). Nevertheless, attachment theory is still evolving (Katz and Katz, 2021) under the influence of a mutual permeation of attachment theory and systemic theory.

DOI: 10.4324/9781003308096-20

In my work, especially that with couples and families, I see that polyamorous relationships are one way for adults to form and maintain relationships. They can even be viewed more broadly as a way of being in the world. This way of being in a relationship can bring challenges. Some of these challenges relate to insecurity. These challenges, like other life challenges that we all face, require reflection and discussion with close others. The challenges faced by people in polyamorous relationships don't appear to be that different from those faced by people in monogamous relationships. The difference, however, is that polyamorous relationships require a more thoughtful approach to these challenges.

While writing this chapter, I became more aware that a sense of security is an important issue for only some of the people who form polyamorous relationships. Researchers exploring the motivation of people who are considering or already engaged in a polyamorous relationship do not single out security as the primary polyamory motivation (Hnatkovičová and Bianchi, 2022).

A relationship or relationships?

Before I move on to analyse a sense of security within polyamorous relationships, I would first like to consider the very concept of a relationship between adults. This term is, in fact, still evolving. Much attention is currently being paid to polyamorous relationships[1] in academic literature, that is, multi-partner relationships based on sexual or emotional non-exclusivity with the consent of all the persons involved (Fern, 2020; Fosse, 2021). Relationships of a highly varied structure are created in this way, where, for example, one relationship may be considered more important (in relationships with a hierarchical structure) or, on the contrary, all relationships possess the same status of importance.

Indeed, these varied forms of relationships (not only mono- and polyamorous) first emerged much earlier than in the 21st century but presently, due to cultural transformations that have taken place in Western society, as well as the established position of gender studies and queer theory in the academic world, relationships other than monogamous are widely accepted and not treated as a sign of deviation. Recent studies in the United States on a sample of almost 3,500 participants have revealed that 1 out of 6 people (16.8 per cent) want to engage in polyamory, and 1 out of 9 people (10.7 per cent) have already done so at some point in their life (Moors, Gesselman, and Garcia, 2021). The results of research conducted in the UK show that almost one in four said they would be open to a polyamorous relationship (Psychreg, 2022). Young people especially are open to the idea of a polyamorous relationship (Levine, 2020).

Due to the diversity of polyamorous relationships mentioned above (a good illustration of which are glossaries of terms describing polyamorous relationships), it is beyond the scope of this chapter to attempt to define them. The interested reader is referred to the literature on the subject (for example, *Rewriting the Rules* by Meg-John Barke or *The Many Faces of Polyamory* by Magdalena J. Fosse).

From the point of view of a psychotherapist, the term polyamorous relationship constitutes a broad category that includes a variety of very different types of relationships between adults. These relationships do not have to be erotic. The line between friendship and polyamorous relationship is also not so clear cut. It seems crucial to me to consider how the people who create these relationships define their relationships.

Security in a relationship from the attachment theory perspective

From the attachment theory perspective, safety is the foundation of a relationship (Dallos and Vetere, 2022), also allowing people in romantic relationships to satisfy their attachment needs and feel safe, where they know that they can count on each other when feeling anxious or tense, or when their psychological well-being is threatened. A sense of security is born in the child-carer dyad (Bowlby, 1988/ 2005). Early good attachment experiences lead to a safe attachment model that underpins the development of adaptive forms of regulating emotions and mentalisation abilities (Holmes, 2001). Cindy Hazan and Phillip Shaver (1987) used an attachment process category to define the romantic feelings binding an adult couple, where there are similar dependencies to the attachment between an infant and their caregiver.

Contemporary attachment theory is developing in several directions, which shed light on different aspects of a sense of security. Attachment theory has also developed as a theory concerning self-regulation and co-regulation. The attachment aspect of regulation is dealt with by Schore (2019), Mikulincer and Shaver (2016), as well as Dallos and Vetere (2020). In this approach, a sense of security in an adult is closely related to the ability to self-regulate one's affective states, as well as co-regulate emotions (coping with tension and stress with other people's help). A sense of security is underpinned by good regulation of emotions (in its two aspects of self-regulation and co-regulation of emotions), and this is the foundation of reflectivity.

Attachment theory has also inspired studies of mentalisation (Fonagy et al., 2005). This construct is broadly discussed in contemporary scientific literature. Reflectivity (Dallos and Draper, 2015) has been written about and valued for a long time now, both within psychotherapy and beyond.[2] The ability to reflect related to the activation of cortical structures in the brain allows a person to consciously choose how they react to danger (contrary to automatic responses related to subcortical centres). Therefore, whether we feel safe or not to some extent depends on the conscious effort that is undertaken.

A different direction of development in attachment theory is proposed by the Dynamic Maturational Model of Attachment and Adaptation (DMM), created by Patricia Crittenden (2016). Within this concept, particular attention is paid to threats and to adapting to them. The term threat entails various forms of emotional deprivation, rejection, neglect, loss of a person with whom one has a close relationship, and physical, psychological and economic violence. The ability to optimally adapt to a threat is more important than a sense of security, which stems from managing to cope effectively with it. A very interesting aspect of DMM is that it points to the psychological costs of coping with threat (or, to put it differently, maintaining a sense of security). These costs result from emotional and cognitive distortions that are key to coping with threats.

Two aspects of a sense of security

In DMM, a sense of security can be treated as the outcome of adapting well to threat (Crittenden, 2016). However, such reasoning is not enough in itself to sufficiently describe the complexity that (having) a sense of security entails. Attachment theory emphasises that a child who feels safe is eager to explore their surroundings (cf. Holmes, 2001). Similarly, an adult who has a sense of security is curious about the world and also ready to explore it. Thus, a sense of security does not only result from effective ways of coping with threat that an individual has worked out for themselves.

Curiosity is often considered to stem from a sense of security; hence, a sense of security should be treated as an essential prerequisite for curiosity. When a person feels safe, they can be curious. Curiosity about the world, then, is rooted in a sense of security, although it sometimes does not seem to depend solely on it. The history of humankind is full of examples of how curiosity prevailed over a sense of threat and led to many discoveries. Perhaps we are not right in thinking that curiosity is something separate from experiencing security.

A sense of security comprises two aspects. The first aspect, which can be considered negative, is security resulting from the absence of threat, while the second, positive aspect, is security as a readiness to explore the world. In both cases, however, a sense of security is created by the attachment experiences collected up to that point in implicit and explicit memory, by how a person regulates their arousal, what knowledge they have about their mind (including knowledge of their own resources) and, finally, how they integrate what they feel with what they think. Thus, the experience of security is the outcome of the integration of cognitive and affective information. It is connected with the fact that an adult can adequately identify threats and knows (implicit or explicit) how to cope with them.

Security as the ability to play

Psychologists have devoted a lot of attention to the role of play, particularly in relation to children. Less attention is paid to play in adulthood, although adults like playing and look for opportunities to engage in play (Brown, 2009). Living close to the ocean, I have the opportunity of observing how adults play: jumping in the waves, splashing each other, collecting pebbles and shells, or adorning themselves with seaweed necklaces. Play not only allows a person to rest and regulate their arousal, it is also a sign of happiness, serving to build relationships and helping a person experience themselves, often somewhat differently to how they do in everyday life. A sense of security is expressed through play, although not every play means that there is a sense of security.

The issue of play among adults and how it relates to attachment requires a wholly separate analysis, but I would like to focus here on just one of its possible manifestations, namely, sex. The relationships between play, sexual behaviour and attachment have been discussed by, among others, Jeremy Holmes (2001). Studies have shown that attachment insecurities are associated with more negative feelings and lower levels of feeling loved and cared for by a partner during sexual activity (Beaulieu et al., 2022). Sexual behaviour also serves to satisfy attachment needs. However, it can also be a sign of play, where adults spontaneously explore new experiences, getting to know themselves and other people. Play in sex combines curiosity with the possibility of experiencing themselves, their bodies, emotions and relationships with others in a new way. Play in sex is not only linked to curiosity (both of oneself, the partner, and their relationship), but also to joy. Joy shared with one's partner is one of those experiences that constitutes the resources of the relationship and is also a personal psychological resource.

The relationship between sex and a sense of security is complex. On the one hand, curiosity about the other person and about oneself in relation to that person can intensify sexual desire and its various manifestations. On the other hand, it seems that a sense of security sometimes lessens desire. Sex combines the two aspects of security discussed above and reveals that security also means a readiness to take the risk of exploring the unknown. Sex allows a person to be present, sensitive and responsive to their partner.

From attachment security to narratives about security

One of the challenges that psychotherapists currently face in psychotherapy is how to combine social constructionism with modernist ways of thinking about the psychological functioning of a person (Dallos and Draper, 2015; Dallos and Vetere, 2022). The experience of a sense of security can also be approached from both perspectives. A lack of security, especially related to experiencing complex trauma, has a negative impact on the development of the nervous system. The experience of security "emerges from internal psychological states regulated by the autonomic nervous system", thus, it has its measurable underlying neurophysiological substrate (Porges, 2022, p. 1). The linguistic dimension of attachment security is, of course, also analysed in attachment theory, which brings it closer in this aspect to the constructionist approach.

The gaining of social constructionism shows just how experience is shaped in language and how language constructs this experience (Dallos and Draper, 2015). Over time, the experience of security begins to depend on the integration of emotional and thought processes and, as a result of this, a growing ability to reflect; reflectivity is also manifest in the ability to create a cohesive narrative about security. The experience of security in adults is also expressed in narratives about security, and both personal experiences and cultural factors affect the shape of these narratives.

Experiencing security in polyamorous relationships

Jessica Fern (2020), based on her own clinical experiences of working with clients, posits the theory that a sense of security in polyamorous relationships is very possible. She also cites research findings that contradict the claim that polyamory is connected with insecure attachment styles. A review of studies carried out by Katz and Katz (2021) comes to a similar conclusion.

Fern (2020) also points to various difficulties that people deciding to have such relationships may encounter. These difficulties primarily concern a sense of security. At the same time, Fern (2020) states that a dyadic relationship does not guarantee a sense of security. People in monogamous relationships experience insecurity in various circumstances. At this point, we can, of course, argue that polyamorous relationships provide more opportunities to feel threat. However, the essence of experiencing security is not avoiding threats but, first and foremost, knowing how to cope with them.

Fern (2020) does not deny that polyamorous relationships can be an attempt to cope with the absence of a sense of security. Simultaneous partners constitute a chance to satisfy attachment needs. However, this may also apply to monogamous relationships, particularly so-called serial monogamy. A change in partners in monogamous relationships at intervals is sometimes motivated by subsequent attempts to find a person who will satisfy their attachment needs even better.

A separate issue remains the degree to which security in the attachment perspective can be experienced in polyamorous relationships. The results of one study have also shown that feeling secure can depend on the structure of the relationship (and its place in this structure). Greater variability in attachment security was found between partners in hierarchical relationships[3] than those in non-hierarchical relationships (Flicker et al., 2021).

The experience of security appears in relationships with close persons to whom we turn when we feel fear and threat, and these persons are attentive, sensitive, and responsive to what is happening to us, their partner, at the time. Attentiveness, sensitivity and responsiveness can appear in many relationships, including polyamorous ones. Perhaps it is not only the characteristics mentioned above that will determine the experience of security in these relationships but also the time that can be devoted to specific partners. Thus, it is not so much about the psychological limitations of the persons creating these relationships but the physical and the easily measured factors that can limit presence and responsiveness.

From traumatic experiences to stories

A particular situation mentioned by Fern (2020) is the experience of complex trauma. It affects the whole psychological functioning of a given person, including the nature of the close relationships they have established. Traumatic experiences reduce a sense of security, although it should be borne in mind that they can be of a varied degree and manner. Dangerous events experienced by a person can lead to trauma responses. These responses may affect the level of security and, as a consequence, the person's overall functioning.

In so much as the experience of security is rooted in early attachment experiences, the most complex sign in an adult is a cohesive story about the experience of security. It is a story about coping with threat, curiosity in relation to oneself and one's surroundings, and joy derived from play. This may involve many stories about the experience of security including, of course, the story of experiencing security in polyamorous relationships. These stories subsequently help to enhance a sense of security, both individually and in a relationship. This phenomenon is also used by narrative therapists.

Stories are also a well-known way of coping with a sense of threat, from the very dawn of humanity. Stories help us to cope with traumatic experiences and threats, and to strengthen our sense of security. However, in non-English literature especially, there are not many examples of stories about polyamorous relationships that are a source of security, care, and allow for thriving. Perhaps such stories are still finding their place in culturally dominant narratives.

The meaning of trust

John Gottman (2011) believes that mutual trust between partners is a key characteristic of good relationships. Trust is the certainty that our partner will be there when we need them. This certainty allows us to feel safe. But what does trust mean in polyamorous relationships? In the classic view of trust, polyamorous relationships carry more risk of attachment wounds. Perhaps in polyamorous relationships, trust takes on a different meaning, that is, talking openly about one's needs and ways of meeting them (and also in dyads, so perhaps that definition of trust applies to all close and simultaneous relationships, e.g. friends, colleagues, lovers, etc.).

An analysis of a sense of security in polyamorous relationships also leads to another issue, namely, the semantic scope of the terms "security" or "trust". An interesting point is how much the scope of these terms should be broadened in line with cultural changes, to an extent that does not make them so wide as to render them useless. Certainly, the experience of psychological security has several dimensions: attachment, narrative, cultural, and social.

What does it mean to trust a partner who has other partners? Do people in polyamorous relationships have to exert a greater effort in order to build their sense of security by referring to their own, individual psychological resources and resilience? These questions deserve to be answered but it is crucial that this is done through methodologically sound research. Perhaps the very term "polyamorous relationship" is problematic in itself. After all, these types of relationships take many different forms that are fundamentally different from each other (Sheff, 2014). There has even been an evolution in the meaning of the term polyamory. In this sense, the question of trust (as well as of a sense of security) in such relationships may be an unhelpful question to ask as it concerns very different relationships. Hence, the term itself is a metaphorical wall behind which lies a wide array of various forms of being together in a relationship.

Age, security and polyamory

When speaking of different forms of polyamorous relationships, it is also worth noting that they can be formed by adults of different ages (Labriola, 2023). This is important in so much as a sense of security, its individual components and the ways of coping with its loss, seem to also depend on the age of a given person (Kubíčková, Rašticová and Hazuchová, 2022). Every life stage has its own developmental specificity that can potentially influence a sense of safety.

Both issues related to ageing and various forms of adult relationships are complex therefore, it is easy to generalise. A network of people in polyamorous relationships can be supportive when facing the challenges of aging. This, in turn, raises questions about when we are dealing with a polyamorous relationship and when with a friendship. If we assume that a polyamorous relationship does not have to be based on an erotic relationship (as in many marriages), how can we define friendship, especially one where a friend becomes an attachment figure?

One of the people I have worked with in the past (who was in a polyamorous relationship), knowing that I was working on a chapter about polyamory for this book, shared her experience of this relationship with me. I will quote here, with her consent, part of her statement: "The older I get, the more time I need to experience everything I experience in relationships. I feel these emotions more intensely. Each person is a new emotion. I can't hold them all anymore."

Polyamorous relationships are form of being-in-the-world. Like any relationship, this one also brings opportunities (for additional support) and risks (suffering attachment injuries) in relation to a sense of security. Constant reflection can help in dealing with the challenges of these relationships.

Community as a source of insecurity and security

A significant source of a lack of security can also be social attitudes towards polyamorous relationships. Rejection is one of the principal threats to attachment. The results of research carried out on a group of 463 Portuguese-speaking adults point to the social stigmatisation of people in polyamorous relationships (Cardoso, Pascoal and Maiochi, 2021). CNM relationships are perceived as serving mainly sexual needs, where feelings and intimacy have a lesser role. Studies carried out in Poland on students participating in psychological support programmes have also revealed respondents to have negative attitudes towards relationships other than monogamous ones (Grunt-Mejer and Łyś, 2019). The studies mentioned earlier were carried out in countries where the dominant religion is Roman Catholicism. Nevertheless, such negative attitudes are present in many societies. Kevin

Patterson, in his book *Love's not Colour Blind* (2018), describes the experiences of black Americans in polyamorous relationships.

As with many groups of people at risk of exclusion, belonging to a community can provide security. This community is made up of other people who prefer CNM relationships. Currently, social media enable the creation of such online communities, which do not have to be based on geographical proximity. Although not without threats, these online communities give them a voice and offer support.

Insecurity as an expression of suffering

A sense of insecurity is linked to feeling mental anguish or suffering. Suffering puts up walls. With time, these walls (which protect a person from suffering) become a source of suffering itself. If the relationship becomes a source of suffering related to insecurity, it ceases to serve the people creating it and can be considered problematic. However, this applies to all kinds of relationships. The decisive factor for creating either a mono- or polyamorous relationship should be the potential suffering of the other person.

Literature on polyamorous relationships emphasises that such relationships should be created on the basis of mutual consent. However, informed consent is not always easy. This agreement should be based on an embodied sense of security and a thorough understanding of one's own mind. A lack of these increases the chances of making decisions that stem from feelings of anguish or heighten them, and can apply to any relationship. Insecurity triggers self-protective strategies. The latter restore a sense of security, though possibly at the price of cognitive and emotional distortions of one's experience. The decision to start a CNM relationship or stay in a polyamorous relationship may, after all, be dictated by such distortions. The importance of open communication in polyamorous relationships is emphasised in various textbooks, but this communication must be based on a clear recognition of one's own emotions, thoughts and needs.

The value of open communication is therefore very high, but sensitivity to the suffering of the other person would seem to be crucial. Some degree of suffering in a relationship is unavoidable. The suffering associated with insecurity, however, affects us in a special way. One of my client said:

> Polyamory sometimes becomes an excuse for meeting one's own needs. From people in polyamorous relationships, I hear: I am free, and the other person must accept it. Such statements make him feel insecure. Polyamory is about love, and love is not only freedom but also the ability to sacrifice.

Searching for new ways of understanding security

Let us now sum up the theses that have been posited in this chapter. Security is not simply a feeling but is underpinned by complex psychological processes. It is secondary in relation to them and not, as it may seem, primary. The way in which a sense of security arises is also sometimes wrongly understood. It is not security that came first (during the course of life), but the relationship. Security is experienced in a relationship and, with time, the nature of this experience becomes more complex. It has its individual and relational dimensions.

A polyamorous relationship can be treated as one of the ways of being in the world. Different developmental pathways and life events can lead to this very way of being in the world. Each of these ways of being in the world is connected with experiencing security or its absence. A polyamorous relationship can be a way of coping with a lack of security and threat. If this is the case, it increases the potential probability of various difficulties, both in the relationship itself and in individual ones.

However, a polyamorous relationship also creates an opportunity for satisfying innate curiosity in relation to oneself in a relationship or relationships with other close persons, and in relation to those people and their way of experiencing. This curiosity can lead to a richer auto-narration and (therefore?) a more comprehensive knowledge of the self. This knowledge in an adult is necessary to foster one's own security and the security of the persons to whom one is closest. A polyamorous relationship (just like a monogamous relationship) is also an opportunity to spontaneously and joyfully play within the relationship with these persons. Such play means experiencing the joys of the activities engaged in with such persons (where such play cannot wound others). Hence, the experience of security is not directly related to the type of relationship itself.

The theoretical and research works concerning a sense of security in adults focus on attachment security and threat to attachment security (especially trauma). Studies on how security is experienced in different kinds of relationship and situations, as well as the meanings given to such experiences, may prove to be crucial in gaining a deeper understanding of what security constitutes. They could help in identifying aspects of security that go unnoticed in attachment theory. An interesting direction of research would be an analysis of the broadly understood sense of security in various groups of people in polyamoric relationships, taking into account gender, relationship status and type of relationship. Another topic that is beyond the scope of this chapter is how love can be understood in polyamorous relationships. It is love that allows us to risk our own safety. Various ways of being in relationships create the metaphorical island of Corfu (or perhaps the whole archipelago) mentioned at the beginning of the chapter. This island spurs curiosity and invites exploratory expeditions.

Notes

1 I will be using CNM as the abbreviation of consensual non-monogamy relationships.
2 These terms are not identical but relate to each other.
3 In the hierarchical polyamorous relationship configuration, people tend to prioritize one or more partners (designated as primary) over others.

References

Beaulieu, N., Brassard, A., Bergeron, S. and Peloquin, K (2020). Why do you have sex and does it make you feel better? Integrating attachment theory, sexual motives, and sexual well-being in long-term couples. *Journal of Social and Personal Relationships*, 0(0) 1–22. DOI: 10.1177/02654075221108759 Available from: https://journals.sagepub.com/doi/full/10.1177/02654075221108759 [accessed Aug 12 2022].

Beaulieu, N., Brassard, A., Bergeron, S. and Péloquin, K. (2022). Why do you have sex and does it make you feel better? Integrating attachment theory, sexual motives, and sexual well-being in long-term couples. Journal of Social and Personal Relationships, 39(12), 3753–3774. https://doi.org/10.1177/02654075221108759

Bowlby, J. A. (1988/2005). *Secure Base. Clinical Application of Attachment Theory.* Routledge.

Brown, S. (2009). Play. *How It Shapes the Brain, Opens the Imagination and Invigorates the Soul.* Penguin Group.

Cardoso, D., Pascoal, P. M. and Maiochi, F. H. (2021). Correction to: Defining polyamory: A thematic analysis of lay people's definitions. *Archives of Sexual Behavior.* Advance online publication. https://doi.org/10.1007/s10508-021-02113-6

Crittenden, P. (2016). *Rising Parents. Attachment, representation, and treatment* (2nd ed.). Routledge.

Crittenden, P. and Landini, A. (2011). *Assessing Adult Attachment. A Dynamic Maturational Approach to Discourse Analysis.* W.W. Norton & Company.

Dallos, R. and Draper, R. (2015). *An Introduction to Family Therapy: Systemic Theory and Practice* (4th ed.). Open University Press. McGraw-Hill Education.

Dallos, R. and Vetere, A. (2022). *Systemic Therapy and Attachment Narratives. Applications in a Range Clinical Settings* (2nd ed.). Routledge.

Eveleigh, D. (2016). What history teaches us about walls. *The New York Times.* Available from: www.nytimes.com/2016/05/28/upshot/what-history-teaches-us-about-walls.html [accessed Aug 12 2022].

Fern, J. (2020). *Polysecure: Attachment, Trauma and Consensual Nonmonogamy.* Thorntree Press.

Flicker, S. M., Sancier-Barbosa, F., Moors, A. C. et al. (2021). A closer look at relationship structures: Relationship satisfaction and attachment among people who practice hierarchical and non-hierarchical polyamory. *Archives of Sexual Behaviour*, 50, 1401–1417. https://doi.org/10.1007/s10508-020-01875-9

Fonagy, P., György, G., Jurist, E. and Target, M. (2005). *Affect Regulation, Mentalization, and the Development of Self.* Other Press.

Fosse, M. (2021). *The Many Faces of Polyamory. Longing and Belonging in Concurrent Relationships.* Routledge.

Gottman, J. (2011). *The Science of trust. Emotional attunement for couples.*W.W. Norton & Company.

Grunt-Mejer, K. and Łyś, A. (2019). They must be sick: Consensual non-monogamy through the eyes of psychotherapists. *Sexual and Relationship Therapy*, 37(2):1–24. DOI: 10.1080/14681994.2019.1670787

Hazan C. and Shaver P. (1987). Romantic love conceptualized as an attachment process. *Journal of Personality and Social Psychology, 52*, 511–524.

Hnatkovičová, D. and Bianchi, G. (2022). Models of motivations for engaging in polyamorus relationships. *Sexologies*, 31, 3, 184–194. https://doi.org/10.1016/j.sexol.2022.03.003

Holmes, J. (2001). *The Search for the Secure Base. Attachment Theory and Psychotherapy.* Routledge.

Katz, M. and Katz, E. (2021). Reconceptualizing attachment theory through the lens of polyamory. *Sexuality Culture*, 26(2), 792–809. https://doi.org/10.1007/S12119-021-09902-0

Kubíčková, L., Rašticová, M. and Hazuchová, N. (2022). What are Czech seniors afraid of? Study on feeling of safety among seniors. SAGE Open, 12(3). https://doi.org/10.1177/21582440221116106

Labriola, K. (2023). *Polyamorous Elders. Aging in Open Relationships.*Rowman & Littlefield.

Levine, N. (2020). This is how many young people are open to a polyamorous relationship. www.refinery29.com/en-gb/young-people-polyamorous-relationship-study   [accessed Feb 14 2023].

Mikulincer, M. and Shaver, P. R. (2016). *Attachment in Adulthood: Structure, Dynamics and Change* (2nd ed.). Guilford Press.

Moors A. C., Gesselman A. N. and Garcia J. R. (2021). Desire, familiarity, and engagement in polyamory: Results from a national sample of single adults in the United States. *Frontiers in Psychology.* 12:619640. http://doi.org/10.3389/fpsyg.2021.619640

Patterson, K (2018). *Love's not Color Blind. Race and Representation in Polyamorous and Other Alternative Communities.* Thorntree Press.

Porges, S. W. (2022). Polyvagal theory: A science of safety. *Frontiers in Integrative Neuroscience.* 16:871227. http://doi.org/10.3389/fnint.2022.871227

Psychreg (2022). 1 in 4 Brits consider polygamous relationship, survey reveals www.psych reg.org/brits-consider-polygamous-relationship/ [accessed Feb 14 2023].

Schore, A. N. (2019). *Right Brain Psychotherapy.* W. W. Norton & Company.

Shaver, P. R., Hazan, C. and Bradshaw, D. (1988). Love as attachment: The integration of three behavioral systems. In R. Sternberg and M. Barnes (Eds), *The Psychology of Love* (pp. 68–99). Yale University Press.

Sheff, E. (2014). The Polyamorists Next Door: Inside Multiple-Partner Relationship and Families. Rowman & Littlefield.

Chapter 17

Dying, death, and bereavement

Jo Wilson

Introduction

One cannot fail to be moved by the American psychiatrist Irvin Yalom's account of his wife's dying and his subsequent bereavement (Yalom and Yalom, 2021), or the actor and comedian Rob Delaney's account of the death of his son (Delaney, 2022), or the journalist Merope Mills' experience of the death of her daughter when the hospital sent "institutional condolences" and admitted "lessons should be learned" (Mills, 2022). The raw suffering of those experiencing the pain of the loss of someone fundamental to their lives years after they have died is almost excruciating to read. For the discussion that is to come "bereavement or loss" refers to the state of having lost somebody or something, "grief" refers to what is felt, "mourning" relates to what is done (Lofland, 1985).

Context

Dying is a natural part of the life cycle. In 2021 there were 586,334 adult deaths in England and Wales (Office of National Statistics, 2023). Many who die are parents, and approximately 111 children are bereaved of a parent every day (Child Bereavement UK, 2022). In 2020, 2,226 infant deaths (aged under 1 year) and 789 child deaths (aged 1 to 15 years) occurred in England and Wales (Quayle, 2022), meaning that 1 in 29 of 5–16-year-olds have been bereaved of a parent or sibling – that's a child in every average class (Child Bereavement UK, 2022). The longer life expectancy of UK residents means many people are adults before they experience bereavement and with many people dying in hospitals, as a society we have lost access to opportunities to watch and learn how to "be with" the dying and bereaved. This means we can be poorly equipped for bereavement, increasing the risk for people to feel very unsafe in their own world.

Attachment

Attachment is a lasting psychological connectedness between human beings (Bowlby, 1997). Our first attachment relationship is usually with our parent/s,

DOI: 10.4324/9781003308096-21

but over our life course we develop relationships with others – our grandparents, friends, teachers, and ultimately our partner, friends, and our own children. How we learn to be in relationship the first time with our parents is often a template for relationships across our life course. If we have been parented in a secure manner, where our needs are responded to and met in a calm and consistent way, then Bowlby describes this as a "secure base" (Bowlby, 2005). We will have had the best opportunity to explore the people and world and understand it and our place in it. We will likely form relationships with our children and parent them similarly.

Not all adults were parented in a secure and consistent way as a child. For multiple reasons, for example, mental health, alcohol, or intense work patterns, the child is unable to have their emotional needs met for such things as reassurance, or soothing. This is estimated to be 10 per cent of the population (Silver, 2013). This speaks to the benefit of the wider family, schooling, and social community, because all children have access to other adults who could provide some of the comfort to a child of having their needs met and learning how to form secure and trusting relationships. When people can recognise and reflect that the attachment pattern, they have learned from their parents is not the quality of care they deserved or wish to replicate, they can learn how to use another secure base to become one themselves (Silver, 2013).

A reflexive stance – my narrative

I now view bereavement as a "tool" that exposes our attachments and challenges our coping mechanisms throughout our life course. It has been a long journey. My mother died when I was eight years old, my gran (her mother, and apart from my father, my mainstay of emotional loving support) when I was 11. It was the most wretched of times and whilst my father remarried and I remained close to him, I am glad of the enabling support of the deputy head in my secondary school. She gave me consistent and kind feedback that has helped me to this day. I am as sure as is possible that I chose the career of a nurse as I had had those skills role modelled to me (my mother was a nurse), and as a connection to my mother.

I have two siblings from my father's second marriage. Recently, as I had the happiest of times with my half sister and children (my nephews) at supper, I was struck by the fact that I would never have had this happiness had my mum still lived. The juxtaposition of the continued loss of my mum alongside the gain of all my siblings and family over the intervening 50 years is hard to articulate. I wondered what my mum would think. I imagine her at the table and being glad for us – she was very much a family person.

I have spent my career leaning into caring for adults who are dying and supporting their families. I now support adults who are caring for their dying child and into bereavement. I have written UK national guidance on how to care for the deceased and to recognise that they are dead, in order that families can feel supported at this critical transition (Hospice UK, 2022). In mountaineering terms, I describe myself as being able to tolerate living above 8000 m – "the death zone" – where most people cannot survive without oxygen. I too need oxygen in the form of counselling, clinical supervision, and to come "off the mountain" regularly for time with those who are dear to me, activities that nourish me and to take care of myself in all dimensions of my life.

Why death causes grief?

The death of a significant person in our lives causes feelings of intense loss and sadness as we have lost our "secure base" and the person we turned to to have fun and pleasure, to help us when we were struggling and for whom we have enjoyed being their secure base. Not all bereavements cause the same level of grief. We are not all attached to those who have died in the same way and as we progress through life we can learn many skills that can help us cope with our bereavements. Niemeyer indicates how these skills can be learned with small unwelcome losses, and then we can use these skills to help us with the larger losses in our lives:

> Human beings … are wired for attachment in a world of impermanence. With the many unwelcome losses of life – of people, places, projects, and possessions in seemingly endless succession, we are called on to reconstruct a world of meaning that has been challenged by loss, at every level from the simple habit structures of our daily lives, through our identities in a social world, to our personal and collective cosmologies, whether secular or spiritual.
>
> (Neimeyer et al., 2014, p. 486)

If it can be identified that a person is likely to be bereaved, then anticipatory work can take place to help them proactively cope, have meaningful conversations, access social support, and make sensible provision for finances, and so on, in bereavement, all of which can help make bereavement more manageable (Rogalla, 2020).

There are bereavements that we know are additionally hard due to the depth of the attachment. These are the death of a parent when the bereaved is a child or young person (Bergman, Axberg, and Hanson, 2017), the death of a life partner, and particularly when a parent is bereaved of a child (Harper, O'Connor, and O'Carroll, 2014). The additional sense of responsibility and desire to care for the child places an additional layer of complexity on the grief. Parents say that being bereaved of a child is worse than losing their own parent or facing their own terminal illness. Bereavements that are also tough relate to the circumstances of the death. Sudden death, or death by trauma or suicide, where there is no ability to prepare psychologically for the bereavement, carry an increased risk for complicated grief, as do those bereavements that are unvalidated by society, called "disenfranchised grief" (Doka, 1999). Examples of disenfranchised grief usually relate to areas of the population who are underserved in terms of bereavement support. This may relate to people who are grieving and in prison, or who are homeless, or people who feel because of the position they are in that they cannot access support, for example, LGBTQ communities. The availability of support also affects the experience of bereavement in all circumstances. Bereavement consistently makes the top ten causes of homelessness cited by homeless people themselves and by those working in the sector (CARIS, 2010).

Some deaths do not involve terrible sorrow but contain relief (Williams, 2016). When a person has had a long illness and suffered, then it can be a relief for the bereaved to know the suffering has ended and the drains of caring are over. In addition, when the deceased has had an addiction, mental health issue, or was abusive, then the death can be a relief, although it does not preclude the bereavement being challenging.

Dimensions of loss

When a person is bereaved, it affects multiple dimensions of a person's life (Walter, 2017). The bereavement can affect the bereaved's identity, emotional equilibrium, their spiritual life, the practical manner of living, their health, their finances, their interaction with their community and, if the relationship involved intimacy, then this too is affected. Whilst the range of grief reactions are well documented (Penny and Relf, 2017), the expression is unique for each person. Our bereaved minds and our bodies can shock us with the strength of our feeling and emotion – they make our own internal world an unsafe place. Yalom describes how in the weeks following his wife's death he had powerful obsessions that he could not halt – about the massacre in Tiananmen Square, thoughts about women's breasts and sexual encounters, and he describes his powerlessness to stop these obsessions. He describes the waves of grief that hit him on days such as her birthday. He also describes his depression – "I've had a strong whiff of depression. I don't think I will ever forget the experience of immobility, deadness, of feeling inert and helpless" (Yalom and Yalom, 2021, p. 214).

Rob Delaney describes how, some months after his baby Henry had died, that he would not have minded if he had died too. At this time, he was married and had three surviving children. He had bought his wife Leah scuba-diving lessons as she had always wanted to learn. One of the things required in the training is to descend to the bottom of the pool and sit in darkness to prepare themselves for the situation of losing visibility. He said they were prepared by the instructor to be fearful, and some of the group were. At the bottom of the pool he describes how he consciously thought:

> I'm quite a bit closer to death twelve feet underwater and without sight than I was a few minutes ago … I won't take the regulator out of my mouth and inhale a lungful of water on purpose, but it if got knocked out … and I panicked and inhaled and they couldn't revive me – well it would be ok … there was a harmony with the knowledge that my son had died and my own death would see me walk through a door he had walked through. We would share one more thing together. And that would be fucking great.
>
> (Delaney, 2022, p. 7)

Merope needed to be physically close to her daughter's grave and so she now lives on the island where she holidayed, and her daughter died. She has made this transition, but for many who are bereaved this can be a time of extreme physical insecurity. Many elderly frail people are cared for by younger members of their families who receive state financial payments for looking after their relative. They can live in the older person's home. If, when the older person dies, the carer has not been prepared, then they can find themselves without a home or income, and it can be a time of great anxiety and insecurity.

It can be a time of social isolation as friends and family withdraw or do not know how to comfort the bereaved. This is described by Cariad Jones

> The social awkwardness we feel when talking about death comes, unsurprisingly, from a place of fear. That might be a fear of upsetting a griever, fear of not saying the "right" thing or making their day worse than it already is. And this leads to people avoiding the conversation, changing the subject, saying nothing at all (so weird), or making the sort of blundering, ill-thought-through comments that a griever has to get adept at handling. We will all die; we all know someone who has died – shouldn't we have got good at talking about it by now?
> (Lloyd, 2023, para. 4)

Bereavement can also cause a spiritual crisis. Klass describes this as "how average, normal people go about reconstructing their lives when one of the foundations they thought they could trust has shifted … when one of their primary attachments has been lost" (Klass, 1999, p. 3) . I argue that grief shows up in the quiet, safe spaces of our lives and renders them unsafe for a while. Yalom describes how in his own home he initially turned his wife's portrait in the sunroom to the wall, because he could not bear the provocation of his grief and his bodily reaction of weeping that was stimulated by looking at her.

Safety and protection

The pain of grief can be overwhelming, and whilst it changes, it never goes away. Losing a parent, losing a life partner, and losing a child is a permanent condition. It is why some professionals do not consider they provide "counselling" support" (Seigal, 2017). In contrast to other counselling situations, where people hope they will ultimately feel better, in bereavement people mainly want to live with their pain and use this to underscore the relationship with the person who has died. The question then is what helps us feel safe and secure in the face of ongoing pain.

Death is not the end of attachment

It is proposed that the bereaved, rather than aiming to come to some place of acceptance with the death of a key person in their life (such as Kubler Ross described), or detachment from the deceased (such as Freud described), can continue to have a relationship with the deceased through the presence of an ongoing inner relationship (Neimeyer, Baldwin, and Gillies, 2006). This has been called a continuing bond (Klass, Silverman, and Nickman, 1996). It is proposed that during the grieving process, the bereaved remain involved and attached to their dead key person through the active construction of inner representations of the deceased. The deceased continues to influence the bereaved, and mourning represents an evolution of adaptation of and transformed connection with the deceased (Root and Exline, 2014).

The nature of a continuing bond

The nature of a continuing bond is somewhat predicated on the fact that the bereaved had a "good quality" relationship with the deceased, and that it is beneficial in some way to self soothe the physical loss of the person by a continued connection, and to build a life where the deceased help our "better self" live in line with their values in some way. We can learn much from Dennis Klass's work with bereaved parents. Whilst respecting the very uniqueness of a bereaved parent's grief, there are similarities with "all grieving". Bereaved parents describe themselves as "newly bereaved", "into their grief", "well along in their grief", and "resolved as much as it will be" (Klass, 1999). The lack of timescales feels helpful to those of us working with the bereaved and we expect this process to occur over years (certainly two) rather than months.

Klass describes how the parent develops the "continuing bond" with their deceased child, and the relationship of this bond to the parents' internal world and social relationships (Klass, 1999). When parents are newly bereaved, in terms of their inner world, they can experience dissociation, being out of touch with their child, and they anticipate a continuing bond, and the need to find a linking object that evokes the presence of their child. In relation to their social world there is isolation from usual support networks and inadequate symbol systems by which to interpret their new reality. As parents move into their grief, in terms of their inner world, they start to separate from their living child, connect with their child's pain and deal with the ambivalences of the parent child bond. With respect to the social world, they start to share the bond with others, they start to "be there" for other bereaved parents, they share practical solutions and validate for others the continuing interactions with their dead child. Once they are well along into their grief in terms of their inner world, they start to exchange pain for positive bond with their child, and they connect their bond with their own wellbeing. Socially, they start to stabilise and share the continuing bond through rituals and customs, by helping other bereaved parents as an expression of the bond and include the bond with wider communities. Once the parent's grief is resolved as much as it can be, the parents will have found a way to live with their sadness and their continuing bond guides the parent's better self as socially they make the child's life count, and they reintegrate into wider communities. There is often an experience of non-ordinary phenomena in the everyday world.

Klass is not proposing a linear progress from one set of experiences to another. It is a complex task to move through finding a linking object, finding the most helpful social support, negotiating the losses of a previous support system, developing, and stabilising their own unique bond, learning to live with their own sadness, helping others, and moving into life with the sense of making the deceased life count in their life. Bereaved parents can, for example, move straight into fundraising in the name of their dead child as soon as they are bereaved. They can, though, find that in time they are exhausted if they have not been able to access support from others and may need to pause their activity to attend to other aspects of their bereavement. However, in the time they have been fund raising, they may have found enough safety and security in other aspects of their lives to tolerate looking at the areas of bereavement that were causing them distress and that provoked the intense fundraising activity as a way to soothe and distract. For example, the bereaved may have returned to work, found financial security, reorganised their home to a home that does not include reminders of the deceased in every area.

Grief is a bodily experience as well as a psychological and spiritual experience. The distress of loss can show itself in symptoms of prolonged physiological stress, for example, headaches, back pain, auto-immune disease. Exercise metabolises the physiological metabolites of stress and helps a person feel calmer and more able to engage in relationships. Many bereaved people initially complete amazing feats of endurance and raise money for a cause. The physical activity temporarily soothes, the bereaved are remembered, communities are formed. This level of activity is rarely sustainable over a lifetime, and after the event the bereaved can need much support. Trauma-informed yoga has been identified to help distressed people regulate and soothe the emotional and bodily experience of distress such that they can start to consider their responses (Kolk et al., 2014). Yoga is helpful for bereaved people (CRUSE n.d.). This is likely due to the inclusion of breathwork to enhance the calming provided by activation of the parasympathetic nervous system, giving participants a sense of control over how their body moves, the opportunity to create beauty through movement, the promotion of care for the person and body, and kind social interactions with others. Even more than this though, over time bereaved people can start to include healthful activity into their daily life and associate the deceased as a guide to the bereaved better self. For example, my father taught me to swim. Later in life we occasionally swam together when I stayed with him, and I enjoyed our early morning time together. Now in bereavement I swim in the morning and am comforted by memories of my father, and I am grateful that he instilled a love of physical activity in my life and for the health benefits it brings. In this manner the continuing bond is expressed through my body feeling soothed and better after physical activity, which I associate with the memory of my father.

What the bond looks like to others can be very varied. The bond maybe expressed to others as a verbal reminiscence about the deceased (Walter, 1996), or involve photographs or possessions of the deceased. It may involve taking on characteristics of the deceased and doing things the deceased would have liked or the bereaved and deceased enjoyed doing together. It may involve special places (Jonsson and Walter, 2017) – either physically the deceased is perceived to be residing in a place such as a funeral plot, or the deceased is remembered at a certain place of significance. It may involve writing about the deceased such as Delaney and Yalom have undertaken. In the 21st century it may involve the memorialisation of the deceased on such things as social media or the intranet.

A very important aspect of being alongside the bereaved as the continuing bond with the deceased is matured is the acceptance and validation of non-ordinary phenomena. The bereaved can experience the presence of the deceased, signs that relate directly to the deceased, or signs from nature that are linked to the deceased and these bring solace (the ability to find comfort or consolation in distress) (Klass, 1999). Klass describes how the dead person is immortalised through the continuing bond with other spiritual realities in the parent's world and in this manner the bereaved remould their bond with their deceased person into one that can continue through their lives. The immortalised person and spiritual reality of which they are a part provides solace in the inner and social world, with a truth that cannot be challenged.

Klass champions the support group, but the maturation of the continuing bond can be via the company of someone who shares a similar experience, and/or who can empathise and validate the bereaved experience (Seigal, 2017). Children and family members can help stabilise the continuing bond by such things as contributing to the narrative or celebrating rituals. For professionals it is truly being alongside the bereaved. This is described by Klass and Siegal as getting to really know the dead person and being with the bereaved in their pain. Siegal described this metaphorically as "rambling" with the bereaved with the companionship of the deceased (Seigal, 2017, p. 136).

It should be noted that whilst the continuing bond is often generated serendipitously through the long relationship between the bereaved and deceased, it can, if a baby or child is likely to have a very short life, be actively generated by creating special events that lead to memory making for parents to draw on. Those who care for families and babies and children offer physical mementoes such as photos, locks of hair, and fingerprint moulding. Parents can spend days with their deceased child in a supported environment.

Are continuing bonds always helpful?

Like all models that try to describe grief, no one size fits all. Recent authors have found that continuing bonds as a therapeutic intervention are unhelpful at soothing bereaved people who have an avoidant nature or who are minimally anxious (Currier et al., 2015). Also, once the bond is internalised it is not static. For example, if a bereaved person moves, and part of the continuing bond was expressed by going to the graveside, it may be that this ritual can be dropped and the sense of the deceased being present transferred to the new home with as much sustenance and feeling of connection and safety. Continuing bonds can need renegotiating if a parent gets pregnant again after the death of a child (Seigal, 2017) or a person gains a new partner.

Implications for those who work with the bereaved

Klass sees it as potentially the role of everyone who comes across a bereaved person to be able to "be with" a bereaved person, to hear their story and the level of attachment to the deceased. He recognises too that not everyone can "be with". We can all think that grief is everyone else's job – such as a religious minister, or a bereavement counsellor. Yet because the bereaved will experience their loss in almost all dimensions of their lives, it is vital that we all develop skills. We can see this compassion related in the "tell us once" campaign (GOV.UK, n.d.) where the bereaved do not have to keep notifying different agencies of a person's death. The complexity of "winding up" someone's physical estate can aggravate their sense of loss and abandonment.

Klass says that if a bereaved person gets stuck in one aspect of the development of the continuing bond and a positive change is made in a different aspect of the bereavement, then it creates conditions for ripples of change. As someone who works with the bereaved, I really appreciate this model. I also value the concept of marginal gains – the theory that multiple small gains can add up – can create a smoother run, in bereavement. I also would argue that the maintenance of physical and mental health, prior experience of the bereaved of significant bereavements, the ability to self soothe (without recourse to excessive alcohol, drugs etc.), and access to financial and social resource also cushions the bereaved in the process of finding a sustenance through the process of establishing a continuing bond that is nourishing.

It's important the bereaved can trust us. The one thing we offer can be safety and continuity so they can trust us even when we cannot do the one thing they want, which is to bring the dead back. As professionals we must make sense ourselves of a world that includes death and senseless deaths. Julia Samuel describes her role as a therapist and how she helps herself:

> Grief is a messy, chaotic, unpredictable, subjective business. It often switches our autonomic nervous system to code red. Part of my professional practice is to find ways to keep myself centred when those I'm working with are suffering. I use habits like exercise to balance me: also, theories as frameworks to turn to help me understand what is going on in the therapy.
>
> (Samuel, 2021, p. 2)

We need to come to an ongoing place about finding meaning in pain and to find a position for constant self-awareness, self-criticism, and reflection with others skilled in this work. We need to understand what are currently thought of as healthy minded bereavements and sick people's bereavements in order that the most appropriate level of support is accessed. We need to practice our own professions well and be critical and reflective of our own world views in order that we can listen to others. We need to find a boundary such that thoughts of death do not pervade our home and social life too impactfully and to actively step into living.

Whilst we can be aware of those who are bereaved who encounter our professional services, we are all attached in one way or another, to greater or lesser-known depths to others. Our challenge is to be graceful to all in society who are bereaved – our friends, families, neighbours, and the wider society. The benefit for us too is that we learn that how people cope can provide a source of awe, inspiration, and challenge to our thinking if we are open to learning. Death is not the end of attachment, but with the appropriate support, and always acknowledging the sorrow of the loss and the unchosenness of this, with time it can be the start of another adventure.

References

Bergman, A.S., Axberg, U., and Hanson, E. (2017). When a parent dies – a systematic review of the effects of support programs for parentally bereaved children and their caregivers. *BMC Palliative Care*, *16*(1), 39. https://doi.org/10.1186/s12904-017-0223-y

Bowlby, J. (1997). *Attachment and Loss. Volume 1: attachment.* Pimlico.

Bowlby, J. (2005). *A Secure Base.* Routledge.

CARIS. (2010). *Influencing Change: Bereavement & Homelessness: Vulnerable People Coping and Struggling with Loss.* 33. https://whatsyourgrief.com/wp-content/uploads/2015/04/Bereavement-and-Homelessness-Study.pdf

Child Bereavement UK (2022). *UK Death and Bereavement Statistics.* www.childbereavementuk.org/death-bereavement-statistics

CRUSE. (n.d.). Yoga for grief and loss. Retrieved March 11, 2023, from www.cruse.org.uk/understanding-grief/managing-grief/yoga-for-grief-and-loss/

Currier, J. M., Irish, J. E. F., Neimeyer, R. A., and Foster, J. D. (2015). Attachment, continuing bonds, and complicated grief following violent loss: Testing a moderated model. *Death Studies*, *39*(4), 201–210. https://doi.org/10.1080/07481187.2014.975869

Delaney, R. (2022). *A Heart That Works.* Coronet.

Doka, K. J. (1999). Disenfranchised grief. *Bereavement Care*, *18*(3), 37–39.

GOV.UK. (n.d.). Tell us once: What to do after someone dies. Retrieved March 11, 2023, from www.gov.uk/after-a-death/organisations-you-need-to-contact-and-tell-us-once

Harper, M., O'Connor, R. C., and O'Carroll, R. E. (2014). Factors associated with grief and depression following the loss of a child: A multivariate analysis. *Psychology, Health & Medicine*, *19*(3), 247–252. https://doi.org/10.1080/13548506.2013.811274

Hospice UK. (2022). *Care After Death Guidance.* 5th Edition of Care After Death: Registered Nurse Verification of Expected Adult Death (RNVoEAD) Guidance. www.hospiceuk.org/innovation-hub/clinical-care-support/care-after-death

Jonsson, A. and Walter, T. (2017). Continuing bonds and place. *Death Studies*, *41*(7), 406–415. https://doi.org/10.1080/07481187.2017.1286412

Klass, D. (1999). *The Spiritual Lives of Bereaved Parents.* Taylor & Francis.

Klass, D., Silverman, P. R., and Nickman, S. L. (1996). *Continuing Bonds: New Understandings of Grief.* Taylor & Francis.

Kolk, B. A. van der, Stone, L., West, J., Rhodes, A., Emerson, D., Suvak, M., and Spinazzola, J. (2014). Yoga as an adjunctive treatment for posttraumatic stress disorder: A randomized controlled trial. *The Journal of Clinical Psychiatry*, *75*(06), e559–e565. https://doi.org/10.4088/jcp.13m08561

Lloyd, C. (2023). You will get it wrong … but you can't make it worse: 16 ways to talk to people who are grieving. *The Guardian*. www.theguardian.com/society/2023/jan/07/ways-to-talk-to-people-grieving-cariad-lloyd-griefcast

Lofland, L. H. (1985). The social shaping of emotion: The case of grief. *Symbolic Interaction*, *8*(2), 171–190. https://doi.org/10.1525/si.1985.8.2.171

Mills, M. (2022). "We had such trust: We feel such fools": how shocking hospital mistakes led to our daughter's death. *The Guardian*. www.theguardian.com/lifeandstyle/2022/sep/03/13-year-old-daughter-dead-in-five-weeks-hospital-mistakes

Neimeyer, R. A., Baldwin, S. A., and Gillies, J. (2006). Continuing bonds and reconstructing meaning: Mitigating complications in bereavement. *Death Studies*, *30*(8), 715–738. https://doi.org/10.1080/07481180600848322

Neimeyer, R. A., Klass, D., and Dennis, M. R. (2014). A social constructionist account of grief: Loss and the narration of meaning. *Death Studies*, *38*(8), 485–498. https://doi.org/10.1080/07481187.2014.913454

Office of National Statistics (2023). *Deaths in registered in England and Wales 2021 (refreshed populations)* www.ons.gov.uk/peoplepopulationandcommunity/birthsdeathsandmarriages/deaths/bulletins/deathsregistrationsummarytables/2021refreshedpopulations

Penny, A. and Relf, M. (2017). *A Guide to Commissioning Bereavement Services in England*. National Bereavement Alliance.

Quayle, G. (2022). *Child and Infant Mortality in England and Wales: 2020*. Office of National Statistics. www.ons.gov.uk/peoplepopulationandcommunity/birthsdeathsandmarriages/deaths/bulletins/childhoodinfantandperinatalmortalityinenglandandwales/2020

Rogalla, K. B. (2020). Anticipatory grief, proactive coping, social support, and growth: Exploring positive experiences of preparing for loss. *OMEGA-Journal of Death and Dying*, *81*(1), 107–129. https://doi.org/10.1177/0030222818761461

Root, B. L. and Exline, J. J. (2014). The role of continuing bonds in coping with grief: overview and future directions. *Death Studies*, *38*(1), 1–8. https://doi.org/10.1080/07481187.2012.712608

Samuel, J. (2021). How was your lockdown? Reflections of a therapist during the Covid-19 pandemic. *Bereavement*, *1*. https://doi.org/10.54210/bj.2022.9

Seigal, C. (2017). *Bereaved Parents and Their Continuing Bonds: Love After Death*. Jessica Kinglsey.

Silver, M. (2013). *Attachment in Common Sense and Doodles: A Practical Guide*. Jessica Kinglsey.

Walter, T. (1996). A new model of grief: Bereavement and biography. *Mortality*, *1*(1), 7–25. https://doi.org/10.1080/713685822

Walter, T. (2017). *What Death Means Now*. Policy Press.

Williams, L. (2016). *Relief After a Death: The Unspoken Grief Emotion*. What's Your Grief. https://whatsyourgrief.com/relief-after-a-death-the-unspoken-emotion/

Yalom, I. D. and Yalom, M. (2021). *A Matter of Death and Life: Love, Loss and What Matters in the End*. Piatkom.

The epilogue

What is a sense of security? Unsurprisingly, working on this book led to even more questions being raised. There probably is no single answer to the question of what constitutes psychological security. Perhaps the question should be phrased differently (which does not mean that we should give up trying to find different possible answers). An alternative phrasing of the question could be: what can I as a psychotherapist do to reinforce a sense of security for my clients? This question, in turn, brings my personal and professional responsibility to the fore.

Arlene Vetere, during one of our supervisions, pointed out that one key objective of psychotherapy is the client discovering their own mind, along with all its specificities and how this allows them to recognise reality. Without going into the intricacies of what the mind is and what cognition means, I, Simon, would like to bring to the attention of our readers a certain metaphor that I have found helpful in my clinical work and is a possible response to the question posited earlier. I chose the sea voyage metaphor for several reasons. First of all, seas and oceans have moved the human imagination for centuries, and many people will find some elements with which they identify in this metaphor. The complex ecosystem of the world's seas is now under threat, and we are all beginning to feel the effects of this threat. The sea is also associated with refugees. Thousands of them die at sea. In their case, the danger takes on terrifying proportions. A number of refugees expose themselves to this threat in an attempt to reach a place where they can feel safe, or to ensure the safety of their loved ones. So the sea also offers hope. Still others embark on sea voyages in search of adrenaline. They deliberately put themselves in danger. Others are curious, and their curiosity outweighs their need for security. Finally, swimming in the sea is also an experience that involves many senses. Similarly, experiencing a sense of safety is a physical phenomenon.

In Porto (Portugal) I have the opportunity of observing ships in a port. I sometimes imagine them sailing across the ocean during very different weather conditions, including storms. Despite not being a sailor or navigation expert, I imagine that the safety of a seagoing vessel depends on many different factors, on how accurately the vessel's captain can read and interpret the displays on the various devices used to navigate the seas, and whether they can identify and assess the threats that a vessel might encounter during its voyage. Hence, the safety of a voyage depends in great part on whether the captain can identify any dangers as they arise, as well as on their ability to rest and relax whenever possible. A captain that either overestimates or underestimates danger on a voyage can put the ship's safety at risk.

Stormy weather can sometimes last many days. Some captains hardly ever encounter good weather, particularly on stormy seas, while others, taught by experience, prefer to always remain over vigilant. Very different and diverse captains "sail in" to my psychotherapy practice. Good psychotherapy can be compared to a safe haven. In this metaphor, the psychotherapist is not the one who knows better what is safe and what is not, or what is or is not a threat. The psychotherapist is the one who helps their client understand and navigate their own situation so that they will be able to see where they are on their own personal voyage as clearly as possible, check if their navigational instruments are not failing them, and what repairs the ship might need. The psychotherapist also helps their client identify their resources.

Thus, security will mean that the client is clearly aware of the situation they have found themselves in (particularly being able to identify the different types of risks that they are exposed to) and is familiar with the resources required to cope in stormy weather. Psychotherapy is helpful in acquiring security but surely every one of us can become a safe haven for others, both those close to us as well as for complete strangers. After all, safe gulfs are filled with subtle but significant currents of compassion and benevolence. Lighthouses also help in navigation. Their light helps you to orientate yourself at sea. It is no coincidence that lighthouses fascinate many people. Discovering your lighthouses is one development task that helps to deal with insecurity.

Sometimes captains of ships can feel very lonely and isolated. These feelings are an inevitable part of some journey(s) and increase insecurity. When a storm is coming (these external and internal storms), it is not easy to notice other ships on the sea/around about. My role as a psychotherapist is to help people spot the other ships, as their captains may well be able to bring comfort and joy. Of course, the crews of some of these ships may prove hostile, but yet other ships might help with navigation.

A sense of security is the foundation of being well aware of the things going on in a person's mind which also means being able to clearly recognise and name one's own thoughts and feelings, and in the world around them. An embodied sense of security allows a person to better cope with their problems, relationships with significant others, and also gives them a greater awareness of everything in their surroundings, neighbourhood, and society. In turn, its absence leads to feelings of being lost and a susceptibility to manipulation, both in relationships and at a social level. A sense of security or insecurity is an expression of various mental processes that take place in a person. They can be compared to the surface of an ocean, which are shaped by various forces, including sea currents. Water is in constant motion, and similarly, our sense of safety is constantly changing.

Security and insecurity are constantly intertwined. They are not completely separate. When one strives for security, one inevitably feels its lack, but also when one feels insecure, one can find security. Metaphorically speaking, security and its lack are like the two sides of the same coin. Security and the lack of it do not create a single dimension whose ends are clearly marked. The ocean is full of dangers, for example reefs threatening the ship, and islands offering safe haven (like the island of Corfu described by Durrell). So, at one and the same time one can simultaneously feel safe in some aspects of life but lacking security in others. While sailing on the sea, we inevitably encounter various dangers, but also on this potentially dangerous sea you can find peace and fulfilment. Sometimes, quite unexpectedly, it is during a storm that you find your own safety.

Salman Rushdie used the metaphor "sea of stories" in one of his books (1990). Broadly understood, stories are another way to deal with insecurity. Małgorzata Mirga-Tas, a Polish artist of Roma origin, presents in her works, among others, Roma who survived World War II. Her artworks are full of colour and ornament while touching on painful wounds. Talking about insecurity is a specific human way of dealing with loss. A method that is neither straightforward nor brings quick results, but it does bring relief. The ocean, especially when you are on an empty Atlantic beach, encourages reflection. Sea travel does not always require leaving the house. Sometimes all you need to do is turn on the radio and listen to the BBC Radio 4 Shipping Forecast (cf. Connelly, 2004).

We would like to say goodbye to our readers with some questions that continue to engage us:

- What meanings can be given to intentions and experiences of safety and security in particular life and working contexts?
- Who defines what safety and security are? What implications does this have for questions of power and control in relationships?
- How are safety and security understood and constructed on individual, couple, family, institutional, and social levels? How do these levels interact to increase or decrease a sense of safety and well being?
- What might be the political, economic, social, and individual factors connected with safety and security?
- How are safety and security connected with and influence the development and functioning of the nervous system?
- What is the relationship between safety and security and curiosity and play? From an attachment perspective, a secure base enables curiosity, but sometimes curiosity is more significant than safety.
- How does the need for safety and security change throughout our life stages and with life events?
- How to build a safe relational environment that enables people to thrive?
- What stories are related to safety and security? How are family and societal discourses around trust, comfort, and reassurance developed and changed in the light of external dangers?

- How are these stories interconnected with other stories about ourselves and our close others?
- When and how are questions of safety and security used for particular political or populistic reasons?
- What are the primary threats to safety and security in our communities in the modern world?
- Who is responsible for protection from danger?
- What happens when we cannot see danger for others?

Reference

Connelly, Ch. (2004). *Attention All Shipping.* London: Hachette Digital.

Index

Note: Endnotes are indicated by the page number followed by "n" and the note number e.g., 217n1 refers to note 1 on page 217. Page locators in *italics* represents figures.

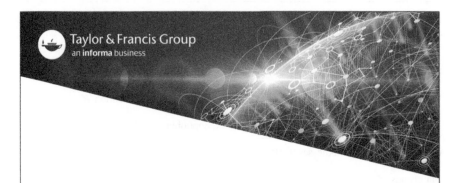